LANDMARKING

LANDMARKING

City, Church & Jesuit Urban Strategy

BY THOMAS M. LUCAS, S.J.

LOYOLA PRESS
CHICAGO

JESUIT
WAY

an imprint of

Loyola Press
3441 North Ashland Avenue
Chicago, Illinois 60657
1-800-621-1008

Cover and interior design: Elizabeth M. O'Keefe and Thomas M. Lucas, S.J.
Cover Art: Facade and interior perspective of the Chiesa del Gesù, Rome;
engraving by Valerién Regnard, 1684; Compass rose by Elizabeth M. O'Keefe.

Library of Congress Cataloging-in-Publication Data

Lucas, Thomas M.
Landmarking: city, church and Jesuit urban strategy /Thomas M. Lucas
p.   cm.
Includes bibliographical references and indexes
ISBN 0-8294-0973-4 (alk. paper)
1. Jesuits--Missions--History. 2. City mission--History.
I Title
BV2290.L83   1997   97-21981
271' .5301732--dc21   CIP

ISBN 0-8294-0973-4

97 98 99 00 01 / 10 9 8 7 6 5 4 3 2 1

BERNARDUS VALLES, MONTES BENEDICTUS AMAVIT;
OPPIDA FRANCISCUS, MAGNAS IGNATIUS URBES.

Bernard loved the valleys, Benedict the mountains;
Francis the towns, Ignatius loved great cities.
                                    —An Old Jesuit Proverb

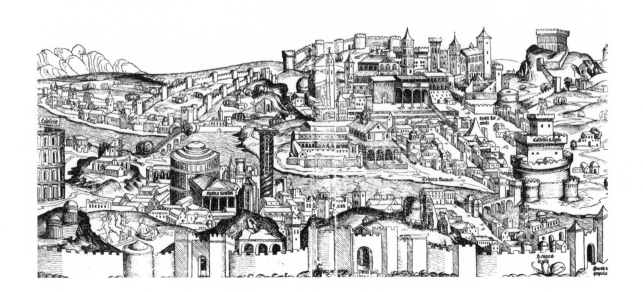

CONTENTS

ILLUSTRATIONS

CHAPTER VII

CHAPTER VIII

CHAPTER IX

FOREWORD

Just when it seems that the personality and life of Ignatius Loyola, and the activities of the Society of Jesus, and their underlying principles have been considered from every possible point of view, at that moment, yet another work appears and sheds new, interesting, and important light on all of those subjects. *Landmarking: City, Church & Jesuit Urban Strategy* is just such a work.

Ignatius plays a central role in the history, over the past four and a half centuries, of the Church as an urban phenomenon. He does so through the decisions he made to locate the heart of Jesuit life and work, as far as possible, in the hearts of great cities. Over and over, in the years between the founding of the Society of Jesus in 1540 and his death in 1556, he made such decisions for the quite variegated places to which he sent the members of this new and, for its time, very unconventional religious order.

The *Constitutions of the Society of Jesus*, of which Ignatius was the principal author, said that the vocation of its members was "to travel through the world and to live in any part of it" [n. 304], and his letters affirmed that vocation at specific sites, carefully chosen in a long-range perspective, as places where Jesuits would establish themselves and their ministries. Movement across the continents of the known world, and stability at the central plazas and major crossroads of cities on all of those continents, were equally parts of a vision of how the Gospel was to be preached to a world caught up then, as it is now, in both the caution and the exhilaration that come with change.

Landmarking is a landmark book. The noun *landmark* can mean a point of orientation in locating other structures, or an event or development that marks a turning point or a stage. The story told here is one way of orienting ourselves, of locating and understanding the structures of the Society of Jesus, both in the lifetime of Ignatius and in the centuries that have followed.

Structures here means, of course, not only physical buildings, but also the social, educational, religious, and even economic, structures that distinguish the internal community life and the external apostolic activities of the Society of Jesus. The book is also a *landmark* in that it marks a turning point or important stage in the way that the history of Ignatius and of the Society can be approached as one formulates a theory or thesis about that history which will or will not be verified by the research that then ensues.

Landmarking–the book–more than amply portrays and documents the urban strategy of Ignatius Loyola himself. That strategy, even if not previously adverted to directly by the Society of Jesus, had a continuing influence on choices and apostolic activities of the Society in the following centuries. Now that this portrait and documentation have made Ignatius' strategy clear, we may well see two reciprocal influences at work in the Society. First, the urban principles and policies of the founder of the Society may in future enter more intentionally and more explicitly into Jesuit choices and activities. Only a prophet, in the popular sense of the word, could give us certainty on such choices and activities. Secondly, choices already and most recently made by the Society of Jesus for its members as "servants of Christ's mission," can be confirmed for their current relevance by recognizing and more deeply understanding the grounding of these choices in this example of Ignatius' "way of proceeding." I refer to the choices made by the "body of the Society," assembled in its representatives at its 34th general congregation in 1995.

Neither the word "city" nor the word "urban" appears in the index to the documentation of that congregation, but the relevance of both concepts is obvious when its first decree talks about "efforts to meet the challenges and opportunities of the modern world" (Decree 1, n.3). Ours is an increasingly urban world where, as the Puebla document of the Latin American Conference of Bishops says, cities are the "motor of the new universal civilization" (n.429) and "in need of a new evangelization" (n.433). What Ignatius said of Seville in a 1547 letter about reciprocal temporal and spiritual help in that city, "because of the concurrence of many people," (*EpistIgn*, p. 601ff.) is even truer today when, by the year 2000, the two largest cities in the world will be Mexico City with 25 million inhabitants and Sao Paulo with 22 million, followed by Tokyo, Shanghai, and New York. It is in those places and in the hundreds of increasingly important metropolitan agglomerations that the Society is "engaged in a variety of ministries at the crossroads of cultural conflict, social and economic struggles, religious revivalism, and new opportunities for bringing the Good News to people all over the world" (Decree 2, n.17).

The 34th congregation recognized that the Society of Jesus is both ineluctably and by choice caught up in that modern world and has to live and work within its contexts. Ineluctably, because, as it well said about Jesuits, "the boundary line between the Gospel and the modern and postmodern culture passes through the heart of each of us" (Decree 4, n.104). By choice, because "a genuine attempt to work from within the shared experience of Christians and unbelievers in a secular and critical culture, built upon respect and friendship, is the only successful starting point, . . . a meeting of equal partners in a dialogue, addressing common questions, or it will be hollow" (Decree 4, n.107). One major such context of the modern world is the city. The first companions of Ignatius and following generations went to the great cities of Europe and Asia and joined in the founding of cities in the new world. In every one of those places they encountered men and women of different faiths, different cultures, different social and economic conditions. They sent back to Ignatius reports of their experiences, their successes, their failures, their questions, their hopes and dreams and plans. In a universal concern for them and for their preaching of the Gospel he saw "the great extent of the circuit of the world, with peoples so many and so diverse" (*SpEx* 103.1). Out of that concern he was able to help the Society adapt its life, its work, its service to the content of the sixteenth-century world.

Today, in the same concern to live and work and serve in the contexts of the world of the twentieth and twenty-first centuries, the Society of Jesus has said that its mission is to be characterized by service of faith, promotion of justice, transformation of cultures, and dialogue with other traditions and experiences. However contemporary the expressions of each of those characteristics may be, one need only move from chapter to chapter of this *Landmarking* to see how those same concerns in different terms and in different expressions played out in the city, the church, and the urban strategy of Ignatius Loyola. In him, "the church in the city found a champion and a conceptual genius, a man who was fully attuned to his urban culture" (p. 21-22). Ignatius, as the head of the worldwide Society of Jesus, lived for sixteen years in small rooms in the great city of Rome. Through all those years and for centuries to come he has marked church and city and Society through vision, imagination, ability and, as Pope Gregory XV said of him at his canonization, "a heart big enough to contain the whole wide world."

John W. Padberg, S.J., Director
The Institute of Jesuit Sources
July 31, 1997

One does not enter a temple,
　　　a shrine that encloses the holy and cuts it off
　　　from a godless and secular world that remains outside.
In the free breadth of a divine world one erects a landmark,
　　　a sign of the fact that this entire world belongs to God,
　　　a sign precisely of the fact
that God is adored, experienced, and accepted everywhere
　　　as the one who, through grace,
　　　has set all things free to attain to him,
and a sign that this adoration takes place not in Jerusalem alone
　　　but everywhere
　　　in spirit and truth.

　　　　　　　–Karl Rahner, S.J.
　　　　　　　Theological Investigations, Vol. 14

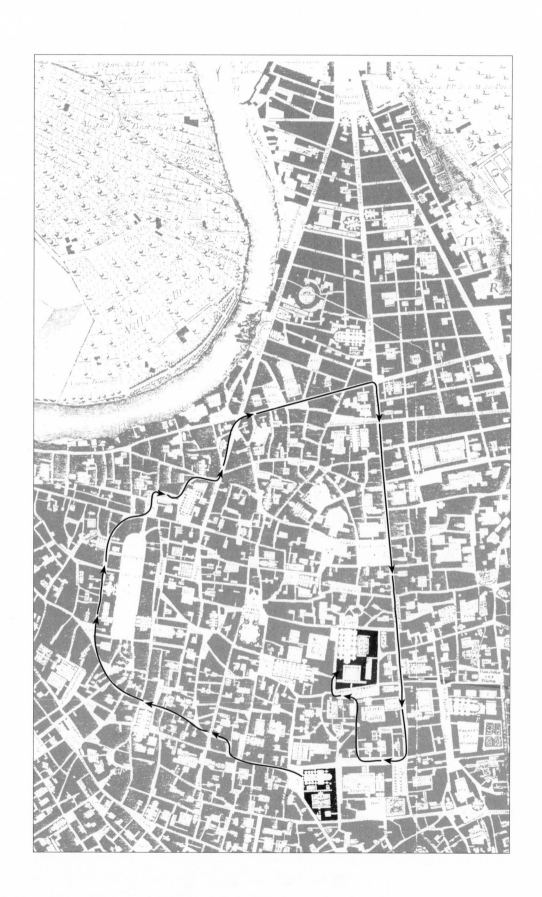

CHAPTER I
LOCATION, LOCATION, LOCATION

 n the twelfth day of March, 1622, the feast of Pope St. Gregory, a Saturday, Pope Gregory XV inscribed among the number of the saints and canonized five Blesseds at the same time. These were Blessed Isidore the Farmer, of the city of Madrid, a Spaniard; Blessed Ignatius Loyola, a Spaniard, founder of the Society of Jesus; Blessed Francisco Javier, a Spaniard, Apostle of the Indies and companion to the same Blessed Ignatius; Blessed Teresa, a Spaniard, foundress of the Discalced Carmelite Nuns and Brothers, and Blessed Filippo Neri, a Florentine, founder of the Congregation of the Oratory at S. Maria in Vallicella. . . . Once the canonizations were celebrated with the requisite ceremonies, there were immediately the most extravagant signs of rejoicing, with the sounds of trumpets, drums, and bells, the firing of mortars and artillery.

That day many alms were given in diverse locations, even by many individual private persons, . . . and the Fathers of the Gesù dispersed to the poor great quantities of white bread, loaves of one pound each.

That evening great bonfires were set in all the streets, and in almost every house of Rome fireworks were set off, and lights placed in the windows, and especially by the fathers of the Society, who not only filled all their windows with light and lit the great cornice of the Collegio Romano, and set fireworks ablaze, and pinwheels; but more so at the Church of the Gesù the entire cupola was covered with torches: it seemed a wonder. And also the whole facade of the church from the great cornice up was full of fireworks, and it was wondrous to behold.

[A few weeks later, on April 6, 1622, the Jesuits staged a celebration to honor their newly canonized saints.] With great solemnity the standard of Sts. Ignatius and Francisco Javier was carried in procession from the Church of the Gesù to the Annunziata of the Collegio Romano. The procession departed from the Gesù towards the [Palazzo dei] Cesarini, straight to the Pasquino, and [passing to] the Church of Santa

Maria dell'Anima at the Torre Sanguigna, on the Ripetta as far as the [Palazzo dei] Borghese, and then returned down the Corso to San Marco, and turned up the street which is opposite the Collegio Romano. There were in the procession 1,500 torches of white wax carried by the Collegio Salviati, and by an immense number of students of the Collegio Romano, of the English and Maronite Colleges, and of the Roman Seminary, and by the Fathers of the Society who carried at the end of the procession the standard. Three bishops surrounded by countless torches carried by diverse people received the standard, amid music and the sound of trumpets, drums and cannonades, and that evening there were grand fireworks and great rejoicing.[1]

–From the diary of Giacinto Gigli, 1622

THE SACRED CIRCLE

Legends relate that on another April day some 2,375 years before, Romulus had read the omens and dug a circular trench in which were deposited "the first fruits of all the things the use of which was sanctioned by custom as good and by nature as necessary." He then traced the sacred circle, the *poemerium*, with a brazen plow pulled by a cow yoked to a bull.[2] Romulus claimed all within that circle as sacred space; his action described the center of a new city, a privileged place where people could live together and commune with their gods.

So too, on that April evening in 1622, the fathers and brothers of the Society of Jesus symbolically delineated a sacred pole. Singing litanies and carrying fifteen hundred blazing torches, they marched clockwise through the spring twilight: the fathers of the Company of Jesus, somber in black capes and birettas, their students bright in linen surplices over their cassocks, and benefactors and friends dazzling in holiday brocades, together they traced a sacred circle with prayer, fire, and music around the Campo Marzio, the military center of ancient Rome. Leaving the church where the newly-sainted bones of Father Ignatius rested under a splendidly decorated altar, their procession staked their claim to the power base that they had been creating for more than seventy-five years in Rome. They did not claim St. Peter's with its relics nor the far-removed Lateran with its history, but the living center of a great city as their sacred place of encounter. This strategic decision would become their trademark, and the heart of their spiritual and temporal presence in the city, the heart of their church. There, in "the free breadth of a divine world," they had set up landmarks, signs that God is to be found and worshiped not on a holy mountain but at the ordinary crossroads of human experience.

THE CHURCH AS
URBAN PHENOMENON

The history of the Christian tradition is inextricably tied to the history of urban society. The first strands of that tradition were spun in ancient cities. Again and again over the past two millennia Christian communities have found form and have unraveled, have grown and have shrunk as Western civilization has reinterpreted urban culture. The Roman Catholic Church is entangled, warp and woof, in the fabric of the city of Rome, where, for good and ill, its leaders have woven much of its history since the time of Peter and Paul.

IGNATIUS: BASQUE AND ROMAN

Ignatius Loyola was a Basque, not a Roman; he was born in a remote valley, not in the center of a great city. He was, however, by training and temperament, by imagination and practical genius, an urban being, a Roman's Roman. There he shaped a resilient and powerful model of religious presence and activity that responded positively to the needs of the Roman Church of his time, when modern urban culture was being born.

Ignatius' Society of Jesus cannot be understood as an abstraction. Rather, to appreciate its inspiration and to comprehend its historical novelty, it must be considered as an element in a continuum: the Church-as-Urban-Phenomenon that began with the first apostolic preaching in the ancient holy city of Jerusalem. That continuum is a complicated dialectic between flight from and embrace of the world, between love of the City of God and rootedness in the City of Man. From its beginnings, the Society of Jesus has willingly participated in the Church's ongoing dialogue with urban culture. Like all great dialogues, it is full of drama, tension, and contradiction. Whether in New York's Lower East Side in 1997 or San Francisco in 1878, in Beijing in 1605 or Goa in 1542, Jesuits have made that dialogue a strategic priority, a characteristic—and even definitive—element of their apostolic program.

GOA, 1542

Praising the Almighty for deliverance after a harrowing thirteen-month odyssey that had begun in Lisbon, Father Francisco Javier debarked in Goa on May 6, 1542, in the company of the new colonial Viceroy Martim Affonso de Sousa. Their journey, like all those from Europe to the Indian subcontinent, had been an arduous one. Seasickness and scurvy racked the crew, and for five months, Father Javier was unable to celebrate mass on board ship for fear that the rolling seas would upset the contents of the chalice. Then, after

3

lying 40 days becalmed in the doldrums south of the Cape Verde Islands, the good ship *Santiago* finally found trade winds and shot across the Atlantic almost to the coast of Brazil before catching a current that drove it to the storm-tossed waters of the Cape of Good Hope. Slowly, the ship then inched up Africa's eastern coast to a four-month layover in Mozambique before beginning the journey's final leg across the open Indian Ocean to lay anchor in Goa.

Javier's missionary voyage marked the beginning of Jesuit outreach to the non-European world, a movement that would eventually develop into an international network of churches, schools, and pastoral centers on every continent. Javier's first target was the commercial center at Goa on the western coast of the subcontinent. Founded half a century before as Portugal's political and commercial capital of the Indies, Goa was the crossroads between east and west, multicultural, rich, bawdy, and vice-ridden. It was the perfect place for the mission to begin.

De Sousa and Javier's arrival was unannounced, and caught the corrupt Dom Estevão da Gama, the soon-to-be-ex-Viceroy of Goa, in his nightshirt. Sometimes the element of surprise is a useful strategy when supplanting one's foes.[3]

FIGURE 1.2
Goa
Church of Bom Jesús.

VALIGNANO'S TACTICS

Alessandro Valignano, Javier's successor as mission superior in the Indies, understood the advantage of surprise. In 1585, when the viceregal government expropriated downtown properties from local Hindus, Valignano had friends of the Jesuits discretely purchase for him houses and gardens on Goa's main square across from the Franciscan Church and the Santa Casa de Misericórdia. Unfortunately, these lots proved insufficient for the projected new Jesuit residence and downtown church, so he had to negotiate openly with other neighbors to round off the site. When Valignano's Franciscan counterpart Gaspar de Lisboa learned of the impending purchases, he lamented in a letter to the King that the Jesuits already dominated Goa with their colleges, chapels, and hospital, and that their "rich and sumptuous" residence would drain revenues from churches of other orders and from the Santa Casa, which served as a kind of religious pawn-shop. By night, Valignano had his Jesuits occupy the disputed territory; possession, then as now, is nine-tenths of the law. Long before the Franciscan's letter ever reached Europe, the archbishop of Goa had solemnly laid the cornerstone for the Church of Bom Jesús. It still stands today at the center of town, a shrine to Javier's remains and to Valignano's determination.[4]

SAN FRANCISCO, 1878

His Grace the Archbishop was not amused when the letter arrived from the Roman Prefect of the Congregatio Propaganda Fidei. Swallowing hard, Joseph Sadoc Alemany, Ordinary of San Francisco and himself a member of the Order of Preachers of St. Dominic, was forced to admit that he had lost another round to the wily Italian fathers of St. Ignatius College.

Jesuits had made their first reconnaissance of Gold Rush California in December 1849, when Giovanni Nobili and Michele Accolti, Italians from the Jesuit Indian missions of Oregon, debarked on San Francisco's Barbary Coast.

> *Arriving on the night of December 8, . . . we were able to set foot on the longed-for shores of what goes under the name of San Francisco but which, whether it should be called a villa, a brothel or Babylon, I am at a loss to determine, so great in those days was the disorder, the brawling, the open immorality, the reign of crime which, brazen faced, triumphed on a soil not yet brought under the sway of human laws.*[5]

SANTA CLARA, 1851

Shortly after Alemany arrived in San Francisco in 1850, he entrusted to the Jesuits the dilapidated Mission Santa Clara, located some 45 miles to the south, near the pueblo of San José. In May 1851, armed with Alemany's blessing and $150 in the treasury, Santa Clara College opened its doors to a handful of students.

SAN FRANCISCO, 1853

Alemany was even more concerned for his burgeoning cathedral city of San Francisco. Writing to Jesuit General Peter Beckx in 1853, he noted that "the number of residents here in San Francisco grows greater each day, and in this city, in which, five years ago, there was not even a thousand persons, there are now forty or fifty thousand."[6] Alemany asked Father Nobili to take charge of an academy founded by the Picpus Fathers at San Francisco's Mission Dolores, an enterprise dubbed "the College of Sorrows" by Accolti, which withered because it was too far removed from the prosperous Embarcadero.

MARKET STREET, 1855

With the arrival of Father Antonio Maraschi and two other Italian Jesuits in 1854, the archbishop resolved that it was time for the foundation of a new college and a church. Waving his hand vaguely over a map in the direction of the unpopulated end of Market Street, Alemany bade the Jesuits to settle in that neighborhood, suitably removed from the city's three parishes. On May 1, 1855, the Fathers purchased a 127- by 275-foot lot on Market Street, and 75 days later St. Ignatius Church, a 75- by 35-foot wood frame hall, opened for worship. On October 15 of the same year, they opened the doors of St. Ignatius Academy and College, a one-room schoolhouse. One of the first Jesuits who lived there, Brother Albert Weyringer, described the site as "a hole surrounded by sand hills"; but Maraschi was more hopeful: "Here let us build and wait," he said. "This will be the center of a great city."[7]

They did not have to wait long. By the early 1860s, a steam train ran along Market Street, bringing students and Sunday worshippers to St. Ignatius Church. Pastors of the other parishes complained that the Jesuits were alienating the loyalties of their flocks, "filling up their vast hall" with activities including Masses, sodality functions, "public blessings and consecrations of old, young, and babies that contribute much to draw the excitable of the other parishes in that direction, " and "the distribution of 'St. Ignatius Water'—this liquid lately has become a beverage, in fact superceding [sic] the Napa Soda Water and the various nostrums guaranteed for the infallible cure of all the maladies of human nature."[8]

About the same time, Archbishop Alemany began a protracted attempt to wrestle the title deed of the Market Street property away from the Jesuits. In letter after letter to Jesuits in San Francisco, Oregon, and Rome and to the Roman Congregation for the Propagation of the Faith that oversaw the American Church, he insisted that, according to the Fifth Decree of the 1852

Council of Baltimore, all church properties must be vested in the person of the ordinary. The Jesuits politely declined, citing ancient precedents and privileges granted to the exempt religious order by the Holy See. Alemany gave the Jesuits one year to tender the deeds to the property or lose their parochial status. The year came and went, and when Alemany finally stripped St. Ignatius of its parochial status, Father Giuseppe Sopranis, a Jesuit "visitor" sent from Rome to look into the Society's dealings in the United States, responded with a legal brief: he acknowledged Alemany's right to revoke the status but at the same time defended "the truth of things, as it is in itself on our side."[9] The Jesuits lost the parish, but the archbishop never won the property.

THE WESTERN ADDITION

    Ten years later, it was time for St. Ignatius College and Church to move. Market Street had indeed become the "center of a great city," with its concomitant problems: high taxes and no room to expand. The fathers determined that the corridor along Van Ness Avenue in the city's "Western Addition" was the next important developing neighborhood. They decided to purchase Block 74, across from the City Hall, the modern site of Davies Symphony Hall, and discretely but methodically set about obtaining the land.

CATHEDRAL OR COLLEGE?

    Archbishop Alemany had other ideas. He was planning to build a new cathedral a few blocks away. He wrote to the Jesuit president of St. Ignatius College, Father Aloysius Varsi:

> *In a country like this, where we have to depend exclusively on the offerings of people attending church, the Cathedral could have no support, if you locate near it or the lot where it has to be. . . . I invited you to San Jose, Santa Clara, and San Francisco to aid me—out of good will because [you were] troubled by bad people elsewhere. I think you might consider a little before establishing yourselves where your church will unintentionally but surely swallow up the congregation and offerings of the Cathedral. Were it not for that I would not object to your choosing the most desirable and central place in this city.*[10]

    Varsi demurely responded that the construction of a new cathedral was news to him and that during Varsi's recent visit to Rome, the Jesuit general had reiterated to him the Society's age-old prerogatives for building churches and colleges anywhere, in any location, in any city in the world. In 1875, in response to Alemany's challenges, the Jesuits had drafted and submitted a document to Propaganda Fidei defending their privileges, and obtained the signatures of the leaders of the fifteen most important religious orders and congregations (including Alemany's own Order of Preachers) in support of it. In a final flurry of closing arguments, Alemany wrote a four-page plea to the Cardinal Prefect of Propaganda Fidei; Varsi countered with a 31-page canonical treatise.

Varsi's weighty document tipped the scales in the Jesuits' favor. On August 20, 1878, Father Varsi received a cablegram from Pope Leo XIII's secretary of state imparting a heartfelt apostolic blessing on the "new building containing the church and college." In a spirit of filial if somewhat frustrated resignation, Archbishop Alemany summoned his real estate broker and began to search for an alternate site for his new cathedral.

FIGURE 1.3
San Francisco
St. Ignatius Church and College, ca. 1890.

LIMA, 1569

In our last letters, we gave an account of our successful voyage and all that occurred in the places we passed through, and how we came to this city; in this we will proceed with what followed.

So that this city might begin to esteem the Society, and as Our Lord willed that it should be appreciated and convey the promise of those great effects which, through its agency, He would accomplish in these kingdoms, the very hour we arrived at the gates, the sun was eclipsed, and it indeed seemed as if it were night. . . . Then [a few days later] on Palm Sunday as Father Provincial ascended the pulpit of St. Dominic's monastery to preach, the very earth trembled, and although [the church] was very large and crowded with people, not one departed, being so desirous to hear Father [Ruiz de Portillo].

These two events were interpreted throughout the Kingdom as portents that Our Lord willed to give, that souls might be favorably disposed—so it is written here and elsewhere by many—and, indeed Our Lord wished to embolden us as well, granting us the hope that he will use us as instruments for the salvation of souls in this kingdom, we who, when we reflect on our miseries and imperfections, reckon ourselves much wanting before such an exalted enterprise.[11]

—Father Didacus Bracamonte
to the Fathers and Brothers of the Society of Jesus.

Eclipses and earthquakes notwithstanding, the Jesuits arrived in Peru in 1568 with strong backing. The King of Spain's letters patent to the viceroy, the local hierarchy, and resident religious ordered them to welcome the fathers "in the principal localities" of the colony to perform "according to their way of proceeding" their usual ministries "of preaching and instruction in Christian Doctrine, in support of and in cooperation with the Prelates and other ecclesiastical ministers." Fourteen months after their arrival, the aged and ailing Archbishop of Lima descended into a trench and with his own anointed hands laid the cornerstone of the Jesuit church and college.[12]

CUZCO, 1571

The Jesuits determined to focus their early efforts in the viceregency on four major cities: Lima, Caracas, Quito, and Cuzco, the former capital of the Inca Empire. When they arrived at Cuzco in May 1571 led by father provincial Hierónimo Ruiz de Portillo, the preacher whose fame outweighed the threat of an earthquake, they were welcomed, at least at first, by the canons of the cathedral who were themselves awaiting the arrival of a new bishop. Portillo wasted no time, and within a few months had obtained property for a new college and church.

CHURCHES
AND CANONS

The canons exploded when they learned where the Jesuits planned to settle. With the help of the viceroy, Portillo had managed to obtain "a very good site on the principal plaza of the city, near the *Iglesia Mayor* [the cathedral]." For the next eighty years, the canons protested loudly every time the

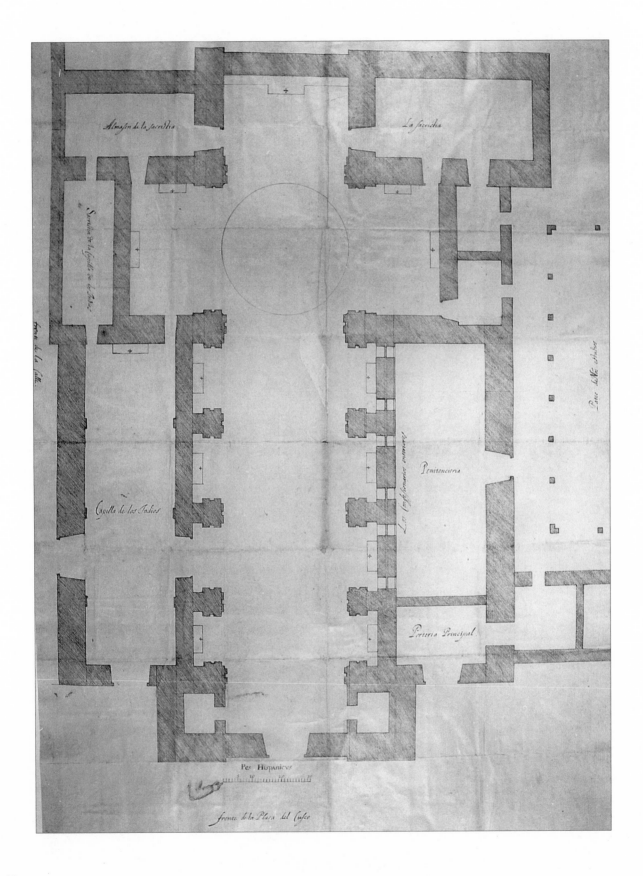

FIGURE 1.4 (LEFT)
Cuzco
"La Compañía."

Jesuits expanded their college or rebuilt after an earthquake. They could have used as their bill of particulars for the alienation of affection of the Cuzco citizenry a letter the Jesuits wrote to their father general in Rome describing the property.

> *On account of this [site], almost all the citizens of the city hear mass in our church; it is in a very healthful location. It has a temporary building that can serve as a residence for 20 persons for a good long time, and space to build for twenty more; it does not yet have a permanent church, but a temporary one will serve quite comfortably where we say mass and administer the sacraments; it is sufficiently large to assemble the whole city to hear a sermon, although not all fit indoors, and given that most of the people come to listen to sermons at our church, there is space enough to build a truly roomy church. It has a patio for classes, large enough and conveniently located outside our residence.*[13]

In the final quarter of the sixteenth century, Portillo replaced the provisional church with an elegant temple of his own design, constructed of stones recycled from an Inca palace discovered in the excavation of its deep foundations. Contemporary accounts tell of Spaniards working alongside feather-bedecked Incas and Cañares, who sang versions of the Psalms of David—"Come, let us build the house of the Lord"—in their own dialects.[14] After a ruinous earthquake in the mid-seventeenth century, Cuzco's "La Compañía" Church rose again, this time modeled after the 1624 Jesuit Church of San Pedro in Lima, which was itself designed by a Jesuit architect who had brought with him from Rome plans of the Jesuit mother church, the Chiesa del Gesù.[15] At its dedication, the complaints of the cathedral canons were drowned out in echoing praise for what the faithful, and centuries of art historians, have considered one of Latin America's most beautiful churches.

THE PORTAL

In the complex dynamic of tension and release, compression and expansion that characterizes baroque architecture and urban planning, the ecclesiastical facade plays a powerful role. The baroque church portal serves as a back-

FIGURE 1.5
Macao
Church of the Holy Mother of God.

drop for processional and civic drama and a *terminus ad quem* for vista corridors slashing through the urban fabric. Its piazza is a monumental transitional zone—a kind of waiting room—between this world and The Next. The portal makes a confident statement about the Church's presence and relevance in this city, in this world, while suggesting at the same time that once one passes through it, wonders unimagined await the pilgrim, the traveler, the adventurer.

The facade of the Jesuit Church of the Holy Mother of God dominates the skyline of Portuguese Macao. Its massing recalls the great facades of Rome's Gesù and Antwerp's Professed Church (now called St. Charles), but its decoration is wholly idiosyncratic. Western theology is literally intertwined with oriental ornament; bronze statues of Christ, the Blessed Virgin Mary, and the Jesuit saints stand on a four-tiered granite wall decorated with chrysanthemums, litchis, poppies, and dragons carved by Japanese Christians expelled from Japan. On the facade—all that remains of the Jesuits' College of St. Paul where Western missionaries trained for service in the Orient and Oriental missionaries learned the ways of the West—two radically different worlds meet and peacefully coexist.

In 1563, when the first Jesuits came to Macao, its Portuguese population numbered about 500, most of whom were middlemen in the lucrative China-Japan silk trade. The Jesuits built a small church of straw and wattle, a house for Chinese catechumens, and a small residence to house missionaries awaiting transit to Japan. In 1572, they opened a primary school for the children of the Portuguese traders. About the time that Michele Ruggieri arrived to study Chinese before entering the mainland (1579), the straw church burned, and a new wooden, tiled-roof church and a school building were erected overlooking Macao's center from a high hill,

> full of very large cliffs, without any land on which to build. . . . On the end of the mountain very large and strong walls were built, within which a large, very flat and comfortable field was graded on which to build the College and the patios that are necessary for it . . . . The college was located in the middle of the mountain, [and it had] a grand view, exposed to all the good winds that come from the sea, and on the other side protected from all bad and unhealthy winds, so that the College was very cool and well situated.[16]

COLLEGE OF ST. PAUL

On that cool and well-situated location, the college grew, and when foreign missionaries were expelled from Japan in 1587, a separate seminary was established there for the training of Japanese clergy. Over rancorous objections from the community of the College of St. Paul in Goa, Alessandro

FIGURE 1.6 Beijing
Church of the Holy Savior
within the Imperial Palace
grounds,
ca. 1700.

BEIJING, 1605

Valignano gave the Macao College—also dedicated to St. Paul—independent status, and in 1597 it granted its first university degrees in liberal arts and theology. At any given time during the expansive half-century that followed, between 30 and 50 seminarians were enrolled there, preparing for work in China and Japan.[17]

When the University's church burned in 1601, Portuguese traders promised a half-percent tithe on that year's Japan trade to rebuild it. By 1603, a splendid new temple designed by Jesuit Carlo Spínola (who died a martyr's death in 1622 in Nagasaki) was dedicated. Its ornate facade was not completed until around 1640. Contemporary visitors, both Catholic and Protestant, compared it favorably to the finest churches in Europe.[18]

In 1605, Valignano wrote that he was ready to "sell the chalices from the sacristy" to help pay for a new residence that Matteo Ricci had just purchased in the heart of Beijing, Just south of the Imperial Palace. Fortunately for the Jesuits (who received a cut for acting as agents and translators in Nagasaki), the Japan trade was lucrative that year, so Valignano had extra funds to send to Beijing for the construction of a second floor and novitiate wing and the excavation of a new well. Ricci complained happily that the fathers were so inundated with important visitors, "acquaintances of Ours from Beijing or from the other houses, or who have heard of the reputation of Ours and of our works, or have seen our printed books or have conversed with Ours . . . that Ours were not given time even for physical refection. . . ."[19]

Some 45 years later, Johann Adam Schall, director of the Imperial Bureau of Astronomy, built a large church and residence nearby, on land granted the Jesuits by the Imperial Court. In addition to his astronomical and linguistic prowess, Schall had won the confidence of the last Ming emperors when he set up a foundry near the palace for the casting of small-gauge cannons. Although reluctant to become a seventeenth-century Krupp, Schall did have experience with firearms. In 1623, he had helped mount a surprise cannonade against invading Dutch traders from the Jesuits' hilltop college in Macao, and had himself captured the Dutch commandant.[20]

France's Louis XIV, jealous of the inroads the Portuguese and Italian Jesuits had made in Beijing and desirous of trade with the Middle Kingdom, sent a delegation of French Jesuits to Beijing in 1688. Unhappy from the start with the prospect of cohabiting with their Mediterranean companions, the French Fathers struck gold when they cured Emperor Kang'hsi's malaria with a new wonder drug, the so-called "Jesuit bark," quinine, exported from the Jesuit missions in Peru. In gratitude, Kang'hsi gave them a lovely house on the west bank of Lake Canchiko, within the *enceinte* of Imperial City on Imperial palace grounds. On the grounds they built a library, an observatory and the Church of the Holy Savior. Over the Chinese-style gateway to the complex, an inscription composed and calligraphed by the emperor himself–"The True Origin of All Things"–was proudly displayed. Behind it on the facade of their decidedly Baroque church, the Jesuits emblazoned the monogram of the name of Jesus, their trademark and their proudest boast.[21]

ST. MARY'S CITY, MARYLAND

The members of this Board taking under their consideration that such use of the Popish Chapel in the City of St. Maries in St. Maries County, where there is a Protestant Church, and the said County Court is kept, is scandalous and offensive to the Government, do advise and desire His Excellency the Governor to give immediate orders for the shutting up of the said Popish chapel, and that no person presume to make use thereof under any pretense whatsoever. Whereupon it is ordered by His Excellency, the Governor, that the Sheriff of St. Maries County lock up the said chapel and keep the key thereof. [22]

—From the Acta of the Lower House
of the Maryland Assembly, 1704

Almost two centuries later and some 60 miles south-southeast of Washington, DC, a team of dedicated archeologists has been laboring for ten years to excavate and interpret what remains of St. Mary's City. In the almost total absence of documentation—the dearth is the result of courthouse fires, religious squabbles, and eighteenth-century recycling—Henry Miller, Timothy Riordan, Silas Hurry, and their crew are trying to decipher the early history of Maryland's first colonial capital from a hieroglyphic composed of broken bricks, pottery shards, and aerial photographs.

BALTIMORE
AND THE JESUITS

Founded in 1634 under a charter obtained by Cecil Calvert, the Catholic Lord Baltimore, the town served as the administrative and social center of an agrarian colony. Calvert's new colony was a novelty in the English-speaking New World, for its proprietor actively espoused religious toleration. At least at first, Catholic and Protestant generally kept an awkward but workable truce. Among the town's first residents was the expedition's Catholic chaplain, Jesuit Father Andrew White, an Englishman who had emigrated to the continent to join the Society of Jesus and take holy orders.

Lord Baltimore's relationship with the Society of Jesus was rocky. He chastised his brother Leonard, the first governor, for granting the Jesuits too many concessions, and in particular for giving the fathers a tract of valuable town land for the construction of a chapel. Haggling over the "Chapel Field" went on for years, but the Jesuits erected a provisional chapel, probably a simple clapboard structure.

During the English Civil War, local Protestants overthrew the Catholic Proprietary Government. White and another Jesuit were sent back to England in chains, and three more Jesuits disappeared forever into the wilds of Virginia. More than a decade of skirmishing was finally resolved with the restoration of both the monarchy and the Calvert family fortune.

In the 1660s, new Jesuit blood flowed into Maryland with the arrival of three priests and two lay brothers, including two men who had lived for several years in Rome. Jesuit plantations were recovered, and timber-frame churches built at Port Tobacco and Newtown.

A BAROQUE PLAN
IN THE WILDERNESS

With peace came prosperity. In 1667 Lord Baltimore ordered the formal incorporation of St. Mary's City. What the archeologists have discovered is that St. Mary's City did not grow as a casual, haphazard waterfront settle-

FIGURE 1.7
St. Mary's City
Baroque city plan, ca. 1680.

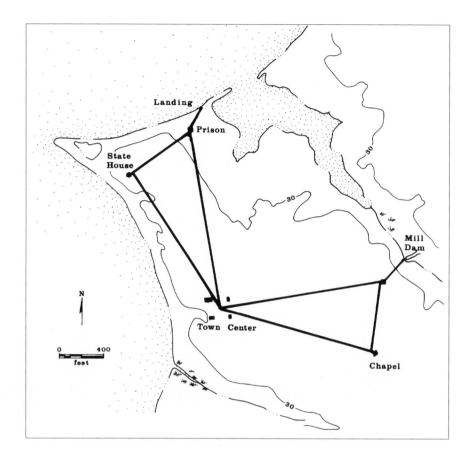

ment. Rather, their excavations have unearthed convincing evidence that a refined baroque urban plan was imposed and implemented in the Catholic tidewater town in the 1660s, 30 years before the capital was moved to Annapolis and that town was given a refined makeover by Protestant Governor Francis Nicholson.

A town square—with three "ordinaries" or taverns and a lawyer's office marking its corners—was located at the converging vertices of two identical triangles whose remote vertices were marked on one side by the state house and brick jail and on the other by a new brick church and a secondary brick building of as yet undetermined function. Each leg measures 1,400 linear feet from the town square to the door of each edifice. The state house and the Church were volumetrically approximately equal. Each was cruciform, and each dominated a key topographic feature: the state house overlooking the harbor, the church crowning the highest point in town, overlooking the main inland access road. The two great brick buildings and their outriggers stood in delicate and what appears to be deliberate counterpoise: church and state balanced against one another on the fulcrum of the town square.[23]

THE BRICK CHAPEL

The story of Brick Chapel remains a tantalizing mystery. Once the Protestants took over the colony in the late seventeenth century, the building was closed; apparently its brick walls, windows, and tiled roof were recycled by its neighbors and the chapel disappeared from the landscape sometime in the early to mid eighteenth century. Its massive foundations—carefully constructed brick footings five feet deep and three feet wide—argue for tall walls. Fragments of paving stones of European origin, bits of imported leaded glass, and carefully formed mullion bricks testify to significant expenditures on its construction. The recent discovery in the left transept of elaborate lead coffins containing the well-preserved remains of a man, woman, and child suggests that perhaps the gubernatorial Calverts (whose male scions had been educated for generations at Jesuit colleges on the continent) were the Church's major benefactors.

The mysteries surrounding the rise and fall of the Brick Chapel at St. Mary's City will probably never be solved. What is not mysterious at all is the fact that "in the free breadth of a divine world" the Jesuits built such a landmark in a city in the wilderness.

The ancients believed that some particular places fall under the sway of malign spirits. If such an evil *genius loci* exists in the New World, its name is "Degradation" and its address is The Bowery in New York City's Lower East Side.

THE BOWERY

The past century has seen scant progress in this archetypal immigrant neighborhood. Poteen gave way to grappa, grappa to rum, as Irish immigrants were displaced by Italians, Italians by Puerto Ricans. Distillates of coca leaf have replaced tinctures of poppy as drugs of choice. Technology has streamlined violence, as Saturday-night specials and semiautomatic weapons have displaced leather-covered lead truncheons and stilettos.

Prostitution has remained one of the neighborhood's constants, although the AIDS epidemic has dramatically accelerated the once leisurely consequences of venery. The other constant is the immensely high risks that immigrant children must navigate just growing up there.

In 1891, Archbishop Michael Corrigan was greatly disturbed by the inroads that evangelical Protestant missionaries were making among Italian immigrants in the Bowery. He asked the Jesuits to open a mission for Sicilian immigrants under the patronage of Our Lady of Loreto. Father Nicholas Russo was recruited, and the former Georgetown professor soon set up shop in a rented barroom at 292 Elizabeth Street. "Without scrip or purse, and with God's blessing, through the hands of our superiors, we undertook the work cheerfully."[24]

The work began auspiciously. A 1917 "Short History of the Mission" published in the *Woodstock Letters* describes the scene:

In order to attract Italians to his church, Father Russo availed himself of a measure that proved effective. The Society of San Rocco, a mutual aid society in the neighborhood, was accustomed to honor their patron saint on the 16th of August by holding a kind of religious festa, as is customary in their own towns in Italy. A brass band, colored lights, and fireworks were important features of the occasion.

Father Russo made arrangements with Mr. Rocco Marasco, the president of the society, to come to his church with his men for the opening mass. Consequently, the men were pressed into service, and at eleven o'clock on the morning of August 16, 1891, about 50 in full regalia, preceded by two policemen and cheered by hundreds of people on the sidewalks, made their solemn entrance into the new basilica, which a month before had been a drinking saloon. The church held about 150 people, and it was filled.[25]

The work grew apace. The barroom chapel was quickly outgrown, and was soon replaced by a temporary church carved out of two tenement houses across the street. The tenement's basement was converted into six classrooms, and by 1895, new and larger quarters were found nearby to house the Loreto School's 500 students. A decade later, the fathers established a "Summer Home" for boys in rural Monroe, New York, where denizens of one of the most densely populated neighborhoods in America were given a two-week reprieve. "The boys have plenty of room to run around, as the property includes about 65 acres. They have a ball field, a swimming pool, a moving picture machine, and everything possible is done to keep them busy, interested, and happy."[26]

Back home, students' lives centered on the Loreto School. They returned after supper in the evening for study hall and attended classes on Saturday. The goal of the school was clear: to move immigrant children out

of danger and into the cultural mainstream. The results were solid, as is evidenced by the many boys who went on to study at the New York Province's Xavier and Regis High Schools and Fordham University.

NATIVITY

As the Italian immigration spilled east of the Bowery, frustrated Irish diocesan clergy prevailed on the archbishop to transfer the Jesuits from their successful mission to Nativity Church on Second Avenue between Second and Third Streets. By 1917, the formerly Irish parish was almost entirely Sicilian. In collaboration with the Mission Helpers of the Sacred Heart, the Jesuits established the Nativity Mission Center, which included a day care center for children of the neighborhood's sweatshop workers.

As the new waves of post–World War II immigration broke on the Lower East Side in the early 1950s, Puerto Rican–born Jesuit Walter Janer began working with the Mission Helpers and lay colleagues to develop a ministry to the Puerto Rican population. Afterschool and weekend programs were established for at-risk youth, and the idea of a "summer home" was resurrected as "Camp Montserrate" on Lake Placid.

BACK TO BASICS

As circumstances continued to change and as the neighborhood continued to deteriorate during the 1960s, Jesuits and their colleagues at Nativity engaged in a process of discernment about the future of the mission's work. They decided that a youth center was not enough: what was needed was an institution that would help at least some young people to break out of the neighborhood's vicious topography. They decided to do what Jesuits have done in troubled cities around the world for the past 450 years. They started a school.

In 1971, the Jesuit mission in the Lower East Side came full circle with the opening of Nativity Middle School. Lay faculty, other religious, and Jesuits live in the dangerous neighborhood where they work, exercising a ministry of presence as well as education. They work with junior high–aged boys and their families, helping them to chart out a path to survival and success before they are detoured into the dead–ends of poverty, drugs, and violence. Following the model of Loreto, Nativity established a strict curriculum, extra tutoring in English and math, afterschool study halls and sports, and a summer camp program. Its small classes and very low student-teacher ratio provide a few lucky, motivated Hispanic children of the 1990s the same chances for success that Loreto School gave Italian children in the 1890s. Nativity gives them a chance to navigate the dangerous urban shoals and move into the mainstream, a chance to discover the landmarks of values, discipline, and community, a chance to transform the evil genius of their neighborhood into a new and shining city.

FIGURE 1.8 (LEFT)
New York City
Nativity school, 1997.

CONTINUITY
AND DISCONTINUITY

The drama of the Roman Church, the oldest continuously administered institution in the Western World, is predominantly set in great cities, is punctuated by great movements and ideas, and is played out in the lives of great saints and sinners. In Ignatius Loyola, the Church in the city found a champion and a conceptual genius, a man who was fully attuned to his urban culture, a man able to adapt—and even abandon—parts of the Catholic tradition in order to shape an instrument uniquely suited for the existential needs of his time and place. *Where* he chose to be—where he located his churches, schools, and residences—clearly incarnates *how* he chose to be and to minister in the Church. That *how* is a conceptual program of great diversity. As it was for Ignatius in his Rome, it has always been, and it still is today grounded in the concrete *where*—in this particular city, among these particular needs, working with these particular people.

From his profound yet practical experience of "finding God in all things" and from his carefully reflected—upon experience of living with and for the citizens of his urban world, Ignatius was able to create a way of life and a pattern of apostolic commitment appropriate to the demands of his historical moment. That way of life and that pattern, lived out by the early Jesuit community in downtown Rome, developed in Ignatius' extensive correspondence, and codified in the *Constitutions of the Society of Jesus,* provided the Church and the Christian urban world with a corps of well-prepared, ready, and eminently flexible religious who could preach, teach, and minister to the various constituencies of the metropolis. It is a pattern that has withstood four centuries of urban trials and undergone infinite variations. It is as sturdy as an ancient hymn, built on the *cantus firmus* of ancient traditions. It is as pliant as a jazz riff, always able to integrate new experience.

THE CITY
AS SACRED THEATER

We can read the drama of Ignatius' life experience and of the early history of the order he founded as if they were operatic texts that are most easily understood when played out on the monumental stage of Catholicism, the historic scenography of the city of Rome. The Society's foundational documents, although necessary for a complete understanding of Ignatius' urban vision, are abstractions, plot synopses of the *Opera Pietatis* which Ignatius and his skilled troupe performed on the particularly well-furnished Roman stage. Just as Greek tragedy cannot be properly orchestrated without its sacred, circular dancing-ground, so too Ignatius' improvisational genius cannot be appreciated if removed from its proper proscenium, the ancient tradition of the Roman Church as *aedificatio aedificans et semper aedificanda,* building in process and ever in need of rebuilding.

This *Opera Pietatis* opens with the overture, an introduction to Ignatius' life (Chapter II). Then we see unfolding the design of the "theater" where it was acted out, a sketch of the Catholic Church as urban phenomenon (Chapters III-V). This scenographic history gives us the context, the fifteen-hundred-year-old tradition of the Church as it negotiated its existence in the developing West. It focuses in particular on the spectacular Roman stage. Once we have met the protagonist and examined the monumental setting from which he drew inspiration and in which he performed for the last twelve years of his life, the Ignatian *opus* unfolds in four parts: the dramatic urban impact of the Roman apostolic adventures of the early Society (Chapter VI); their thematization into its foundational documents (Chapter VII); Ignatius' letters—recitatives and arias that expose what was happening in his mind and heart (Chapter VIII); and a coda that draws together and recapitulates the various themes of Ignatius' creative and practical attunement to his changing world, Jesuit continuity and discontinuity with the Christian urban tradition, and the impact of Jesuit building on the early modern city (Chapter IX).

Ignatius was the first founder of a major religious order in the history of the Church to locate his headquarters in Rome and the first to opt deliberately for complete insertion of a religious order's works and residences in the center of the urban fabric. Those decisions, both politically and religiously motivated, were not casual but definitive: they placed the emerging Society of Jesus intentionally in the psychological center of Catholic Christendom, within the sacred circle at the heart of the human city. There, at the crossroads within the circle, Ignatius Loyola staked his claim. There he erected his landmark.

In great cities on every continent, Jesuits have done the same ever since.

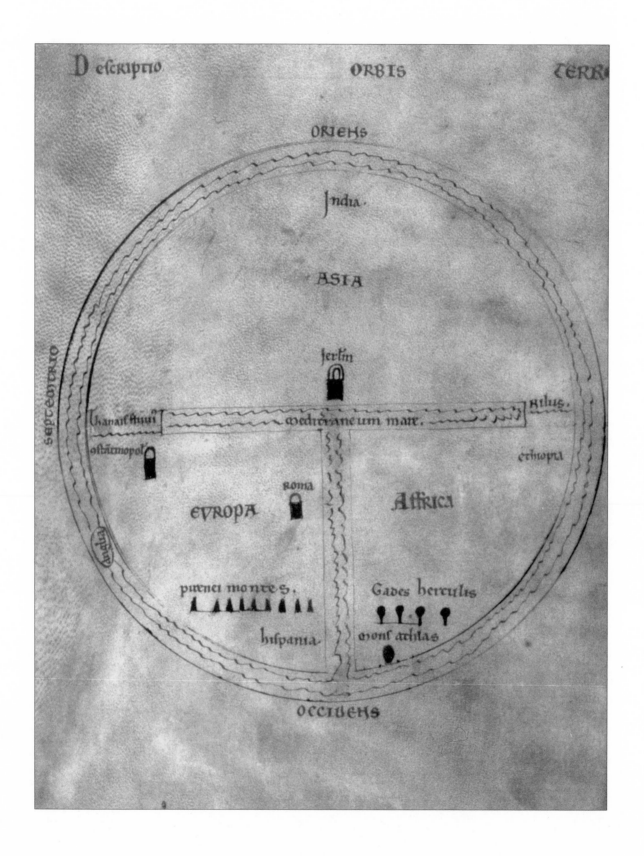

CHAPTER II
BETWEEN TWO WORLDS

T he valley of Loyola is narrow, and deep enough to give the sense of encompassing security. In spring the air smells of apple blossoms; the valley is a rich provider. In summer, though, there are tastes of the not-too-distant sea on the wind. The valley seems small then, even claustrophobic.

In 1491, Iñigo Lopez de Loyola was born in a remote valley in northern Spain, between two worlds: between the stable and circumscribed world categorized by the medieval synthesis and the apparently limitless horizons of expanding knowledge and experience of the Renaissance.

The medieval world was a place of hierarchically ordered relationships where science, both secular and sacred, served theology. Nowhere is this subordination so clearly shown as in the work of the medieval map-maker. The cartographer did not attempt to make a topographically precise rendering of the world but to show how the world revealed the orderly plan of the divine intelligence that had created it and the saving initiative of the divine son who entered into its history. The map, then, was not so much a guide for getting from one place to another as an icon, teaching a moral and spiritual truth to the person who contemplated it. Medieval "T-O" maps, based on ancient Ionian models from the fifth century before Christ, are mandalas, sacred circles with Jerusalem at the center. A tau cross unites the waters and divides the lands, just as the cross of Christ standing at the center of the human world was believed to be the sign of unity among Christians and the absolute demarcation between believers and non-believers.

The medieval world never entirely lost touch with the scientific lore of antiquity; in the eighth century the Venerable Bede described the world as "round like a shield, but also in every direction, like a playground ball."[1]

FIGURE 2.1 (LEFT)
Parchment "T-O" map
from Paulus Orosius's *Historia*
13th century.

When Ptolomey was translated from Greek into Latin in the early 1400s cartographers were furnished with the essential conceptual tools of latitude and longitude for projecting a spherical surface onto a two-dimensional plane. With the Portuguese explorations of the African coast in the fifteenth century, a new era of mathematically and commercially based cartography evolved at the school of Prince Henry the Navigator.

SHIFTING HORIZONS

The Spanish monarchy's desire to undercut Portugal's expanding empire led to the funding of Columbus' westward voyage in 1492. Although it took almost 20 years before the full commercial ramifications of Columbus' discovery were fully appreciated in Spain, the discovery of the New World changed the horizon for all time. The world was no longer circumscribed by divine design but circumnavigable by ordinary sailors. The stable circle gave way to undefined coasts and continents. The shifting horizon changed human perception of the physical world, and challenged Europe's epistemological certainties.

IÑIGO BORN, 1491

Iñigo Lopez de Loyola was born in 1491, the thirteenth and last child of a family of petty nobility in the rugged Basque region of Guipúzcoa. The *casa torre* of the Loyola clan dominated the intersection of the narrow, mile-long valleys of Azpeitia and Azcoitia. The stronghold was a blockhouse, a simple construction of thick stone walls, 16 meters square and four stories high. The lower floors were used as an armory and kitchen, while the upper stories, rebuilt of brick in the Moorish-influenced Mudéjar style by Iñigo's grandparents, served as the residence of the family. From small windows piercing the upper floors, one could gaze on surrounding orchards and dense woods. In the near distance lay the town of Azpeitia and its parish church of San Sebastián, over which the Loyola clan exercised more authority than the local bishop. Visually, the site recalls the subalpine valleys of Ticino, or the American Ozarks: the small, rich valleys are hemmed in by tall but not imposing mountains. At the beginning of the sixteenth century as today, the Basque province was a closed world, whose geography, unique language, and customs bred fierce regional loyalties.

IÑIGO'S FAMILY TREE

Iñigo's father was Beltrán Ibáñez de Oñaz, a local clan chief and stalwart loyalist who fought for the crown for more than 20 years. His union with Doña Marina Sáenez de Licona, a member of the most important family of Azcoitia, solidified his position and standing in the region. Iñigo's eldest brother, Juan Peréz, commanded his own ship in the Spanish war for the conquest of Naples, where he died in 1496. Another brother, Hernando, renounced his inheritance to take part in the colonization of the New World, disappearing in the Americas in 1510. Martin López, the second eldest brother and future lord of Loyola, was well known as both a warrior and a gentleman in the court of Castille and married one of Queen Isabella's favorite ladies-in-waiting, Magdalena de Araoz. Another brother, Ochoa Pérez, was a gentleman in the court of Doña Juana "La Loca" in Flanders and Spain. Pero López, who had accompanied Iñigo in adolescent revels in 1515, became the pastor of the parish church of Azpeitia, where the Loyola children were christened. Little is known about Iñigo's five sisters.[2]

ARMY, CHURCH, OR COURT

As the last son of a family of provincial gentry, three career paths were open to Iñigo: the army, the Church, or the court. Sometime between 1504 and 1507 (the year of his father's death), Iñigo was sent as a page to the household of the *contador mayor,* the royal treasurer of Castille, Juan Velázquez de Cuellar. De Cuellar served as a member of the Royal Council, and his services required him to follow the peripatetic court of King Ferdinand and

FIGURE 2.2
Young Iñigo Lopez de Loyola
Anonymous 17th Century,
in the Casa Professa, Rome.

Queen Isabella. After the death of Isabella in 1504, he served as one of the executors of her will. De Cuellar's wife, Maria de Velasco, was a particular favorite of Ferdinand's second wife, the bibulous Germaine de Foix. Iñigo traveled around Spain in high court circles for at least ten years, until de Cuellar's death in 1517.

Religiously and socially, the Spain of Ferdinand and Isabella was still a medieval kingdom. At the urging of their confessor, Tomás de Torquemada, *los reyes católicos* instituted the Inquisition throughout their realm and conducted a long and successful domestic crusade against the Moors who had occupied parts of the Iberian peninsula since the eighth century. In 1492, the same year they routed the Moors, Ferdinand and Isabella exiled from the realm all Jews who would not convert to Christianity.

Politically, though, Spain was already inclining toward the Age of Absolutism. After more than a century of civil wars, the *hermandades*, confederations of local towns, were willing to forgo hard-won independence in favor of political stability guaranteed by a strong central monarchy. The forging together of Isabella's Castille and Ferdinand's Aragon, the retaking of Granada in 1492, and the conquest of Naples in 1503 marked Spain's successful entry into Mediterranean power politics. During the first quarter of the sixteenth century, the acquisition of the Kingdom of Navarre, the first harvests of riches from the colonies of the New World, and the creation of the Hispano-Hapsburg empire under Charles V gave Spain super-power status.

Ignatius' *Autobiography,* dictated near the end of his life to Luis Gonçalves da Câmara, evocatively depicts the waning years of medieval chivalry in Spain. Addicted to popular romantic novels, well known at the gaming tables, and a favorite of the ladies, "given over to the vanities of the world, [Iñigo] took special delight in the exercise of arms, with a great and vain desire of winning fame."[3] There is some evidence that the particular object of his romantic attentions was the Infanta Catalina, daughter of Juana "La Loca" and Ferdinand of Austria. His friend and biographer Pedro de Ribadeneyra described Iñigo as a lively and trim young man, very fond of court dress and good living.[4] Although he never renounced his Catholic faith, his practice was casual.

After de Cuellar's death, Iñigo served for four years as a gentleman-in-waiting to Don Antonio Manrique de Lara, duke of Nájera and Viceroy of Navarre. During this period he acted as a messenger for the Viceroy and sometimes served as a kind of under-sheriff or justice of the peace.

In 1521, Iñigo's comfortable world of medieval romance and chivalry was destroyed forever by a French cannonball. During a battle for control of the border town of Pamplona, the young hidalgo's right leg was shattered.

During a long and painful convalescence at the family manor at Loyola, only two books were available to help fill his tedious days: a life of Christ by the Carthusian Ludolphus of Saxony and the *Flos Sanctorum,* the legends of the saints by the Dominican Jacobus de Voragine. Iñigo discovered that when he contemplated returning to his former life he was satisfied while the thought lasted, but that it brought no lasting contentment. When, however, he thought of following the example of the saints and giving his life in service to Christ, lasting consolation followed.

Like all intensely personal experiences, Iñigo's conversion was contextualized, filtered, and fitted out with his own personal conceptual furnishings. When Iñigo read the lives of the great preaching saints Francis and Dominic, he decided that he himself would become a preaching knight-errant in the service of Christ, "the eternal prince of all the knights of God, who are the saints."[5] He daydreamed of outdoing the holy penitents with the severity of his mortifications. The drama of the medieval quest and the romance of the grand chivalrous gesture informed his desire to embark on a single-handed crusade to reconquer Jerusalem for the Faith.

Some 75 years before Cervantes' Don Quixote appeared, a lame former knight made a vigil-at arms before the Lady of Montserrat. There he laid down his sword at her feet and after swapping his rich clothes for a beggar's rags, set off toward Jerusalem. The pilgrim quest for Jerusalem, the longing for the crusade, became the *leit motif* for the next 15 years of his life, until it was supplanted in his imagination by the dominant image of another religious capital, Rome.

MANRESA

Iñigo got as far as Manresa, a village not far from Barcelona on the banks of the river Cardoner. There he spent almost eleven months. Those months marked the beginning of his pilgrim's crusade through time, space, and experience that would end at Rome in 1537.

At Manresa, Iñigo underwent a broad range of experiences, attacks of scruples, ill health, dramatic mood-swings, comatose raptures, and suicidal episodes. He suffered a kind of psyco-spiritual breakdown, the sort of liminal experience that characterizes all great initiation rituals. At the end of this period he received the greatest mystical graces of his life, and from this period date the most important insights and the first jottings that developed into the *Spiritual Exercises.*[6]

Iñigo himself later called this period "my primitive Church."[7] In a certain sense, he retreated in time, as surely as he distanced himself physically from the courtly world that no longer allured him. What he did, in fact, was unconsciously to mirror the actions and experiences of the first Christian monks who rejected the urban world of the late Roman Empire and fled into the Egyptian desert. Iñigo the medieval courtier, like Anthony, Pachomius, and Jerome a millennium before him, abandoned the glitter of an ambiguous world, and retired into the solitude of the cave. He did not, however, remain fixed in that remote past. Rather, focused by his experience, he moved through it toward the next epoch, the next great rite of passage, the Crusade.

In 1523, Iñigo set out in deliberate poverty on his journey to the Holy Land, traveling first to Rome to receive a pilgrim's safe-conduct and the customary papal blessing. In his *Autobiography*, Iñigo captured the contemporary Spanish attitude toward Renaissance Rome when he recounted his conversation with a benefactor in Barcelona:

> *When he begged from a lady, she asked where he wanted to go. He hesitated a bit whether he would tell her, but at last he resolved to say no more than that he was going to Italy and to Rome. Surprised, she said, "Do you want to go to Rome? Well, I don't know how those who go there come back." By this she meant that in Rome they profited little from the things of the spirit.*[8]

FIGURE 2.3
Iñigo's pilgrimage to Jerusalem 1523.

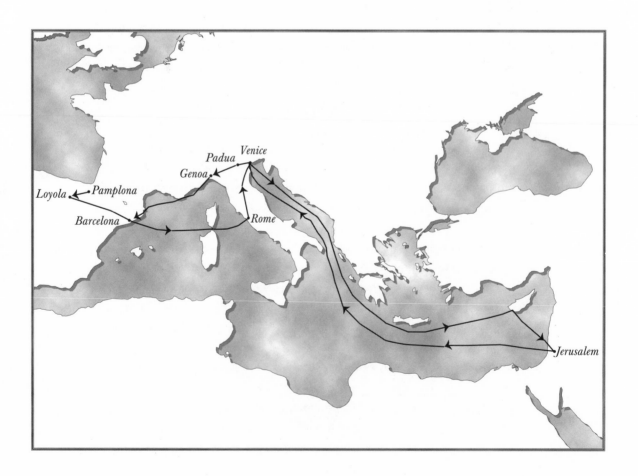

The Rome Iñigo found in Holy Week of 1523 was basking in melancholy twilight after the worldly noonday splendor of the pontificates of Julius II (Della Rovere) and Leo X (Medici). The ascetic Dutch Pope Hadrian VI (Dedal), himself a former tutor and regent of Charles V, had hoped to reform the Church but was distracted by threats of war with the French and the real possibility of a Turkish invasion. During his stay in Rome Iñigo probably lodged in the Spanish hospice of S. Giacomo in Piazza Navona.

After receiving a safe-conduct, Iñigo continued his journey on foot to Venice. He often slept in doorways and outside city gates because of the guards set up against the pestilence. Upon arriving in Venice he begged his bread and camped out in St. Mark's Square.

Iñigo traveled to the Holy Land via Cyprus in the summer of 1523, arriving in Jerusalem on September 4. He fervently made the usual pilgrim round of the Christian shrines and resolved to stay and wage his own *reconquista* to convert the "infidels" who occupied the holy places. The Franciscan Guardian of Mount Zion, Angelo da Ferrara, however, knew trouble when he saw it. Invoking a mandate of governance from the Holy See that included the power of excommunication, he forbade Iñigo to remain, ordering him, for his own safety and because of the volatile political climate of the moment, to return to Europe on the next boat.

Thus Iñigo's romantic vision of a crusade collided with the harsh realities of the wider world he began to encounter in his travels. Ever one to learn from experience, he realized that he needed more training and a more credible platform from which to launch his inchoate apostolic work. During his return journey to Spain, he made a crucial decision: "After the pilgrim realized that it was not God's will that he remain in Jerusalem, he continually pondered within himself what he ought to do. At last he inclined more to study for some time so he would be able to help souls, and he decided to go to Barcelona."[9] The 33 year old's audacious yet humble decision to return to the benches of elementary school "so he would be able to help souls" marks the beginning of his passage into an adult comprehension of a post-medieval world whose focus was increasingly professional and urban. It was his first practical step away from his childhood realm of medieval romance toward the real and complex modern world.

From 1524 through 1535, Iñigo's pilgrimage continued as he systematically acquired the educational and professional tools he needed for his future work. He returned to Barcelona, where for two years he studied Latin, the indispensable tool for scholarly work in his times. There, under the tutelage of Jerónimo Aredévol, he encountered for the first time the newer, more humanistic trends in pedagogy: his Latin studies included excerpts from Vergil, Seneca, and Dionysius Cato as well as from the Fathers of the Church.

ALCALÁ

After his examinations, Iñigo was admitted to the new University of Alcalá, the center of humanistic learning in Spain. There he studied scholastic philosophy and theology for 18 months. At Alcalá his private work in spiritual direction and counseling caused Iñigo to run afoul of the Inquisition. He was briefly imprisoned and was examined on three distinct occasions. Although in each instance the charges were dismissed, Iñigo and his companions were ordered "not to speak about matters of faith until they had studied for four more years, because they had no learning. For in truth, the pilgrim was the one who knew the most, though his learning had little foundation."[10]

SALAMANCA

With his situation at Alcalá untenable, Iñigo moved to the other great Spanish university at Salamanca—and more trouble. Shortly after his arrival Iñigo languished in chains for 22 days at the Dominican convent while the Inquisition examined his orthodoxy and, in particular, his *Spiritual Exercises*.[11]

PARIS

As at Alcalá, no error was found in his life or teaching, although the requirement of four years of theological studies was again imposed before Iñigo could teach about controversial technical matters like the distinction between mortal and venial sin. When Spanish doors slammed behind him, Iñigo

> decided to go to Paris to study. When the pilgrim was reflecting at Barcelona, he was considering whether he should study and how much, his entire concern was whether, after he had studied, he should enter religion or go about in the world. . . . Now at the time of his imprisonment in Salamanca the same desire to help souls, and for that reason to study first and to gather some others for the same purpose and to keep those he had, did not fail him.[12]

Iñigo's sojourn at Paris lasted seven years, from February 1528 to March 1535. For seven years, he lived in the intellectual capital of Catholic Europe and attended the University of Paris, which numbered 50 colleges and 4,000 students. For seven years he lived downtown in Europe's largest city: Paris had an immense population of more than 200,000 inhabitants.[13]

During his student years at Paris, Iñigo traveled at least three times to Spanish-dominated Flanders where, in Antwerp and Bruges, he encountered both Spanish benefactors and the followers of Erasmus. Most probably in 1531, he also visited London, where he received large gifts from Spanish courtiers for his own and other needy students' expenses. By the time Ignatius settled definitively in Rome in 1537, he had visited, with the exception of those in Germany, most of Western Europe's major cities.

Iñigo first studied humanities for a year and a half at the ultra-traditionalist Collège Montaigu, which had been bitterly satirized by its alumni Erasmus and Rabelais. As Iñigo arrived at the Collège Montaigu, John Calvin was finishing his philosophical studies there, but there is no evidence that they ever met. In 1529 Iñigo transferred to the more progressive Collège Sainte-Barbe, then a center of Catholic humanism.

In the records of the University the name "Ignatius Loyola" appeared for the first time in 1529.[14] He received his licentiate in philosophy in 1534, which he followed with courses in scholastic theology at the Dominican Collège Saint-Jacques, also known as the "Collège des Jacobins" for their large convent located by the city walls at the Porte Saint-Jacques.

During his Parisian years, Ignatius attracted an international group of companions who formed the nucleus of the Society of Jesus. Spaniards Francisco Javier, Diego Laínez, Alfonso Salmerón, and Nicholás Bobadilla,

FIGURE 2.4

Paris
Woodcut from Sebastiano
Munster's *Cosmologia Universalis*,
1550.

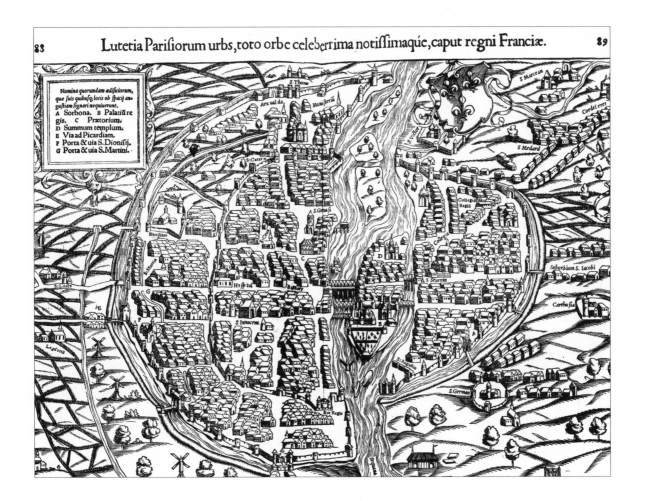

Portuguese Simão Rodrigues, and Savoyard Pierre Favre all made the Spiritual Exercises and frequently joined Ignatius for prayer and companionship. As their studies drew to a close in 1534, this loose fraternity formalized itself by a promise or informal vow:

> to go . . . to Jerusalem to spend their lives in the service of souls; and if they were not given permission to remain in Jerusalem, they would return to Rome and present themselves to the vicar of Christ, so that he could make use of them wherever he thought it to be to the greater glory of God and the service of souls.[15]

Although the image of the crusade to Jerusalem still loomed large in his consciousness, Ignatius' prior experience, and, it can be argued, his maturing perspective of the needs of the Church acquired in his years of study and travel, caused him to build into the first sketch of the Society of Jesus a particular focus on the person and office of the Roman pontiff.

Shortly after receiving his master of arts degree at the age of 44, and

FIGURE 2.5

Travels of Ignatius, 1524–1537.

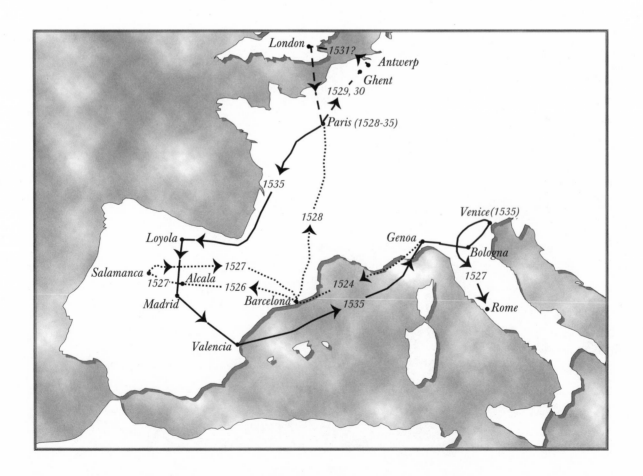

after another brush with the Inquisition,[16] Ignatius' health—he suffered severe abdominal pain from chronic gallstones for the last 25 years of his life—forced him to leave Paris to seek a cure in his "native air" of Guipúzcoa. Before his departure, his companions promised to meet him in Venice in 1537 once they had completed their studies in Paris.

"HIS NATIVE AIR"

Following the traditional pilgrim route from Paris towards Compostella, Ignatius arrived in Azpeitia in April 1535. He refused to live at his family manor because one of his nephews was living there in open concubinage, and resided instead at the Hospital of Santa Maria Magdalena, a hospice for beggars. During his three months in Azpeitia, he engaged in a variety of apostolic works. He preached and taught catechism. Through the authority of his brother Martín, the protector of the local Church, Ignatius promulgated 53 *ordenanzas* for the reform of the clergy and organized a permanent charitable foundation that took up a collection each Sunday and saw to the equitable distribution of alms to the truly needy.[17] This initiative for the rural poor who came into the relatively wealthy town of Azpeitia to beg was perhaps modeled on the ideals of social welfare enunciated in humanist Juan Luis Vives' well-known *De subventione pauperum,* published in Bruges in 1526. Ignatius had, in fact, met and dined with Vives on his first begging trip to Bruges in 1529.[18]

Departing from Azpeitia in July, 1535, Ignatius traveled to Javier, Almázan, and Madrid, where he met the ten year old Crown Prince Philip, later Philip II, who vividly recalled the encounter 51 years later.[19] Ignatius continued on to Toledo and Valencia. After a stormy sea passage to Genoa, he went on foot to Bologna to continue his studies, but the climate there proved unhealthly for him. At the end of 1535 he moved to Venice, where he continued his studies in private while awaiting the arrival of his companions in 1537.

VENICE

Prior Andrea Lippomano, "a man very learned and good,"[20] welcomed Ignatius at the Priory of the Holy Trinity, a hospice for reform-minded churchmen and scholars. Girolamo Emiliani, founder of the Order of Clerics Regular of Somasca that was dedicated to the care of orphans, had spent 1534 under Lippomano's roof. Lippomano's spiritual father, Bishop Gian Pietro Carafa, co-founder of the Order of Clerics Regular or "Theatines," probably first encountered Ignatius there.[21] Lippomano was to become one of the Society of Jesus' most ardent supporters, founding a residential college for Jesuit students in Padua in 1541; Carafa, as Pope Paul IV, was one of its most implacable foes.

During 1536, the year of Erasmus' death and Calvin's publication of *The Institutes of the Christian Religion,* Ignatius pursued his theological studies privately, taking advantage of Lippomano's extensive library. It is clear from an autograph document of that year, however, that Ignatius was seriously considering the shape and design of religious life.

IGNATIUS
AND THE THEATINES

The document is a letter or copy of a letter, unaddressed but almost certainly directed to Carafa, in which Ignatius provided an uninvited and unwelcome critique of the recently-founded "Theatines."[22] Although there is some doubt as to whether the letter was ever sent, Carafa's animosity towards Ignatius from as early as 1537 suggests that even if the text was not physically delivered, its contents almost certainly were communicated.[23]

The letter is of major importance. It is the earliest written document in which Ignatius sketches out his ideas of an aggressive, interactive urban ministry. The core of Ignatius' criticism of the Theatines is that while they reside in the city they do not converse with it. From their beginnings (1524), the Theatines lived in pious retreat from a world they condemned as tainted by sin and corruption. In a letter of October 9, 1532, Carafa summarized their inward-turning tendency: "Because it is necessary in these evil days, we gladly stay in the house, with wondrous love, fleeing from every practical engagement."[24]

IGNATIUS' CRITIQUE

Ignatius' critique is grounded on his own personal commitment to the "*greater* praise and service of the Lord." Even at this early stage in his own theorizing, his understanding of that *greater* or the *"magis"* is one of the characteristic notes of Ignatian spirituality, an explosive rather than implosive principle that precipitates a confrontation with the world and requires active engagement with it for the "good of souls."

He criticized the Theatines on three counts: that their closed-minded attitude would discourage others from joining them, thus limiting the good they could accomplish; that Carafa's episcopal life-style was a potential source of dissension within a congregation not only pledged to poverty but forbidden to beg; and finally, and centrally, that the totally contemplative focus of the Theatines, while admirable in theory, cut them off from the necessary business of the Church, the preaching of the gospel and the works of mercy. Implicit in all three points is Ignatius' own incarnational optimism that would shape the Society of Jesus in an essentially positive missionary stance toward the world, rather than in retreat from it.

Ignatius' companions, whose number had swelled to ten with the addition of Paschase Broët, Claude Jay, and Jean Codure, arrived in Venice early in 1537, and during the interval between late winter and an anticipated summer departure for the Holy Land they decided to live in various hospitals and to work serving the sick. Toward the middle of March, the "masters of Paris" traveled to Rome. Only Ignatius remained in Venice, perhaps fearing that a Roman encounter with old adversaries from Paris and with

Carafa, recently named a cardinal, might jeopardize the companions' chance of obtaining permission for priestly ordination and the requisite safe-conduct for the pilgrimage.[25] In fact, they were warmly received by Pope Paul III (Farnese, pope from 1534-1549) and received the permissions and a monetary gift from members of the Papal Court. After their return to Venice, they were ordained priests (except for Favre, Jay, and Broët, who were already priests, and Salmerón, who was not yet 23 years old) under the dual *titulus* of voluntary poverty and sufficient learning.[26]

THE FIRST DIASPORA

In Venice, the newly ordained companions engaged in street preaching and during the summer they scattered to the major cities of the Veneto. The voyage to Jerusalem, in fact, proved impossible that year. Mounting tension between the Republic of Venice and the Turks closed the sea lanes to the eastern Mediterranean. For the first time in 38 years no pilgrim ship sailed to the Holy City.[27] Their pilgrimage blocked, the companions gathered once again, this time in Vicenza, and there formed a plan of focused apostolic work. The cities chosen were either strategic centers of population like Venice, Vicenza, and Ferrara or important university towns like Bologna, Padua, and Siena "in order to see if Our Lord would deign to call some students to our institute."[28] Before dispersing, they decided on a name for their group: "given that they had no other superior except Jesus Christ whom alone they desired to serve, it seemed to them most fitting that they should take the name of him whom they had as their head, by calling themselves the 'company of Jesus.'"[29]

LA STORTA

Late in 1537, Ignatius himself, accompanied by Laínez and Favre, set out on the last leg of his pilgrim journey. On the outskirts of Rome, in a ruined roadside chapel at La Storta on the Via Cassia, Ignatius had his second great mystical experience, a vision that clarified his mission. In that vision, he saw Jesus carrying his cross and heard God the Father ask Jesus to take Ignatius beside him into his service. In the vision Jesus told Ignatius, "I want you to serve us."

Diego Laínez, Ignatius' companion and the second superior general of the Society, recalled the event in this way:

> As we were coming along the road from Siena here to Rome, it happened that our Father [Ignatius] received many spiritual consolations. He told me that it seemed to him as if God the Father had imprinted the following words in his heart: "Ego ero vobis Romae propitius: I will be propitious to you in Rome." Since our father did not know what these words might mean, he remarked: "I do not know what will happen to us: maybe we will be crucified in Rome." Another time, he said that he seemed to see Christ with the cross on his shoulder, and the Eternal

Father said to him "I will that you take this man for your servant." And so Jesus took him, and said "I will that you should serve us." Because of this, seized by great devotion to this most holy name, he [Ignatius] wanted the congregation called "the Company of Jesus."[30]

After more than 15 years of pilgrimage, Ignatius Loyola experienced in a new and more profound way the call to service he had first heard at the time of his conversion. At the gates of the Holy City of Catholicism, he exchanged his pilgrim's staff for the preacher's cross and went in search of crossroads where he could preach his crucified Lord.

FIGURE 2.6

The Vision at La Storta,
Engraving from Ribadeneyra's
Vita Beati Patris Ignatii, ca. 1610.

CHAPTER III
"BUT OF YESTERDAY"

In many ways, the Rome Ignatius entered in 1537 resembled the Jerusalem Jesus entered 1500 years before. Rome and Jerusalem were sites of strategic importance and intense psychological resonance for their peoples, and both shared a tradition of theocratic leadership. Each was an important cultic capital whose history was bound up in sacred traditions of theophany and epiphany. Finally, neither Rome nor Jerusalem had a population proportional to its cultural and socio-religious importance: Rome of 1537 A.D. and Jerusalem of 30 A.D. each numbered somewhere between 40,000 and 50,000 inhabitants.[1]

OLD TESTAMENT IMAGES Two physical images dominate the iconic landscape of the Old Testament: the Promised Land and the Holy City, Jerusalem. The entry into the Promised Land marked a psychic as well as a sociological shift, as a nomadic people became a settled population. After the long struggle for domination of the land in the period of the Judges, David's establishment of Jerusalem as his capital city and Solomon's construction of the permanent Temple of Yahweh to replace the wandering Tent of Meeting (ca. 1000 B.C.) marked Israel's coming of age.

The image of the city and of Jerusalem in the Old Testament is highly equivocal. A positive theology of Jerusalem as City of God is found in the book of Psalms:

> On the holy mount stands the city God founded; the Lord loves the gates of Zion more than all the dwelling places of Jacob. Glorious things are spoken of you, O city of God. (Ps. 87. 1-3)

> Some wandered in desert wastes, finding no way to a city to dwell in; hungry and thirsty, their soul fainted within them. Then they cried to the Lord

in their distress; he led them by a straight way, until they reached a city to dwell in. (Ps. 107. 4-7)

In the sacred texts, then, the city can represent the fulfillment of God's promise to the people of Israel, a symbol of refuge and sanctuary.

In the writings of the prophets Jeremiah and Ezekiel, however, the city is portrayed as a negative vortex that sucks its inhabitants into idolatry and unfaithfulness:

> *This is the city which must be punished; there is nothing but oppression within her. . . . Be warned, O Jerusalem, lest I be alienated from you; lest I make you a desolation, an uninhabited land. (Jer. 6.6, 8)*

> *Because the people have forsaken me, and have profaned this place by burning incense in it to other gods whom neither they nor their ancestors nor the kings of Judah have known . . . therefore the days are coming, says the Lord, when this place shall be called the valley of slaughter . . . and I will make this city a horror, a thing to be hissed at, every one who passes by it will be horrified and will hiss because of all its disasters. (Jer. 19. 4, 6, 8)*

The destruction of Jerusalem and the deportation of the Hebrew people to Babylon in the sixth century B.C. gave rise to an immense nostalgia for the Holy City and to an important secondary strand of apocalyptic prophecy that foretold destruction and the raising of the eschatological "New" Jerusalem (e.g. Ezekiel 48). This strand later provided the fundamental imagery for the last canonical book of the New Testament, the Book of Revelation of John the Evangelist.

JESUS AND JERUSALEM

Jesus' mission was focused on Galilee: he "went about in all their towns and villages, teaching in their synagogues and preaching the gospel of the kingdom, and healing every disease and every infirmity" (Mt. 9. 35). The culture of Palestine at the time of Jesus was essentially rural and agrarian, although frequent pilgrimages to Jerusalem punctuated the devout Jew's religious life. Jerusalem, rebuilt by Cyrus the Great, fell first to the Greeks and then to the Romans, who allowed the temple priesthood to arbitrate the social and cultic life of the nation. Jesus' crucifixion and death, choreographed to take place in the Holy City at the time of the most important feast of the religious year, can be interpreted as a hierarchical attempt on the part of both the Roman civic and Jewish cultic leadership to put down a troublesome small town sect leader who disrupted their carefully crafted coexistence.

THE APOSTOLIC PREACHING

Although Jesus' personal mission was largely addressed to Galilee, the Acts of the Apostles recounts that the focus of the apostolic Church was firmly fixed on cities. On the day of Pentecost, Peter's inspired preaching converted a large number of Jews of the Diaspora gathered in Jerusalem from all over the world:

> *Parthians, Medes, and Elamites, residents of Mesopotamia, Judea and Cappadocia, Pontus and Asia, Phrygia and Pamphylia, Egypt and the parts of Libya belonging to Cyrene, visitors from Rome, both Jews and proselytes, Cretans and Arabians . . . hear them telling in their own tongues the mighty works of God"* (Acts 2. 9-11).

Even allowing for rhetorical exaggeration, the accounts in Acts of large conversions—the Church quickly growing from 120 to 3,000 to 5,000 to "many thousands"—suggest that "the Way" was followed by significant numbers of Jews in the period of its early preaching at Jerusalem.

CITIZEN PAUL

The greatest of the preachers and travelers of the Apostolic Age was, of course, Paul of Tarsus, whose conversion on the road to Damascus marked the remote beginnings of the mission to the Gentiles. A rabbi himself, of the Pharisee faction, and a Roman citizen by birth, Paul exploded the earliest understanding that the message of Jesus was addressed only to the Jewish world. Through persuasive argument—and inspired bullying—he persuaded the first eye witnesses of the "Jesus event" to allow him to preach to and baptize Greek-speaking "gentiles" without forcing them to accept circumcision and complete adherence to the Mosaic law. Paul traveled more than 10,000 miles as he crisscrossed the Mediterranean, preaching in the most important cities of Syria (Antioch), Asia Minor (Ephesus), Greece (Athens and Corinth), and Italy (Rome).[2]

Paul was proud of his Roman citizenship and taught that there was no inherent contradiction between the Christian message and civic requirements of life in the Roman world (Rom. 13.1–7). Using civic language, he called himself an "ambassador" to the local churches (Eph. 6.20, Philem. 1.9). Indeed, he used his citizenship to appeal his case when accused of impiety by his fellow Jews in Jerusalem and thus received a safe-conduct to Rome, where he preached under loose house arrest for more than two years (ca. 60 A.D.). Persistent traditions date the Roman martyrdom of Paul and Peter to Nero's persecution after the city burned in 64 A.D.

THE URBAN DIASPORA

Paul's audience included the Jews of the Diaspora—some five to six million scattered throughout the cities of the Roman empire, who often composed up to 15 percent of the urban populations—as well as gentile members of all but the highest social classes. His largest following, and the most significant early growth of the Church in general, occurred among members of his own class, that of free artisans, humble city folk who occupied the stratum just above slaves in the social pyramid.[3]

In its first centuries, Christianity had no centralized organizational structure, and hence no programmatic missionary or evangelizing works were carried out. The Christian "Way" or message traveled, rather haphazardly, with traders and travelers who traversed the Empire.[4] In 110, Pliny the Younger, Trajan's legate to Bithynia and Pontus on the southeastern shores of the Black Sea, described the composition and diffusion of the Christian communities he encountered there: "Persons of all ages and ranks, and of both sexes are, and will be, involved in this prosecution. For this contagious superstition is not confined to the cities only, but has spread through the villages and rural districts; it seems possible, however, to check and cure it."[5]

Sporadic persecutions of the Christian community were the exception rather than the rule. For most of its early history, Christianity was generally tolerated by the Romans, at first as a sectarian offshoot of Judaism and later as an independent cultic group that organized its own *collegia* for social services like feeding the hungry and burial of the dead. Each urban community was usually based in a house or *domus ecclesiae,* and they often held title to their own cemeteries.

ESCHATOLOGY VS. REALITY

From its beginnings, a tension existed in the Christian community between the eschatological promise of Jesus and the reality of life lived in the here-and-now. Jesus had promised to return soon to establish the Kingdom of God, but he himself professed not to know "the day or hour." This eschatological tendency, most fully developed in the extravagant imagery of the book of Revelations, called for a flight from the world in order to prepare for the Second Coming of Christ. Rome was identified with Babylon, and any compromises with "the world" were seen as defections or betrayals.[6]

ESCHATOLOGY
AND APOLOGETICS

Although sympathetic to such tendencies, Paul was himself the first of the great Christian apologists, attempting to translate the Christian message into the cultural idiom of the Graeco-Roman world. In his sermon at the Areopagus in Athens, he attempted to show that the God of Christian revelation was the "unknown god" of the Greek philosophers (Acts 17:19ff.). The great apologists of the second century, in particular Justin Martyr and Clement of Alexandria, followed his lead: they attempted to show that Christianity recapitulated the best of the learning of Graeco-Roman culture, that Plato and the Sibyls were pointing the way, albeit unknowingly, to Christ.

On the other side were writers like Tertullian and Tatian, rigorous integralists who denied any intellectual *rapprochement* between Christian revelation and secular wisdom. Tertullian summarized the discontinuity in a famous passage:

[Paul] had been at Athens, and had in his interviews become acquaint-
ed with that human wisdom which pretends to know the truth, whilst it
only corrupts it, and is itself divided into its own manifold heresies, by
the variety of its mutually repugnant sects. What indeed has Athens to do
with Jerusalem? What concord is there between the Academy and the
Church? What between heretics and Christians?[7]

In spite of the discontinuity between Christianity and secular culture, Tertullian was quick to point out the demographic fact of the community's quick growth and its integration into every level of society:

We are called to account as harm-doers on another ground, and are
accused of being useless in the affairs of life. How in the world can that
be the case with people who are living among you, eating the same food,
wearing the same attire, having the same habits, under the same necessi-
ties of existence. We are not Indian Brahmins or Gymnosophists who
dwell in woods and exile themselves from ordinary human life. . . . We
make sojourn with you in the world, abjuring neither forum, nor sham-
bles, nor bath, nor booth, nor workshop, nor inn, nor weekly market, nor
any other place of commerce. We sail with you, and fight with you, and
till the ground with you; and in like manner we unite with you in your
traffickings—even in the various arts we make public property of our
works for your benefit.[8]

If we desired, indeed, to act the part of open enemies, would there be any
lacking in strength, whether of numbers or resources? . . . We are but of
yesterday, and we have filled every place among you—cities, islands,
fortresses, towns, market-places, the very camp, tribes, companies, place,
senate, forum—we have left nothing to you but the temples of your gods.[9]

URBAN CHRISTIANITY

In the third century, Christian communities continued to grow, predominantly in urban settings.[10] Their ubiquity, as Tertullian had pointed out, was complemented by the fact that their lives were outwardly not different from the ordinary citizen's. The third–century Epistle to Diognetus developed an important theme, the Christian as "sojourner":

Christians are not distinguished from the rest of humanity either in local-
ity or in speech or in customs. For they do not dwell off in cities of their
own, nor do they practice an extraordinary style of life. . . . They dwell
in their own countries, but only as sojourners. . . . Every foreign country
is fatherland to them, and every fatherland is a foreign country.[11]

It was their very ubiquity, the "cockney" nature of their culture, which allowed them to spread throughout the empire, and which led to the last persecutions late in the third century.[12]

In a letter of 251 A.D., the Roman bishop Cornelius claimed jurisdiction over 46 presbyters, seven deacons, seven subdeacons, 42 acolytes, 52 exorcists, readers, and doorkeepers, and more than 1,500 widows and others were supported by Church collections. Extrapolation from these figures suggests a community of between 30,000 and 50,000 persons.[13] Shortly thereafter, Bishop Dionysius established parochial structures in Rome, and the model was used throughout the empire.[14] When the Emperor Diocletian reorganized the Empire into smaller administrative units called "dioceses" at the end of the third century, that terminology was adopted for the local epicospal "sees" (see = *sedes,* city where the bishop's teaching seat or *cathedra* was located).

Although it is impossible to measure the relative density of local congregations, rosters from local church synods of the mid to late third century report that there were Christian churches scattered in cities, towns, and villages throughout the entire Roman world. Neo-Platonic philosopher Porphyry loudly lamented the fact that Christians were building large meeting halls to rival traditional temples; indeed, when Diocletian built a palace in Nicomedia, one of the imperial capitals, a Christian church crowning a nearby hill was clearly visible from it.[15] Eusebius, writing half a century later, rhapsodized about the growing strength and numbers of Christian adherents: "How could one describe those mass meetings, the enormous gatherings in every city, and the remarkable congregations in places of worship? No longer satisfied with the old buildings, they raised from the foundations in all the cities churches spacious in plan."[16]

A SENSE OF BELONGING

The reasons for the rapid spread of Christianity throughout the Empire are complex: as the Empire began to contract, there was a generalized move toward spiritual introversion that supported the expansion of Christianity and other Eastern mystery cults. In a world defined by bonds of association and patronage, the Christian community provided a ready-made "solidarity group" that transcended class and caste lines. Cultural historian Peter Brown describes the climate:

> *The Christian community suddenly came to appeal to men and women who felt deserted. At a time of inflation, the Christians invested large sums of liquid capital in people; at a time of increased brutality the courage of Christian martyrs was impressive; during public emergencies such as plague or rioting the Christian clergy were shown to be the only united group in town, able to look after the burial of the dead and to organize food-supplies. . . . Plainly, to be a Christian in 250 brought more protection from one's fellows than to be a* civis romanus. [17]

In spite of this rapid growth and to a certain extent because of it, tensions arose within the early Church. Lengthy, bitter controversies arose over the issue of readmission of the so-called *lapsi,* those who had denied the faith during the persecutions of 250 and 257–60. Theological arguments– attempts to define orthodox teaching as opposed to heresy–split many communities. Finally, general acceptance of Christianity caused many to fear that the pristine splendor of the Church of the Martyrs would be polluted by commerce with the secular world.

EARLY MONASTICISM

One response to these challenges was a radical turning-away, a rejection of the urban world, its pomps, and works. Following the example of the Anthony of Egypt (251–356 A.D.), who took literally the gospel's injunction "if you would be perfect, go, sell what you possess and give it to the poor . . . and follow me" (Mt. 19.21), thousands fled into the deserts of Egypt, Palestine, and Syria to seek individual perfection away from the temptations of the world. A more archaic, apocalyptic suspicion of the world challenged the ordinary Christian attitude of indifference to it. A focal point of that suspicion was the organizational Church itself as it became increasingly politicized.[18] The monk, "the solitary one," deliberately chose the silence of the desert far removed from the roar of gladiators in the coliseum and the bickering of bishops and theologians in the cathedral.[19]

CIVIC RECOGNITION

Constantine's recognition of Christianity early in the fourth century moved the Christian church solidly into the center of public life. Particularly in the declining Western Empire, Catholic clergy took on roles of leadership and public responsibility: its bishops, (*episkopoi,* literally "overseers") became imperial civil servants, and its presbyters or elders often became civic as well as religious aldermen. Huge imperial-sponsored building campaigns erected Christian cultic centers in the major cities of the Empire, a public works program larger than any undertaken since the time of Alexander the Great.[20]

In Rome itself, residual pagan influence, particularly in the Senate, led Constantine to site the Christian holy places outside the *pomoerium,* the traditional center of the city delineated by the Servian Wall.[21] The large episcopal complex at the Lateran and the site of S. Croce had previously been private holdings of the imperial family, and the *martyria* of Ss. Pietro, Agnese, Lorenzo (fuori le mura), and the Apostles (S. Sebastiano) were all outside the city limits. Opposition from the conservative pagan bloc in Rome was a strong factor in Constantine's decision to move the imperial capital east to the new city of Constantinople. There, the catechumen emperor was free to design a new city in which palace and patriarchal basilica were side by side, and his sarcophagus was planned as the thirteenth in the monumental *Heroon* of the Twelve Apostles.[22]

CENOBITES AND HERMITS

Even after the official recognition of Christianity in the fourth century, eastern monasticism, particularly in the cenobitic form developed under Pachomius (†346), continued to attract large numbers. With the close of the age of the martyrs and confessors, organized monastic life proposed to the virtuous a new model of Christian heroism, and to the pragmatic, a relatively secure and tax-free haven in a very insecure world. As interpreted by Basil (†379), the monk's ascetic life was not an end in itself but a way of opening the heart to the love of God and neighbor taught in the gospels. Thus, Basilian monasteries tended to be located near towns where the monks could perform apostolic works, particularly in service to the poor.[23]

In the first century of Christianity's official establishment in the West, two forms of religious life emerged. Inspired by Athanasius' immensely popular *Life of Anthony*, many hermits took to the hills around the Mediterranean basin. Martin left Ligugé, Honoratus (Lerins), John Cassian (Marseilles), Ambrose (Milan), and Jerome (Rome, Jerusalem, and Bethlehem); all established quasi-eremitical communities in the fourth century. Germanus, a disciple of Martin, carried monastic practices to Britain, and Patrick, who had studied at Lerins and Auxerre, brought them to Ireland early in the fifth century.[24] In a tangential development, North African clerics in the episcopal *curia* of Hippo lived a common life under the leadership of their bishop Augustine.

In 410 A.D., only 15 years after all pagan cults were outlawed, Rome fell to Alaric and his Visigoth invaders. The psychological damage caused by sack of the *caput mundi* was even more devastating than the physical toll it exacted on the urban fabric. Even the acerbic Jerome, who had left Rome in high dudgeon late in the fourth century, lamented, "my voice fails . . . fallen is the city to which the world once fell."[25]

INTERPRETING THE FALL

It fell to Augustine of Hippo to make sense of that fall and to interpret it for the new Christian majority. Pagan critics—as Gibbon did centuries later—attributed the collapse of the empire to the rise of Christianity. In his immense and meandering *De Civitate Dei*, Augustine set out, in the first 12 books, to counter the pagan contention that the abandonment of the "old" gods led to the collapse. In the second half of the work, Augustine explored uncharted terrain: the theological implications of Christian life lived in historical time and space.

THE TWO CITIES

Augustine's early Neo-Platonic and Manichean training left him with a residual distrust of the physical world and, by extension, its institutions. Faced with the reality that the eschatological advent of Christ seemed permanently delayed and with some in the Christian community who read the triumph of Christianity as a sign of the coming of the kingdom of God on earth, Augustine posited two societies or "cities," the City of God and the City of Man. Neither is exactly co-extensive or identifiable with ordinary human society.

> *Now, the first person born of two parents of the human race was Cain. He belonged to the City of Man. The next born was Abel, and he was of the City of God. . . . The fact is that every individual springs from a condemned stock and, because of Adam, must be first cankered and carnal, and only later to become sound and spiritual in Christ. So, too, with the human race as a whole, as soon as human birth and death began the historical course of the two cities, the first to be born was a citizen of this world and only later came the one who was an alien in the city of men but at home in the city of God, a man predestined by grace and elected by grace. By grace an alien on earth, by grace he was a citizen of heaven.[26]*

SOJOURNERS
AND PILGRIMS

Augustine's division of the two cities is strongly grounded in the symbolic language of "sojourning" and "pilgrimage" that described a fundamental dynamic of the Judaeo-Christian religious experience. It is a culture "at its very roots, about experiences of spiritual dislocation and homelessness. The terrors of exposure are at the heart of our religious imagination. Our faith began at odds with place, because our gods themselves were disposed to wander."[27]

Continuing the parallel of the two sons of Adam, Augustine insists that the City of God itself moves on pilgrimage through human time and space, while never being compromised by them:

> *Now it is recorded of Cain that he built a city, while Abel, as though he were merely a pilgrim on earth, built none. For the true city of the saints is in heaven, though here on earth it produces citizens in whom it wanders as on a pilgrimage through time looking for the kingdom of eternity.[28]*

This understanding marked a radical conceptual shift and had sweeping political implications. The *res publica* of good citizenship was supplanted by the *res privata* of individual salvation; the inner quest became more important, more real, than outer diversity. The walls of mighty Rome had failed to protect her citizens from the chaos that lurked just outside. Christians, sojourning in such an uncertain world and on pilgrimage towards the City of God, could at best look for a refuge, a stronghold wherein Church and State would collaborate, howsoever uneasily, to protect them.

CHAPTER IV
RENEGOTIATING THE PERSPECTIVE

he millennium between the fall of Rome and the Italian Renaissance has often been characterized as a dark age, a middle or middling period between two great cultural flowerings. The Fall of Rome—what Cassiodorus called the *communis patria,* the common homestead of humanity—marked the end of an awesome conceptual structure: the idea and ideal of a world empire governed by a single law, ordered by a single cultural vision, ruled from a single place.

The reality was, of course, much more complex. The Western Empire's disintegration was neither complete nor totally unexpected. Since the third century, a complex of social, economic, and political factors had been eroding the West. Once the empire was fully extended in the late second century, there were no new sources of slave labor, on which industry and particularly agriculture depended. Production dropped, and systems of distribution of goods deteriorated. Shortages of precious metals and wage and price controls fed an inflationary spiral. Overextension of borders, increased reliance on mercenaries, and constant, harrowing pressure from the German tribes weakened the army's strategic capabilities. Finally, late antique society suffered an enervating spiritual malaise that sapped creative energies and will. The cumulative result of these and other factors was a sense of "loss of the center."[1]

More and more people retreated as urban centers became less and less viable. The rich fled to country villas, the poor to the countryside where at least food supplies were near to hand. Cities became towns, towns became villages, villages became hamlets. Many former population centers were entirely depopulated, particularly on the fringes of the Empire.

This is not, of course, to say that city life completely disappeared. Rather, throughout Western Europe, horizons narrowed, the scope of public

THE URBAN FABRIC
UNRAVELS

life was drastically reduced, and focus on the local and the circumscribed—a fundamental social descriptor of the feudal world—replaced the Roman notion of citizenship in a world empire.

Cities contracted. Rome herself had once been crowded with upward of one and one half million inhabitants.[2] By the time of Constantine and through 400 A.D., that figure stabilized at about 800,000. After the Visigoth and Vandal invasions, the population fell to about 500,000, and by 500 A.D. to about 100,000. During the Gothic siege perhaps fewer than 30,000 remained; at the time of the sack of Totila (546 A.D.), only 500 able-bodied men were found in the city. Legend has it that for 40 days thereafter the city lay completely empty. By Gregory the Great's time (ca. 600 A.D.), constant migrations of refugees had returned the city's population to about 90,000.[3]

For the next thousand years, Rome's population also fluctuated dramatically because of physical factors: the suburbs died of thirst when imperial aqueducts were ruptured; the failure of the imperial sewage and swamp-drainage systems contributed to widespread diseases, particularly malaria and fevers; periodic floods of the Tiber, earthquakes, fires, and natural disasters checked population growth; and, as always, limited local food supplies necessitated expensive importation, often from as far away as Sicily. Moreover, in the absence of a single unified government and defensive army, central Italy continually fell prey to foreign invasions.

SEES AND MONASTERIES

Until around the beginning of the twelfth century, what "civilization" there was in the West—understood here under the broadest rubrics of social order, minimal economic stability, and at least some access to learning—tended to center around two foci: cities and towns that were episcopal sees, and monasteries.

Particularly in the Mediterranean basin, many Roman towns were continuously occupied, although populations were generally much smaller than during imperial times. Invading tribes, attracted by their wealth and by the residual administrative structures of the Late Empire, often made uneasy alliances with local bishops. Local diocesan *curiae* maintained contact with other bishoprics within their "metropolitanates" and often provided the only sure means of communication with other regions and with the Byzantine imperial court. The Roman See held pride of place in the West, not only because of its historical importance as the former *caput mundi,* but especially because its bishop, as successor of Peter, "prince of the Apostles," claimed precedence over all over patriarchs and metropolitans.

THE SEE OF PETER

Constantine's largesse to the bishops of Rome, Miltiades (311–314) and

Sylvester I (314–331), was legendary. By conferring civic dignities on them and on other bishops, Constantine and his successors prepared a political and social infrastructure that eventually evolved into the imperial papacy. That process, far too long and complicated to detail here in anything but the most schematic outline, saw a millennial ebb and flow of papal political power in the west as invading Goths, Byzantines, Lombards, Franks, and Germans vied for control of Italy and of the Church that provided the West with its only principle of unity and organization. The City of Rome provided the proscenium for many of those struggles.

Once Constantine abandoned "Old" Rome for his "New Rome," Constantinople, the bishop of Rome became the most significant political and social leader in the Western Empire. Caesars came and went, Ostrogothic and Byzantine "dukes" rose and fell, Gothic princes, Frankish "patricians," and "Holy Roman Emperors" crossed the Roman stage, but the bishops of Rome, according to their talents and with varying degrees of success, occupied its center.

THE LATERAN COMPLEX

The physical fabric of the city still shows the impact of the early centuries of papal ascendancy. Constantine's most important gift to the Roman bishop, the Lateran complex (along with S. Croce in Gerusalemme, erected in the palace of the Dowager Empress Helena in the nearby Sessorian Palace) was located just inside the Porta Asinaria, as far as possible from the pagan cultic center in the Roman Forum. His other important constructions for the Christian community were *martyria* and covered cemeteries outside the city walls. As Christianity consolidated its hold on the old imperial capital, its buildings quickly invaded the center of the *pomoerium*. As early as 336, Pope Mark I dedicated the first basilica of S. Marco in the shadow of the Capitol. His successor Julius I (337–352) erected the first Marian church (S. Maria in Trastevere) in the heart of the crowded–and probably largely Christian–neighborhood of Trastevere. Damasus I (366–384), a skilled diplomat and fund raiser, raised a large church dedicated to St. Lawrence (S. Lorenzo in Damaso) and a church archive on the site of his family house in Campo Marzio (present day Palazzo della Cancelleria), as well as S. Anastasia below the Palatine and the immense basilica of S. Paolo fuori le Mura on the Via Ostiense. The building of S. Paolo crowned Damasus' campaign to underscore the apostolic origins of the Roman See and to transpose imperial imagery into an apostolic, and hence papal, register.

The shock of the Sack of Rome in 410 only briefly distracted the emerging papacy from its building programs. Only 15 years later, S. Sabina began to rise on the site of an Aventine villa burned during the sack. Sixtus III (432–440) and his Archdeacon Leo (later Leo I) were responsible for construction of S. Maria Maggiore, the building perhaps most representative of the architectural fusion of late Roman civic and Christian cultic spaces. Its solemn proportions and rich mosaic decorations made a confident visual statement about the permanence and power of the Christian church. No less striking was the architecturally innovative and refined Lateran baptistery, remodeled about the same time.[4]

The fifth century saw an attempt, albeit abortive, to create a "sacred pole" around the remote Lateran complex. Because the shrine of St. Peter was closer to the center of Rome and possessed a rich hoard of relics, it attracted the lion's share of pilgrims and tourists. The Lateran cathedral and the papal palace were increasingly isolated as the declining urban population retreated into the elbow of the Tiber. Close to the Lateran, the building of very large (S. Maria Maggiore and S. Stefano Rotondo) and moderately sized (S. Bibiana and S. Martino) non-parish churches, renovations of S. Croce, and the scheduling of important papal stational liturgies in them, all point to a deliberate attempt to entice the urban population out of the center of town to worship around the episcopal headquarters.[5] This strategy, however, was not successful, and with the passage of each century, the Lateran became ever the more isolated from the life of the city.

LEO AND GELASIUS

The fifth and sixth centuries saw fuller development of the claims of the papacy. Popes like Leo the Great (440–461) and Gelasius I (492–496) insisted that Petrine apostolic succession was grounds for universal religious authority over the entire Church; they took their political role for granted,

FIGURE 4.1

Rome,
Papal quarter around the Cathedral of S. Giovanni in Laterano, showing fifth century churches, detail from Cataro's Large Plan of Rome, 1574.

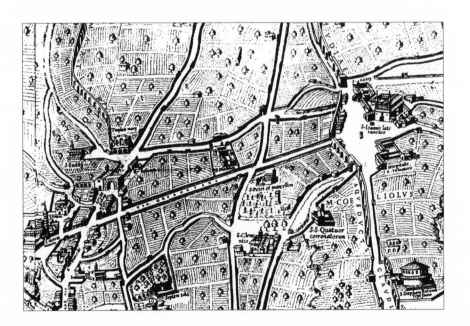

particularly in the governance of the West. Gelasius, the first self-styled "Vicar of Christ," confidently wrote to the Emperor: "there are two powers which for the most part control this world: the sacred authority of priests and the might of kings. Of these two, the office of the priests is the greater in as much as they must give account even for kings to the Lord at the divine judgment."[6]

GREGORY THE GREAT

After more than a century of confusion that saw the rise and fall of the Ostrogothic kings, the Byzantine reconquest of Italy, the Gothic wars, the Longobard invasions, and a long series of natural calamities, the powerful personality of Pope Gregory the Great (590–604) was the only effective governing force in Italy. Gregory ruled not only the devastated city (reduced to about 90,000 inhabitants) but large portions of central Italy (the so-called "Patrimony of St. Peter"), Tuscany, and Sicily.[7] In the century that followed, the church took over a number of imperial buildings. The Pantheon was transformed into the Church of S. Maria ad Martyres, the guardhouse of the Palatine residence of the Byzantine viceroy became the church of S. Maria Antica, the Roman Senate house was consecrated as the church of S. Adriano, and Hadrian's mausoleum near the Vatican was crowned with a chapel dedicated to St. Michael the Archangel. During the same period, an integrated social services network of *diaconiae* was developed throughout the various neighborhoods of the City, under the administration of seven deacons.[8]

Gregory the Great is probably best remembered for sending his own monks to bring the Celtic churches of Britain back into line with Rome. In the brief interval between his tenure as City Prefect and his mission as papal ambassador to Constantinople, Gregory had founded a monastery in his parents' mansion on the sparsely populated Coelian Hill. In doing so, he followed a pattern of withdrawal from the cares of disintegrating city life that was adopted by many disillusioned Christians.

BENEDICT

Foremost among those refugees was Benedict of Nursia, who abandoned his studies in Rome for a cave on Mount Subiaco in the 520s. As had happened with the Desert Fathers, Benedict soon attracted disciples who wished to follow him in his chosen way of life. Although little is known about Benedict's life, his legacy is immense. His adaptation of an earlier anonymous rule (the so-called *Rule of the Master*) was a masterpiece of practical spiritual organization and applied common sense. It centered on the relationship of the community to its *abbas* (father) and provided a stable and structured life integrating prayer, work, and study for its adherents. In doing so, Benedict laid the cornerstone for a structure characterized by moderation, durability, and flexibility.[9]

In the same year that Justinian suppressed the pagan School of Wisdom in Athens, Benedict founded his monastery at Monte Cassino.[10] His *Rule* and way of life envisioned the monastic community not only as family but as school and new society. As such, it raised a new paradigm that challenged family, traditional schools, and civic society as the primary *loci* for integral human formation. Peter Brown points to the depth of the conceptual shift:

> *In the monastic paradigm, the city lost its identity as the distinctive cultural and social unit. . . . Monasticism not only destroyed the particularity of the city, it threatened the city's hold on its notables at one of its most intimate points: it threatened the role of the public spaces of the city as the primary locus for the socialization of young males.*[11]

Benedict envisioned each monastery as a self-sufficient, self-contained social unit where members of the monastic family could work out their own personal salvation removed from the temptation of the city. The *Rule* imposes the obligation of stability on its followers, an obligation that requires a large— and preferably quiet—foundation for a permanent resident community. The *Rule* is as specific as the zoning regulations of modern gated suburban communities: "The monastery should, if possible, be so constructed that within it all necessities, such as water, mill, and garden are contained, and the various crafts are practiced. Then there will be no need for the monks to roam outside, because this is not at all good for their souls."[12]

FIGURE 4.2
Cluny
Drawing by Kenneth Conant.

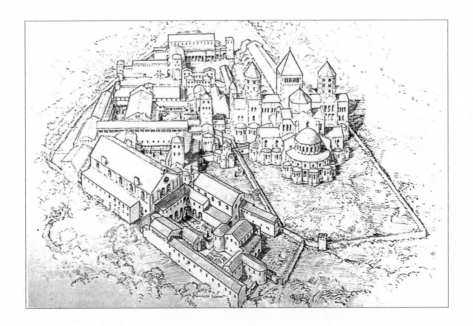

For both practical and ascetic motives, such foundations tended to be located in the countryside or at least outside city walls. The Benedictine "type" of extramural and rural monasteries that gradually spread over the European landscape evolved as a kind of "counter-city," a place where those seeking the City of God could do so together, safely removed from the City of Man. Monasteries also served as important regional agricultural centers, as hospices providing refuge for travelers, and as depositories and production centers for the written word.

EASTERN INFLUENCE

From the seventh through ninth centuries, Rome was inundated with several waves of refugee Greek and Syrian monks and nuns. The lightning spread of Islam across the Mediterranean basin caused widespread dislocation of Eastern religious and clergy. Many settled in suburban monasteries around Rome, and others were charged with servicing the large, extra-urban basilicas and shrines directly under papal control.[13] In the interval between 672 and 752, 11 of 13 popes were Syrian or Greek; ritual and architectonic development of the Western liturgy during that period, as well as emphasis on the cults of Eastern saints, clearly demonstrate Byzantine influence.[14] In the mid eighth and again in the early ninth centuries, significant numbers of religious fleeing from the persecution of the Iconoclast movements were welcomed in Rome.

In the eighth and ninth centuries, dogmatic disagreements and political tensions strained the already fragile bonds between the Byzantine Empire and the Western Church. Faced with the constant threat of invasion from the Lombards (who had conquered the Byzantine capital of Ravenna and laid siege to Rome in 753), the bishops of Rome made alliances with the increasingly powerful Frankish monarchy, granting it viceregal status and bestowing such titles as "patrician of Rome," *subregulus,* and *princeps.*[15] In return, the pope was recognized as the temporal ruler of most of Italy: Pepin and Charlemagne addressed title deeds to St. Peter himself. Rome herself became the capital of the *Sanctae Dei ecclesiae res publica Romanorum,* the "Republic of the Holy Church of God of the Romans."[16] Leo III's coronation of Charlemagne as the Holy Roman Emperor in 800 cemented the Franco-Roman alliance, symbolically cut the ties with the Byzantine Empire,

"RENOVATIO ROMAE"

and looked wistfully to the *renovatio Romani Imperii,* the renewal in the West of the Roman Empire.

In Rome that *renovatio* was celebrated with the building of a number of new churches (among them S. Prassede, S. Maria in Domnica, S. Cecilia, and Ss. Quattro Coronati) that took as their architectural and artistic exemplars the great Constantinian basilicas. Renovations and expansions of the Lateran Palace sought to equate it with the Imperial Palace of

Constantinople. Such building programs reiterated in brick, mortar, and golden tesserae the same political statement found in the fraudulent *Donation of Constantine*. That forged document (ca. 754) purported that Constantine had conceded to the Roman Pontiff powers, honors, and dominion more exalted than his own, as well as "all provinces, places, and towns of Italy and the Western regions."[17] By reprising late imperial and early Christian architectural models, the papacy sought to reinvest itself with Constantinian splendor and so to legitimize its claim to be the central, living link between the old Roman empire and the new.

Just as the Church used the Frankish kings, Charlemagne and his successors did not hesitate to use the structures of the Church to help them rule their widely-extended empire. Episcopal *curiae* provided a well-integrated communications network, and the monasteries, particularly those of the Benedictine observance, provided clerks and educators for the palatine courts and schools. Charlemagne's zeal for centralized organization led him to attempt—unsuccessfully—a gathering together of all monks under a single Benedictine rule.[18]

FIGURE 4.3

Plan of St. Gall, redrawn with identifications translated ca. 820.

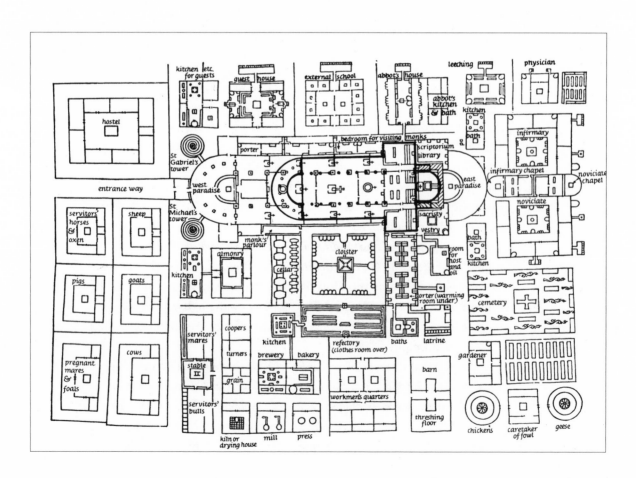

FIGURE 4.4
Monastic and collegiate
churches of Cologne
Redrawn from a 16th Century
sketch by Anton Wonsam.

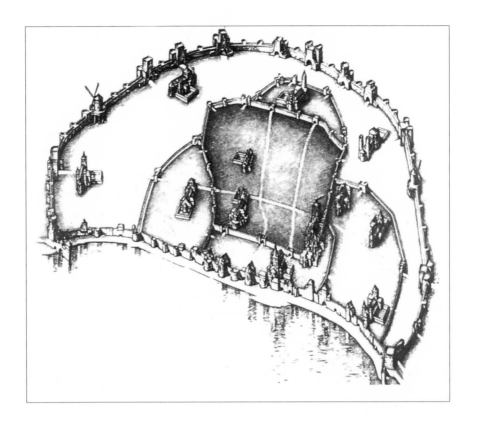

SACRED AND
SECULAR SPACE

Monasteries grew in size and intricacy: monastic communities of 300 clerical monks and 150 or more *conversi* (lay brothers who performed the menial work of grange and kitchen) were not uncommon. Immense construction projects were likewise common. At Fulda, a monastery church was planned that would have been larger than the Basilica of S. Pietro in Rome. The ninth century "Plan of St. Gall," although never realized, gives a clear indication of the sophisticated and integrated planning that characterized monastic life.[19]

The modern visitor to important European cities might wonder at the number of ancient monasteries found not far removed from the historical centers. With the exception of communities of cathedral canons and some cloistered women's convents, most "urban" monastic communities of the early Middle Ages were located on the edge of town, close to the curtain of defensive walls. Clustered around the walls for protection but keeping at least a spiritual eye turned away from the city center, the early medieval monastery could claim the protection of being "in" the city while not being "of" the city. Their centrifugal siting, moreover, often gives a clear indication of how much the urban centers had contracted from Roman times.

COLOGNE

Statistical surveys have showed a clear correlation between the number of monastic establishments and the relative size and importance of the city or town.[20] Monastic life required large cloister complexes as well as easy access to the monastery's agricultural holdings outside of town. Wolfgang Braunfels' lucid analysis of the situation in Cologne, an important trading center on the lower Rhine, shows a pattern that prevailed in many European cities. By the year 1074, 14 major religious institutions had been built in and around Cologne. The cathedral, the collegiate church, and two convents were located within the original Roman wall. Just outside, on the roads leading into the city, were four important cemetery churches. Three Benedictine monasteries and three more collegiate churches rose in the region beyond the wall. With the first expansion of the wall in 1074, five churches were incorporated into the city limits, while the construction of the third wall (1180-1210) brought all but S. Heribert in Deutz (across the Rhine) into the burgher city.[21]

"Incorporated" monasteries and collegiate churches helped to hold open spaces within densely crowded urban fabrics while controlling vast rural agricultural estates. Those feudal holdings grew over the centuries, often to immense proportions: by the twelfth century, the Parisian monastery of S. Germain-des-Prés governed estates totaling 12,000 hectares, an area nine times larger than Rome within the Aurelian walls.[22]

MONASTIC LIFE-CYCLE

Many monastic communities were victims of their own success and followed a predictable life-cycle. Primitive simplicity and stability attracted large numbers; the focused hard work of the monks and, later, of their retainers, led to great wealth, corruption, and decadence. Finally a new reform wing from within the community itself or a visionary leader from outside it would call for a reform, most often in terms of strict observance of the original rule, and attract both old and new members. Yet in spite of these almost tidal fluctuations—Cluniac papalism giving way to a whole constellation of semi-eremetic congregations that inspired Cistercian rigorism—monasticism remained one of the most determinant Western cultural forces up until the early thirteenth century.

In the period of instability caused by the dissolution of the Carolingian empire, Rome was sacked by Arab pirates (846), inspiring Leo IV (847–855) to wall the Vatican and create the *Civitas Leonina*, an extension of Rome across the Tiber.[23] While the papacy passed, in the tenth century, to the playboy sons and lovers of Theodora and Marozia, matriarchs of the corrupt Theophylact dynasty, a series of extraordinary abbots began a reform of the Benedictine rule at the Abbey of Cluny in Burgundy. The strength and genius of the Cluniac movement was its transposition of the feudal model of fealty into the religious sphere. At its height, the monks of more than 1,500 different abbeys were under direct obedience to the Abbot of Cluny, who was himself directly linked to the pope without episcopal intermediaries. Cluniac monks were instrumental in the reform of the papacy. When one of their number, Hildebrand, became Pope Gregory VII (1073–1085), he proved a strong champion of papal authority in the investiture controversies with the German emperor.[24]

In reaction to the wealth and power of Cluny, a rigorist reform flowered at the Abbey of Cîteaux. The principle of this reform was a return to a purer, less centralized form of monastic life. Stark monasteries were located in lonely wooded valleys, in places not likely to encourage the development of a parasitic village. Chronicler Odericus Vitalis in his *Historia Ecclesiae* recorded that "all Cistercian monasteries were built in remote places in the midst of woods and were constructed by the monks with their own hands."[25] The Cistercian focus was inward rather than apostolic, "[for] while it may be sanctifying to sacrifice oneself to the needs of others, it may not be *monastically* satisfying."[26] St. Bruno's Grand Chartreuse and St. Romuald's Camaldoli provided the ultimate in such "monastically satisfying" structures: monasteries where the inhabitants could live as hermits, in minimal contact with each other and entirely removed from the world.

The greatest works of architecture in the early medieval period were sacred spaces, solid centers that towered over the confusion of the secular world. Order was found within the cathedral's sheltering wall, and meaning in the eye's instinctive upward movement. The cathedral parvis, like the monastic cloister garden, was a place of sanctuary and refuge, an intermediary, a buffer zone between this world and the next, a sacred theater where communal and individual salvation could be worked out, where mercy was obligatory.[27] The market, which sometimes nestled haphazardly under the cathedral's buttresses, bespoke another world entirely: the horizontal, unplanned world of contingent secular reality. Two worlds shared an uneasy coexistence: the sacred, inner world of the Church, protecting and protected, towered vertically over the messy, threatening horizontal world of human intercourse. As the horizontal quickly expanded in the later Middle Ages, Church and city were forced to renegotiate their perspectives.

CHAPTER V
RESURGENCE AND RENAISSANCE

A cluster of social, economic, and political phenomena no less complex than those that contributed to the near demise of urban life in late antiquity contributed to its resurgence in the later Middle Ages. Good weather and technological advances like the use of the water mill, the heavy plow, horseshoes, and improved horse collars led to surpluses of foodstuffs and goods. As production rose, so did population. Slowly, towns became affordable again. With trade of surplus goods, it was possible to sustain both merchants and artisans who were not directly engaged in production of the necessities of survival. The limited, autochthonous self-sufficiency of the manor paled in comparison with the variety offered by fair and market.

THE CROSSROADS IN THE CIRCLE

Politically, the town presented a paradox: the crossroads within the circle of walls was closed off from the rural realm of production, but intensely open to the wider world, a crucible where compaction increased creativity. The "open city" of the tenth and eleventh centuries, the town dominated by episcopal or royal buildings, gave way in the twelfth and thirteenth centuries to the "closed city" of the burghers. The feudal prince and bishop—whose wealth and well-being had depended on those bound in fealty to them and to the land—were eventually forced to rely upon autonomous, freely associated citizens, whose overall literacy level rose because of the demands of commerce. Market and guildhall arose as powerful centers to counterbalance and challenge cathedral and castle, and the market economy made the great cathedral building campaigns possible.[1]

PASTORAL IMPLICATIONS

The renewal of urban life caused the emergence of great pastoral needs within the Church and led to major innovations. While the structure of traditional monasticism was ideally suited to a feudal, agrarian society, it was ill-adapted to respond to the demands of an urban population. New forms of religious life evolved, and old forms of lay organization permutated to fill the voids.

An ill-defined, barely thematized longing for religious life within the urban context led to informal groupings of people under the wide umbrella of the so-called "Rule of St. Augustine." Most commentators hold that the "Rule" is based on a letter of Augustine to a group of religious women (ca. 423).[2] It lays out very general guidelines for a common life based on charity and moderation, similar to that lived by the clerks of Augustine's diocesan *curia* at Hippo. Rarely observed in the early Middle Ages, the Augustinian rule reappeared with town life and provided a loose, semimonastic structure for "canons" who staffed cathedrals and collegiate churches. Urban II (1088-1099), himself a Benedictine, used a scriptural metaphor to highlight the conceptual differences between the followers of the Augustinian rule and traditional monks: he likened the canons to Martha who worked while her contemplative sister Mary prayed.

R.W. Southern explains the canons' impact. They

> *picked up the pieces in an already settled world, rebuilt ruined churches, restored religious life in broken-down or half formed communities, provided a framework of life for diffused religious impulses, gathered together large quantities of misappropriated ecclesiastical tithes and applied them to religious impulses for the relief of the poor, the sick, the infirm, and the endowment of a modest religious life. . . . The Augustinian canons as a whole lacked every mark of greatness. They were neither very rich, nor very learned, nor very religious nor very influential: but as a phenomenon they are very important. They filled a very big gap in the biological sequence of medieval religious bodies. Like the ragwort which adheres so tenaciously to the stone walls of Oxford, or the sparrows of the English towns, they were not a handsome species. They needed the proximity of human habitation and they throve on the contact which repelled more delicate organisms. . . . They were ubiquitously useful. They could live on comparatively little, yet expand into affluence without disgrace. They ran many small schools, many hospitals and places of retirement for the sick and aged, for pregnant women, for the blind, for lepers. In an increasingly busy and practical age, they appeared to give more than the Benedictine monks.*[3]

Ubiquitous yet low-profile, the canons and the many offshoot groups following the Augustinian rule provided an important intermediary ecclesiastical structure between highly structured monastic life and re-emerging lay confraternities.

One of the most important genera of social structures that survived the fall of Rome was the lay collective association. In imperial times, *collegia,* pagan and Christian social groupings of various occupational and religious constituencies, were widespread among the middle and lower urban classes, even among slaves.[4] Such groups had diverse, though not necessarily mutually exclusive ends: they shared religious celebrations, socialized at regular banquets, and provided social services for their members. Almost all required payment of some kind of dues and imposed moral obligations of solidarity on their members.

CONFRATERNITIES

Although almost impossible to document in the early Middle Ages, Christian "confraternities"[5] of pious lay folk grew in strength and importance during the Carolingian era. As the Christian cult focused increasingly on intercession for the dead and the cult of the saints, religiously inspired "corporations" performed suffrages for their deceased members and organized celebrations in honor of their local or occupational patron saints. In feudal villages such groups often endowed masses at local monasteries. As town life reasserted itself in the eleventh and twelfth centuries, parish divisions and boundaries were subsumed as civic administrative units, and confraternity chapels and chaplaincies often served as the foundations for parochial structures.[6]

"FRATERNITAS ROMANA"

In Rome, the documented history of medieval confraternities dates to the tenth century, when the *Fraternitas Romana,* a mutual assistance group of local clergy was constituted, probably during the pontificate of John XIV (ca. 984). At first organized to guarantee dignified funerals and annual suffrages for members of the Roman diocesan clergy, the urban clergymen used the confraternity as a kind of college of presbyters, particularly during times when the papacy was weak. Through this organization, they sorted out personnel problems, defended the material interests of the clergy, and saw to the naming of pastors. The "rectors" of the fraternity were among the most important clerics in the city. During the papacy's "Babylonian Captivity" in Avignon, the fraternity effectively dominated Church life in Rome, and the absentee popes wrote a series of briefs emphasizing its jurisdiction and precedence over all lay confraternities.[7]

Throughout Europe, the early thirteenth century saw the emergence of large numbers of lay confraternities whose scope was both religious and secular. The activities of religiously motivated lay groups ranged from the conventional "works of mercy" and prayer to the exuberant fervor of the flagellants and the heterodox teaching of the Albigensians and Cathars.

Given the highly charged religious atmosphere of the medieval world, it is all but impossible—and perhaps irrelevant—to make a clear-cut distinction between purely religious and economically motivated corporations: the bylaws of arts and crafts guilds usually included provisions for annual masses and devotions for the spiritual welfare of their members. In the epoch of the communal movement, trade guilds and craft-oriented fraternities increasingly assumed social responsibilities like health care and sustenance of the poor that had once been undertaken by the hierarchical church, and also gave rise to popular movements that focused on Church reform.

FRANCIS OF ASSISI

Early in the thirteenth century, an Umbrian mystic and inspired minimalist named Francis of Assisi founded a spectacularly successful popular movement, an order of mendicant "little brothers" or *fratres minores*. At least initially, Francis led a lay movement, a loose fraternity of people from every part of the social spectrum who were attracted by the simplicity of the evangelical message he preached in absolute poverty. Although begun without a clear-cut intention to found a new religious order, Francis' way of life was quickly recognized by pope and people alike as an attempt to return to the integrity of Church life in the apostolic age.[8]

James of Vitry, an early chronicler of the Franciscan movement, located Francis' innovation solidly within the living tradition of the Church:

> *There had already existed for a long time three religious orders: hermits, monks, and canons, but the Lord willed that the fourth corner of the foundation should be firmly established on those who live according to a Rule, and so he added in these days a fourth religious institution, the beauty of a new order, the holiness of a new rule. But if we observe attentively the manner of living of the primitive church, we must conclude that not so much did he add a new Rule as renew that ancient one, raise up that which had been laid low, and resurrect that religion which has become moribund, in this eventide of the world as sunset approaches.[9]*

The Franciscan lodestone was the simplicity of life that spiritual and actual poverty imposed. Francis proposed a literal following and universal preaching of the gospel of Christ by devout lay folk who had forsaken all possessions for the sake of the kingdom of God. Freedom from possessions meant freedom from *stabilitas loci* that was at the heart of the Benedictine Rule, and at least implied in the way of life of the Augustinian canons. For Francis, the wide world was the friar's cloister, where he lived as a pilgrim and sojourner.[10] Himself the son of a wealthy burgher, Francis paradoxically rejected the stability offered by urban capitalism to embrace a peripatetic urban ministry.

Such idealism, of course, was bound to suffer when confronted with the hard realities of life. When huge numbers joined his apostolic fraternity of "pilgrims and sojourners," huge numbers had to be fed, clothed, and trained. A model relying entirely on divine providence worked well for a group of 40 in the early 1200s, but was impossibly taxed by a membership of upwards of 40,000 in the fourteenth century.[11] Much to Francis' personal consternation, reinterpretations and relaxations of the rule of absolute poverty began almost immediately. After two centuries of conflict within the order, this fundamental dispute over the meaning of poverty and possessions eventually led to a fifteenth-century canonical split within the order between the "Observant" and the "Conventual" factions.[12]

DOMINIC OF GUZMAN

While Francis' movement of "little brothers" sprouted from the seeds of lay confraternities popular in the thirteenth century, the second great mendicant congregation of the Middle Ages, Dominic of Guzman's Order of Preachers, had its roots in the monastic and clerical canonical traditions. Dominic's innovation was to establish a clerical order that combined the poverty of the Franciscans with the learning of the universities. In an era when the laity, due to the indifference and corruption of the local clergy, often assumed the traditional clerical offices of preaching and teaching, Dominic's religious preachers were an extraordinary novelty. Such novelty attracted many recruits. Founded in 1215, the Order of Preachers grew to 10,000 members in 1256 and to about 20,000 in 590 priories ca. 1300.[13]

Organized under the Rule of St. Augustine, the semimonastic life of the Preachers had built into it a large measure of flexibility. Although bound as monks were to choral office and contemplative living, the apostolic dimension of the Dominican's life was safeguarded by the local superior's extensive powers of dispensation, "especially in those things that are seen to impede study, preaching, or the good of souls, since it is known that our Order was especially founded from the beginning for preaching and the salvation of souls."[14]

TENSIONS

Quite early on, the exigencies of new works made harsh practical demands on the ideal poverty espoused by the new mendicant orders. Francis had espoused an essentially eremetic life interrupted by apostolic labors: "By day they go into the cities and villages to win souls to God, dedicating themselves to active ministry; at night, they return to deserted or remote places to give themselves to God."[15] The lack of any domestic organizational structure, even for new recruits or novices, proved impractical almost from the start. An early critic arched a rhetorical eyebrow at the Franciscans:

> *The Friars Minor are in part merely youths and boys. If, then, the flexibility of their years makes them changeable and fickle, this is only to be expected. However, they have gone to extremes of madness, since they wander about cities and towns and solitary places imprudently, enduring horrible and inhuman sufferings.*[16]

Many recruits, raised in the encapsulated world of the medieval town or manor, found Francis' model of itinerant mendicant preaching psychologically dislocating:

> This order of perfection and the extension of its spacious cloister [spatiosi claustri amplitudo] does not appear to suit the weak and immature, for if they go down to the sea in ships and labor in many waters, they may be overwhelmed by the waves and the storms, unless they have first remained in the city until they be endowed with virtue from on high.[17]

Even before Francis' death, necessity compelled the order to accept the *usus simplex* of donated houses whose ownership was vested in the papacy, local benefactors, or the commune.[18]

A NEW STABILITY

Dominic eliminated the vow of stability as a definitive note of clerical religious life. In doing so, he relocated the focus even as he dislocated the individual: the order itself and its international works, and not a particular monastery or house, became the stable center of the preacher's life. Such an international body, however, needed fixed centers, particularly for those engaged in academic preparation and scholarly research. Such requirements, as well as those imposed by choral office, demanded large, rather traditional cloister complexes. Dominic rejected outright ownership of any immovable property save the priories and their attached churches and imposed strict rules for austerity in building.[19]

URBAN MINISTRY

Urban ministry, addressed particularly to the expanding artisan and mercantile classes, was the focus of the apostolic works of both the Dominican and Franciscan movements. Through orthodox preaching, the Preachers sought to counteract the heretical tendencies of many of the urban lay movements; their schools, universities, and great scholars described the philosophical and theological road map to reality followed by the Catholic tradition up to the Second Vatican Council.

In the early thirteenth century, the Franciscans generally concentrated on itinerant evangelical preaching to the artisan classes and the urban poor. The progress of the century, however, saw decided shifts in mainline Franciscanism toward clericalism, academic pursuits, and ministry to the mercantile class. The 1257 election of the *Doctor Seraphicus* Bonaventura of Bagnoregio as Minister General of the Franciscans, his subsequent appointment as a cardinal, and his nonrigorist reading of Francis' *Testament* in regard to property are indicative of these shifts.[20]

COMPETING FOR SITES

As the thirteenth century advanced, in fact, the Dominicans and Franciscans (with the exception of the hard-line "spiritual" Franciscans, who often preferred remote hermitages) often found themselves in competition for urban sites. Even as the differences between two congregations became less pronounced, the rivalry between them increased and very often focused on control of important urban neighborhoods.

The first Dominican and Franciscan installations tended to be haphazard and temporary: lack of funds and an insufficiently large constituency to support a building campaign often inhibited solid growth. By the mid-thirteenth century, however, the mendicants were well known and quite popular, particularly among the mercantile and artisan classes. That popularity, coupled with the decreased power of the episcopacy, led to a century of phenomenal growth.

ARCHITECTURAL
IMPLICATIONS

Rapid mercantile advances of the early thirteenth century accelerated the deterioration of already tenuous aristocratic and episcopal authority. Emerging communal organizations and the mendicant orders quickly moved to fill the power vacuum on the civic and ecclesiastical levels. While ambitious cathedral projects remained half-built in Florence, Perugia, and Siena, huge yet simple hall churches (*chiesa fienile* or *chiesa capanna)* and cloisters were built in those same cities–and all over Italy–for the popular Franciscans and Dominicans.[21] Although the relative simplicity of the hall churches was consistent with the mendicant ideology of poverty, the churches' immense volumes gave silent yet indisputable testimony to the friars' power.

Neither Francis nor Dominic left detailed descriptions or master plans for the churches and houses of their orders. In general, their followers adopted the traditional Benedictine form of church with attached cloister, refectory, chapter house, and dormitory. Quite early on, the open dormitory gave way to individual cells where the friars could pursue their studies and prepare for their apostolic works in some degree of privacy. This innovation led to very large complexes, often comprising several discrete cloisters.

SITING ON
THE URBAN EDGE

Large properties in the heart of the old downtown areas proved to be prohibitively expensive, and, moreover, it was often considered politically inopportune for the new mendicant foundation to invade episcopal or collegiate neighborhoods. The mendicants therefore tended to locate their foundations at or near the city gates, where lively *faubourgs* were expanding outside the narrow confines of the old city. In those areas open property was still available, and it was possible to obtain sufficient land not only for a church and ample cloister but also for a large *piazza* or square for preaching. Such *piazze*–those of S. Maria Novella and S. Croce in Florence are classic examples–became centers of new urban neighborhoods when city walls were expanded in the late thirteenth and early fourteenth centuries. The property was often the gift of a local bishop or the city government itself,

FIGURE 5.1

Florence,
showing the relationship of the
medicant churches to the 12th
century wall.

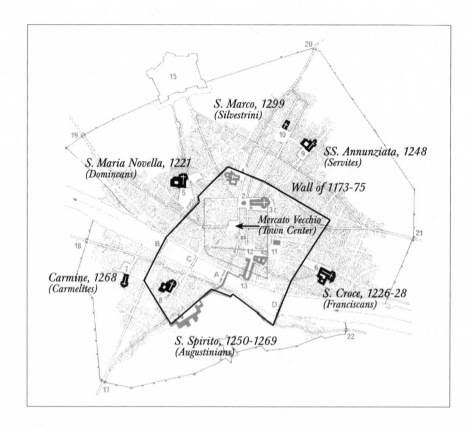

and civic and ecclesiastical authorities frequently joined the guilds in sponsoring the construction of mendicant complexes.[22]

The mendicant complexes were sometimes incorporated into the defensive works of the walls. Important examples include the Basilica of S. Francesco in Assisi, S. Domenico in Siena, and the mendicant foundations in Hagneau, Colmar, and Wiener Neustadt. In Paris, the Dominican priory at the Porte Saint-Jacques (the famous convent of the "Jacobins," where Ignatius later studied) actually broke through the city wall in order to expand its refectory.[23]

A CENTURY OF GROWTH

By 1350, almost every important city and most good-sized towns in continental Europe had both Dominican and Franciscan friaries. By 1277 there were 414 Dominican priories; in 1358, more than 635. The Franciscan expansion was even more dramatic: by 1358, there were 567 friaries and 198 nunneries in the Italian province, 247 friaries and 47 nunneries in the French province, and 203 friaries and 47 nunneries in the German province.

In general, the Dominicans tended to favor middle-sized to larger towns that could sustain their houses of study, while the Franciscans spread like wild flowers, covering entire regions with small refuges called *romitori*, chapels, and larger urban emplacements often located a day's walk distant from one another. Just as the number of suburban monasteries was an index of a town's importance in the early Middle Ages, the presence of various mendicant foundations served as an indicator of economic health for a thirteenth-century town and its outlying regions. Large numbers of convents implied a significant basis of urban wealth that could support the mendicant enterprises of the friars and provide the large endowments required to sustain the strictly cloistered Franciscan and Dominican womens' congregations.[24]

The nearly simultaneous appearance of the Franciscans and Dominicans and the emergence of the Reformed Augustinians, Carmelites, Servites, and other groups shortly thereafter set off a flurry of building that absorbed much of the liquid capital generated by the burgeoning mercantilism of the thirteenth century. The mendicants, forbidden by their constitutions to hold income-producing properties, were the grateful recipients of large cash gifts as a currency-based economy grew in the late thirteenth and early fourteenth centuries.

PAPAL INTERVENTION

Since capital was limited, it was necessary to parcel out the new construction so that the same neighborhood would not be burdened with building too many churches or supporting too many friars. It became necessary to impose mandatory minimum distance restrictions—a kind of religious zoning—between mendicant foundations and any new convents, hospitals, or oratories. In a series of papal bulls dated 1265 governing construction in Ascoli as well as in Bologna and Assisi (the respective burial places of the founders of the Dominicans and Franciscans), a standard distance of 300 *canne di quattro braccie* (approximately 650 meters or about 2,150 feet) was to be observed. The measure was to be taken *per aeram,* in straight line of sight rather than following the meandering street grid.[25]

FORMULAE EMERGE

Practical formulae emerged in the thirteenth century:

> *A single installation—a single site, usually Franciscan, in less important places—generally favored the choice of a very important or elevated place, or the privileged position outside the main gate. The position of two convents is however generally balanced in respect to the city center; often these were disposed taking into account the requirements of the overall equilibrium, both when they were located outside the walls or when they were found within. For the same motives, three principal convents tended to be placed planimetrically at the vertices of a triangle, while four convents were often coordinated according to a cruciform schema.[26]*

The triangular pattern of mendicant emplacements was particularly widespread in central and northern Italy and in other parts of Europe as well: Perugia, Siena, Riete, Narni, Todi, Pistoia, Castiglione Fiorentino, Cortona, Montefalco, Prato, San Sepulcro, Lucca, Bologna, San Giminiano, Orvieto, Città di Castello, Massa Marittima, Florence, and Colmar. The epicenter of the triangle varied in different cities, sometimes coordinated with the Duomo or principal church of the town (Bologna and Colmar), the Palazzo or Piazza Comunale (Perugia and Montefalco), or some important civic building (the Loggia dei Mercanti in Siena and the Palazzo dell'Arte della Lana near Orsammichele in Florence). In the sixteenth century, this triangular patterning was, moreover, exported to the New World in the development of the Spanish capital cities, including Mexico City and Cuzco.[27]

Foundation of the mendicant orders corresponded with a brief yet important moment of papal supremacy that followed almost three centuries of

CONSTRUCTION
AND RECONSTRUCTION

FIGURE 5.2
Siena,
Triangular relationship of the mendicant churches to each other and to and the Loggia dei Mercanti.

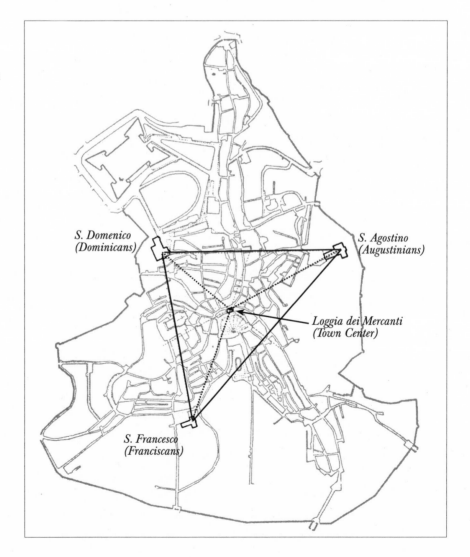

FIGURE 5.3
Bologna,
Triangular relationship of the
mendicant churches to each
other and to the Piazza S.
Petronio.

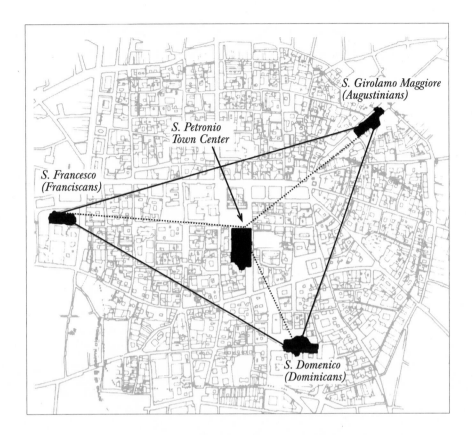

international conflict between the papacy and the German empire and a simultaneous period of domestic rivalry among the pope, the Roman nobility, and the emerging merchant and artisan classes. Under Innocent III (1198-1216) and Honorius III (1216-1227), the papacy was a dominant force in European politics. Papal approval of the mendicant orders, which paid, through their superiors, direct allegiance to the pontiff and not to the local bishop, can be interpreted as a significant attempt by the papacy to consolidate its influence over local church life.

THE MENDICANTS IN ROME   In Rome, both the secular clergy and established religious orders greeted the establishment of the mendicants with hostility. As early as 1219, Honorius III gave the Convent of S. Sisto Vecchio near the baths of Caracalla to Dominic as a dwelling for reformed sisters following his rule, and Dominic assigned a number of friars there as chaplains. In 1222, a year after Dominic's death, Honorius gave the preachers his own Savelli family palace on the rural Aventine as their Roman headquarters. The success of the Dominicans' preaching inflamed the secular clergy of the *Fraternitas Romana*, and in 1248 Innocent IV had to intervene with the *Fraternitas* to allow the Dominicans to preach in parochial churches. After that controversy was successfully resolved in favor of the Dominicans, the preachers began to lament the remoteness of their foundation on the Aventine from the medieval city center, and they began to seek a convenient site on the edge of the *abitato,* the city's populated core. One chronicle records that the preachers appealed to Innocent IV, complaining that the papal court's move from the Aventine, the fetid air, and the distance from apostolic opportunities impeded their work. Offered both S. Maria in Ara Coeli and S. Maria Sopra Minerva, they chose the Minerva site near the Pantheon "for its commodity to the people."[28] The site had been occupied by a convent of Greek nuns and was on the very fringe of the *abitato* in a decidedly suburban neighborhood.

Construction of the new S. Maria Sopra Minerva, attributed by Vasari to the Dominican architects of S. Maria Novella, Florence, did not begin until 1280, after almost 30 years of acrimonious negotiations with the Greek nuns and the secular clergy of the parish church of S. Marco. It was funded in part with gifts from the papacy and the Roman Senate.[29]

In 1231, Gregory IX gave the Franciscans title to the abandoned Benedictine hospice of S. Biaggio, where Francis had lived during a visit to Rome in 1219. On the remote edge of Trastevere, S. Biaggio, renamed S. Francesco a Ripa, represented a typical case of an early Franciscan installation. The rustic neighborhood was poor, sparsely populated, and far from the urban core.[30] More typical of the later pattern of Franciscan engagement

FIGURE 5.4

Rome, S. Maria in Aracoeli, the Campidoglio, and the *disabitato.* Illuminated Initial from Giacomo da Fabriano's version of St. Augustine's *De Civitate Dei,* 1456.

in urban life was the choice of S. Maria in Aracoeli on the Campidoglio.

The oratory and monastery of S. Maria in Capitolio had been built during the eighth century amid the ruins of the Temple of Juno Moneta, and the Benedictines owned and controlled most of the hill until the mid twelfth century. A civic uprising established a short-lived communal government in 1143-1144, and the commune's use of Roman senatorial nomenclature and its siting of its headquarters on the Campidoglio have endured through multiple mutations until the present day. The revived Senate met in the fortress of the Corsini, built into the ruins of the ancient Roman civic archive, the Tabularium. The Benedictines rebuilt S. Maria in Capitolio at about the same time but were forced to give it over to the Franciscans in 1250.[31]

Renaming the church S. Maria in Aracoeli, the friars almost immediately began a radical reconstruction that reoriented the facade westward, overlooking the *abitato* in the bend of the Tiber. Richard Krautheimer describes the choice:

> In France, England, the Rhineland, North Italy, and Tuscany, where cities and communes had evolved early and placed their civic buildings in the center of town, the order had settled on the periphery in the slums; in Rome, the late rise of a civic movement as well as the emotional values and traditions of the Capitoline Hill has forced the civic center to the edge of town, and thus impelled the Franciscans to settle close by. Indeed, as early as 1242 if not before, the old church of S. Maria in Capitolio and its convent functioned collaterally as civic buildings: edicts were publicized in front of the church and the city council, which assisted the Senatore, met at the convent, possibly in one of the cloisters. . . . The Capitol, however, notwithstanding its great traditions and its renewed importance as a political focus in medieval Rome, topographically remained on the outskirts of town, a last outpost on the rim of the disabitato.[32]

Indeed, even into the sixteenth century, the Campidoglio was known as *Monte Caprino* for the goats that grazed on its hillsides, and the Roman Forum was called "the cow pasture," *Campo Vaccino*.

Political pressures from without–the papacy was being squeezed between the resurgent Hohenstaufen emperors and France–and local discontent with high war taxes quickly eroded the imperial papacy of Innocent and Honorius. The commune flexed its muscles again, imposing taxes and claiming jurisdiction over clergy and church properties. Under Senatore Brancaleone of Andalò (1252-1258), the civic faction dominated the papacy and the Roman barons: 140 tower-citadels of the nobility were razed. Almost half a century of intermittent three-way warfare among the papacy, the nobles, and the burghers followed Brancaleone's death, and in the midst of it, the papacy fell under the protective mantle of the French royal house, which also controlled Sicily and Naples. Despite the immense wealth generated by papal tithes, the sale of offices, and the Holy Year of 1300, Boniface VIII's claim to universal sovereignty in *Unam Sanctam* was a hollow rhetorical echo of the *realpolitik* of Innocent III a century before. Boniface's humiliation at the hands of the French in 1303 set the stage for Rome's disgrace: for 70 years, the Bishop of Rome was to live on the Rhone and not the Tiber.

AVIGNON

The "Babylonian Captivity" in Avignon and the Great Schism that followed it deprived Rome of its economic and psychological center. Rome was, for all practical purposes, a one-industry town: the papal court with its allied service trades, banking, construction, and pilgrimage-tourist operations had dominated the social, economic, and political life of the city for a millennium. Although tourism in the form of pilgrimages continued, loss of papal revenues impoverished the city. The fabric of the city decayed. The fourteenth century saw only one major building project: the construction of the huge staircase in front of S. Maria in Aracoeli.[33]

During the period of enforced papal absence, the population plummeted to fewer than 20,000 inhabitants.[34] The Latin Patriarchate at the Lateran was abandoned, the Constantinian basilicas were badly damaged by fires and earthquakes. Petrarch lamented the degradation of Rome even as he doggedly insisted on the city's centrality: "though exhausted and unkempt, Rome is without doubt the head of the entire world."[35]

COLA DI RIENZO

The abortive and ultimately pathetic attempts of Cola di Rienzo to found a new Roman republic and the ongoing trauma of multiple claimants to the Throne of Peter once the papacy returned to Rome in 1367 further destabilized the city and the Church. The Great Schism ended in 1417 when the Council of Constance, after invalidating the claims of three papal contenders, finally elected Oddo Colonna as Pope Martin V. The Colonna prince was the first Roman to occupy the See of Peter in more than a century.

MARTIN V

After more than a century's neglect, the Eternal City was in sorry shape. The Lateran was uninhabitable and, because of its distance from the *abitato*, impossible to defend. Illuminated miniatures of Rome from the mid fifteenth century (see Fig. 5.4, p.72) show a vast greensward separating Rome's cathedral from the Campidoglio. During the winter, wolves were killed within the Vatican walls; the tiny Vatican Palace, begun by Innocent III at the beginning of the thirteenth century and never a regular papal residence, was inadequate for the needs of the papal court. Martin V chose to live in his family palace on the eastern edge of the *abitato* at Ss. Apostoli.[36]

Although Martin did no significant building, he reasserted the papacy's concern for the urban fabric by reinstating the powers of the *magistri aedificiorum*, Rome's urban building superintendents, bringing their office under the authority of the Camera Apostolica. A statute of 1363 charged them with "opening up, repair, and superintendency of buildings, streets and roadways in the city."[37] In 1452 their brief was enlarged to include demolition ("to break down, trim, cut and demolish whatever may occupy streets, piazze, alleyways, canals, riverbanks, and other public places").[38] Under Sixtus IV (Della Rovere, 1471–1484) they were given extensive authority to expropriate or condemn property for the public good, and their title was changed to *magistri stratarum* or *maestri delle strade* ("superintendents of streets"), a shift in terminology that reflected a growing concern for the reorganization of the street grid as classical Vitruvian principles of urban design took hold in Rome.[39]

ALBERTI

On his way to the Council of Constance in 1415, Roman humanist Poggio Bracciolini discovered a complete copy of Vitruvius' *De Architectura* in the monastery library at St. Gall. The discovery proved a rich mine for the architects and aestheticians of the early Renaissance, particularly for Leon Battista Alberti. Absorbing the architectural and design principles of the Augustan Age from Vitruvius' wide-ranging and often difficult text, Leon Battista Alberti, court architect to Eugenius IV (Condulmaro, 1431–1439) and Nicholas V (Parentucelli, 1447–1455), integrated them together with his own theories in his *De Re Aedificatoria* of 1452.[40]

Alberti's work on St. Peter's and the Vatican Palace served Nicholas V's anti-conciliar ideology by stressing the claim to papal authority through Petrine succession, rather than relying on the Constantinian donation symbolized by the Lateran complex.[41] Likewise, by focusing on the Campidoglio, Alberti served his papal master's claim that Rome was the *caput mundi* by identifying papal Rome with imperial Rome, even as the popes were finally and definitively by-passing the power of the commune and diffusing the power of the nobility.

Around 1444, Alberti composed his *Descriptio urbis Romae*, a treatise describing how to draw an accurate map of Rome. He took precise measurements using an astrolabe-like device mounted on the Campidoglio. His choice for the center of his map is of iconic importance. For an accurate rendering of the city, he ignored sacred Christian topography and recognized the Campidoglio as center of the city. His choice of the Campidoglio for his platform was based not only on convenience but also on Vitruvian and Renaissance principles of urban planning that related all parts of the body politic to the center just as the proportions of the human body are related to the umbilicus. On the conceptual level, if not on the political, the

FIGURE 5.5

Rome,
View from the Campidoglio
looking northward,
Detail from a drawing by
Marten van Heemskerck,
ca. 1535.

center of gravity of the city was shifting back toward the traditional civic and cultic center of the *umbilicus mundi*, the Campidoglio.[42]

THE FACE-LIFT BEGINS

Once the papal court resettled definitively in Rome in 1443, the city got an overdue face-lift. Construction of great cardinals' palaces like the Palazzo d'Estouteville at S. Agostino and the Palazzo S. Marco (modern Palazzo Venezia) signaled the end of a building hiatus that had lasted more than 125 years. When Cardinal Pietro Barbo (later Paul II) began his Palazzo S. Marco in 1455, the Via Lata (dubbed "Via del Corso" for the horse races the Barbos sponsored during the reinstated *carnivale*) marked the remote eastern edge of the *abitato*. The new palace at the foot of the Campidoglio remained more an immense suburban villa than a princely townhouse.[43]

As Rome emerged from its medieval decrepitude, a procession of builder popes in the late Quattrocento and early Cinquecento undertook individual campaigns of urban renewal that opened up the heart of the medieval city to accommodate the economic, propagandistic, and cultic needs of an imperial papacy.

SIXTUS IV

Much of the street work in early Renaissance Rome, initiated to ease the flow of annual and Jubilee processions, had important commercial overtones. Sixtus IV's construction of the Ponte Sisto not only eliminated the dangerous bottleneck at Ponte S. Angelo but also forged a link between the busy commercial neighborhoods of Rioni Ponte and Trastevere.[44] The urban program of Sixtus also included reorganization of the Campo dei Fiori and the transfer to the Piazza Navona of the open market that had been held on the western slopes of the Campidoglio since the fifth century.[45] He widened the Via Papale from the Banchi to Piazza Pasquino and opened and paved the Via Recta Iuxta Flumen (Via Coronari) from Platea Pontis (at Ponte S. Angelo) to modern Piazza Nicosia. This straight street allowed the pope easier access from the Vatican to S. Maria del Popolo, rebuilt in 1477 as his family church, and set in motion development of the area of the northern Campo Marzio in the direction of Porta Flaminia. With Sixtus IV, self-styled *Restaurator Urbis,* Rome finally began to lose its picturesque medieval character. Wider and straighter streets opened up vistas and eased traffic patterns.[46]

ALEXANDER VI

Under Alexander VI (Borgia, 1492–1503) a major reordering of the Borgo took place with a deliberate focus on the defenses of Castel S. Angelo and its environs. Borgia's repair of the *passetto,* a defensive escape route atop the Leonine wall connecting the Vatican Palace to the papal fortress set into the ruins of Hadrian's tomb, is perhaps more indicative of the Borgia pon-

FIGURE 5.6
Rome,
Renaissance reorganization and
new streets.

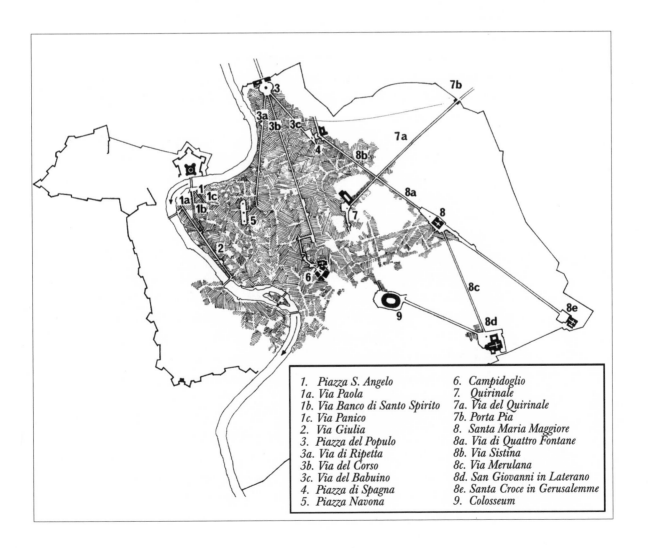

1. Piazza S. Angelo
1a. Via Paola
1b. Via Banco di Santo Spirito
1c. Via Panico
2. Via Giulia
3. Piazza del Populo
3a. Via di Ripetta
3b. Via del Corso
3c. Via del Babuino
4. Piazza di Spagna
5. Piazza Navona
6. Campidoglio
7. Quirinale
7a. Via del Quirinale
7b. Porta Pia
8. Santa Maria Maggiore
8a. Via di Quattro Fontane
8b. Via Sistina
8c. Via Merulana
8d. San Giovanni in Laterano
8e. Santa Croce in Gerusalemme
9. Colosseum

tiff's concerns than the processional Via Alessandrina he had built for the Jubilee of 1500.[47]

The *terribilità* of Julius II (Della Rovere, 1503–1513) expressed itself in his Roman building campaigns as well as in his military and political exploits. His decision to replace the Constantinian Basilica of S. Pietro often overshadows his ever more radical urban policy. He ordered the daring slash of the Via Giulia across the heart of the *abitato*. He constructed its parallel in the Via della Lungara on the opposite side of the Tiber, (originally planned to connect the Port of the Ripa Grande to the Borgo). His comprehensive masterplan for the unbuilt Palazzo Giulio and a new bridge to connect his two new thoroughfares provided Rome with a vision of grandeur and expansiveness unknown since the time of the Caesars. The city itself became an emblematic tapestry of the imperial papacy.[48]

If Julius II styled himself after the *Divus Iulius*, then his successor Leo X (Medici, 1513–1521) presided over a brief Augustan age. The Campidoglio became an imperial banqueting hall for a dazzling humanistic court that effectively insulated itself from disharmonious cries for reform that echoed in Northern Europe. A report to Leo, variously attributed to Raphael or Bramante, described the ancient urban framework as it awaited its Renaissance completion: "the structure exists, without the ornament; the bones without the flesh."[49]

Ever more entangled in the web of Valois-Hapsburg rivalries and intrigue and lacking a sufficient power base of its own, the papacy floundered about during the pontificates of Hadrian VI (Dedal, 1522–1523) and Clement VII (Medici, 1523–1534). Clement's repeated double-dealings earned him the contempt of French and imperial factions alike.

A half-century-long dream of an imperial papacy collapsed in the nightmare of the Hapsburg sack of Rome in 1527. In May, unpaid and disgruntled Spanish veterans and German *landsknecht* of Charles V's Imperial Army–Catholics and Lutherans together–descended on the Holy City for a month of rapine and destruction. The pontiff and his court, including Alessandro Cardinal Farnese (later Paul III), barely escaped across the *passetto* to Castel S. Angelo. From the battlements they watched impotently as Lutheran troops paraded by in looted papal vestments and played ball with the heads of Sts. Peter and Paul.[50]

The toll was immense. Perhaps as many as 10,000 Romans died in the month of plundering and looting, while another 10,000 fled the city or died as a result of the sack. A papal census of 1526 numbered 55,053 inhabitants, already a decrease from the 65,000–70,000 estimated residents at the end of Leo X's reign. By 1530, though, the population probably did not exceed 30,000.[51]

PAUL III

It is tempting but not altogether accurate to look on the extraordinary pontificate of Paul III (Farnese, 1534-1549) as a simple reprise of the Roman Renaissance after the ugly interruption of the sack. Gone forever, however, was the exuberance—the euphoria—that had characterized the reigns of Julius II and Leo X. Replacing it was the hard-headed wisdom of the aged Farnese, a *barone* from nearby Bolsena who considered himself a Roman. He confronted the geopolitical, religious, and urban scenes with cool determination, balance, and resolve.

Paul III's work on the urban fabric demonstrated three major concerns: the aggrandizement of the papacy and his own family apparent in his continued work on S. Pietro and the construction of his own Palazzo Farnese; the security of the city's defenses; and the opening up and expansion of the street grid to encourage growth.

FORTIFICATION

Early in his reign, Paul III initiated a comprehensive program of defensive works. It included the building of curtain walls and bastions from the Aventine to the Tiber and the walling of the Gianicolo from Porta S. Pancrazio to the Vatican. He refortified the Città Leonina and the Vatican and constructed a massive bastion at the Belvedere. He had Andrea Sangallo the Younger draw designs for a new fortified wall within the Aurelian walls.[52] That plan would have effectively halved the urban defensive perimeter, leaving the sparsely populated neighborhoods around the Lateran and S. Maria Maggiore outside the circle of the walls. This huge work, which included 18 bastions with intervening cannon emplacements, was never realized.[53]

On a much smaller scale and closer to home, Papa Farnese ordered a tower and enclosed garden constructed on the northern slopes of the Campidoglio overlooking the Corso and his preferred residence at Palazzo S. Marco. The Torre Farnese was connected to the papal residence by a covered *passetto,* just as Castel S. Angelo was linked to the Vatican. Serving both as a retreat and an emergency defensive refuge, the tower dominated the skyline of the Capitol. It also served as "an urbanistically tangible sign of the usurpation of former municipal liberties."[54]

OPENING THE GRID

Paul III's concern with revitalizing the center of the city and extending its commercial areas is seen in the several diverse, yet homogeneous, works of urban planning he ordered from Latino Giovenale Manetti, his trusted lieutenant, ambassador, and *maestro delle strade*. Although documentary evidence of Manetti's role is sketchy, his 19-year term as one of the two *maestri* began in 1535, a year after Paul III's accession, and lasted until his own death, four years after Paul III's.[55] As commissioner of antiquities and *maestro,* Manetti's artful stage-managing of the hated Charles V's 1536 visit to

FIGURE 5.7
Campidoglio,
ca. 1552.

FIGURE 5.8 (RIGHT)

Rome,
from the Pantheon to the
Campidoglio
From Leonardo Bufalini's *Pianta
di Roma*, 1551.

Rome won Manetti great renown. His routing of the imperial cavalcade through the Roman Forum (his plan for the reorganization of the Campidoglio—which clearly presaged Michelangelo's—could not be realized in the six months between its conception and the Emperor's visit) was a triumph of papal propaganda. "The path chosen by Manetti was a veritable monumental route through the major surviving antiquities of the city: it reveals him to be a planner capable of dealing with the city's topography in broad, sure strokes . . . a true precursor of Sixtus V."[56]

Together Manetti and Paul III revised the confusing medieval grid. They opened up sclerotic arteries in the heart of the Banchi with the cutting through of the Via Paolina and the Via del Panico to form the elegant mini-trident linking the Ponte S. Angelo with the fashionable Florentine commercial quarter of the Via Giulia. The Via Paolina Trifaria (modern Via del Babuino) opened from Trinità dei Monti to Porta del Popolo completed the framework of the great trident, while Via Trinitatis (Via Condotti) linked the new neighborhood to Rione del Ponte and Campo Marzio.[57]

Manetti's work on Farnese's own neighborhood, the Rione della Pigna, and the approaches to the Campidoglio are of particular interest. Via del Gesù linking Piazza Altieri (modern Piazza del Gesù) and S. Maria Sopra Minerva was opened to allow carnival processions to pass from the Campidoglio to the Pantheon, whose piazza was also paved.[58] An ideological rerouting of the traditional route of the Via Papale created the Piazza Altieri–Via Aracoeli–Piazza Aracoeli–Cordonata–Piazza del Campidoglio axis. Alan Ceen cogently describes the development:

FIGURE 5.9

Rome,
street work in the Rione della
Pigna and Campidoglio areas
designed by Latino Manetti
for Paul III.

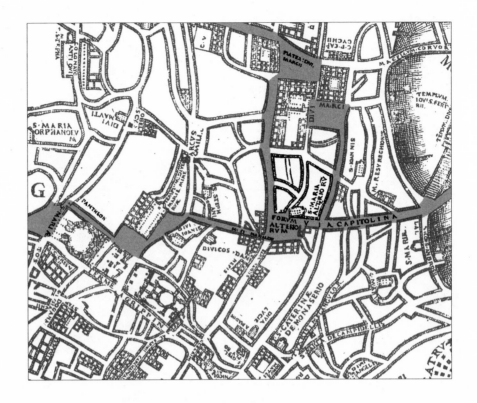

*Standing in front of the Gesù and looking up the Via Capitolina [Via
Aracoeli] one can see the Campidoglio framed by the buildings along the
street. Michelangelo's mid-century plan for the reorganization of the
Campidoglio followed closely upon the beginning of the cut for the Via
Capitolina. Since both projects dragged on until the end of the century,
they can be considered to be practically concurrent. It is hard to avoid the
notion that they were both part of one large urban scheme for connecting
the Campidoglio with the Forum Alteriorum [Piazza del Gesù] while
simultaneously embellishing the Via Papale. Certainly all the elements
are there: the straight, comparatively wide street, the Piazza Aracoeli,
part of which is trapezoidal, the Cordonata which is similarly trapezoidal, and the Piazza del Campidoglio which is also trapezoidal.*

*Whatever planning scheme was in operation, the simultaneity of the
change of papal route during the reign of Paul III and the reorganization
of the Campidoglio clearly point to a development in the processional
aspect of the Via Papale. It coincides with a period when . . . secular government was dependent on the* Camera Apostolica *and the prefect of
Rome [was] appointed by the pope. It now became possible and desirable
for the pope to assert his secular authority by passing through the
Campidoglio, seat of the secular government, on his way to the Lateran.
Formerly when the government was more powerful or independent, the
processions had carefully gone around the Capitoline, as the older route
indicates.*[59]

The rerouting was begun in 1538, the year Ignatius' companions began their work in Rome. It was completed in 1544, the same year Ignatius moved into the house he had built in the shadow of the Campidoglio on the Via Papale, at the intersection of Piazza Altieri and Via Aracoeli, one block from the papal residence at Palazzo S. Marco. From the windows of his simple apartment overlooking the largest open space on the parade route between the Vatican and the Lateran, Ignatius, champion of the papacy, could salute his neighbor the pope passing below in solemn procession.

CHAPTER VI
"A GOOD AND TRUE JERUSALEM"

arefoot, hungry Romans leaned into the bitter wind, and shopkeepers shoveled snow from the doorways of their depressed businesses. Everywhere commerce slowed. Neighborhood prostitutes hid indoors: the unseasonable freezes cooled the ardor of even their most regular clients.

The cold, at least, cleared the air somewhat. Slops thrown into the narrow streets quickly rimed over. Ordinary horse traffic—and its residue—was reduced to a minimum because of the famine. The 1538 autumn harvests in the papal states had been very meager, and from Christmas 1538 until May 25, 1539, there were terrible, battering storms: "intolerably intense cold periods, frequent snowfalls, and extraordinary rains . . . in the very heart of winter there was unseasonable thunder . . . things horrendous indeed to see and hear."[1]

In the shadow of the Campidoglio, the poor died of exposure by night. By day they huddled for warmth around the neighborhood kilns, where ancient Roman marbles were reduced to powdered lime for cement. In spite of the unusual cold and famine, raw materials for construction were still in demand: even during the hard winter of 1538–1539, the Rome of Papa Farnese continued to grow.

That winter, the ermine-wrapped papal court was distracted from its usual curial ennui by curious news: Ignatius of Loyola and his "Masters of Paris," some of the best-educated priests in Italy, were operating a Salvation Army–style mission and soup kitchen in their rented house only three minutes' walk from the pope's residence at Palazzo S. Marco. There the "reformed fathers" attended to the needs of groups of up to 400 hungry, sick, and frost-bitten Romans, providing not only food, fire, and beds but also

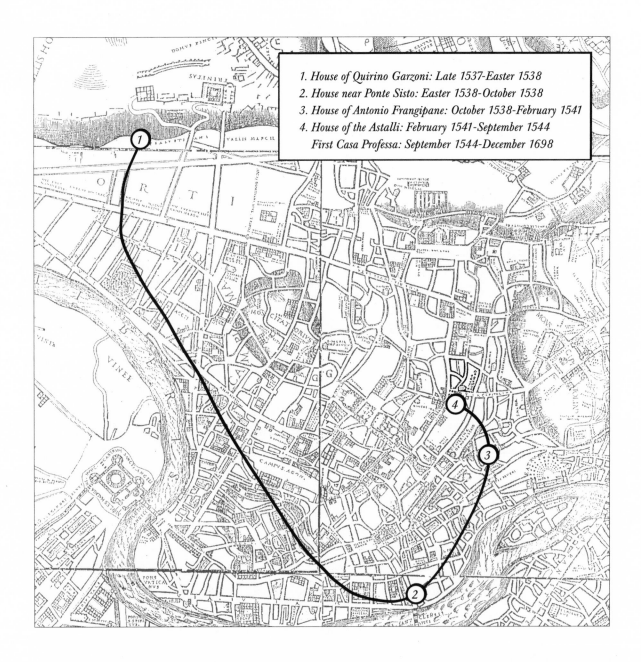

1. *House of Quirino Garzoni: Late 1537-Easter 1538*
2. *House near Ponte Sisto: Easter 1538-October 1538*
3. *House of Antonio Frangipane: October 1538-February 1541*
4. *House of the Astalli: February 1541-September 1544*
   First Casa Professa: September 1544-December 1698

FIGURE 6.1

Circling towards the center. Moves of the early Jesuits' community in Rome, overlaid on Bufalini's 1551 *Pianta*.

spiritual refection in the form of homilies and lessons in Christian doctrine. Important people, including members of the papal court, soon began bringing alms to assist the fathers' work. Space in their rented house at Torre del Melangolo was tight, so Ignatius diverted much of the assistance to other hospices in the city. In all, more than 3,000 of the destitute would be cared for through his intervention.[2]

When Ignatius, Favre, and Laínez arrived in Rome late in 1537, they took up residence in a small house in the vineyard of Quirino Garzone, not far from Trinità dei Monti.[3] Ignatius set to work giving spiritual direction and the Spiritual Exercises, while Favre and Laínez were immediately engaged to lecture at the Roman university, the Sapienza. The Dean of the Sacred College, Cardinal Gian Domenico De Cupis, tried to prevail upon his friend Garzone to evict the fathers after they were accused of being crypto-Lutherans. Ignatius pleaded his case before De Cupis, and received an abject apology from the Dean. Fearing that the companions' apostolic effectiveness might be compromised by such slanderous rumors and armed with glowing affidavits from church officials in Siena, Ferrara, and Bologna, Ignatius went to see the pope himself. At Ignatius' insistence, Paul III ordered Benedetto Conversini, the secular governor of Rome, to conduct a thorough investigation of the charges and to deliver a written judgment. The judgment (dated November 18, 1538) found the companions innocent of all charges and declared them victims of calumny. Ignatius sent copies of the acquittal to cities around Europe where he and his comrades were known.[4]

"A MORE CONVENIENT LOCATION"

At Easter 1538, the other companions arrived from a series of successful pastoral missions in cities of northern and central Italy. "Soon after [their arrival], seeing that this first house was inconvenient, they moved to another house close to the Ponte Sisto and that of Doctor Ortiz."[5] At least in part, the inconvenience of the first house was its distance from the densely-populated center of town: Bufalini's icnographic plan of Rome—drawn 13 years after Ignatius lived in the Garzone vineyard house—shows the neighborhood still empty, given over to orchards and vines. The vineyard house that Ignatius persuaded his companions to leave was not far from the site the Theatines had occupied most contentedly from 1525 until the sack of Rome.[6]

The companions' first Roman move, from rural peace to urban bustle, occurred two and a half years before the formal foundation of the Society. One of his companions recalled that Ignatius had a sense of place shaped by apostolic need even at this early stage:

> *Some months later they [the companions] moved to another, larger house and a more convenient location; persuaded by Ignatius, they left their old residence, remote from the concourse and traffic of people, and moved to the central part of the city [to the house near Ponte Sisto], which was seen as more appropriate for the ministries of the Society.*[7]

URBAN PREACHING

During the 50 days between Easter and Pentecost, the companions broke with the local custom that mandated preaching only during Advent and Lent.[8] They embarked on a concentrated blitz of urban preaching that focused on the churches in the medieval core of the city.

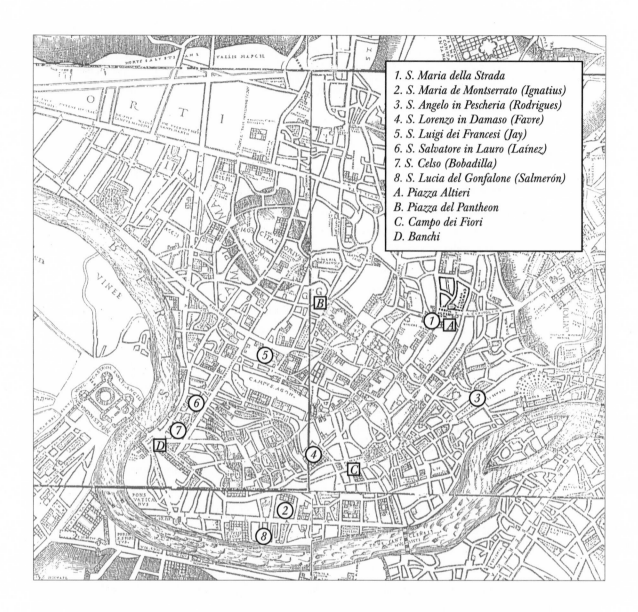

1. S. Maria della Strada
2. S. Maria de Montserrato (Ignatius)
3. S. Angelo in Pescheria (Rodrigues)
4. S. Lorenzo in Damaso (Favre)
5. S. Luigi dei Francesi (Jay)
6. S. Salvatore in Lauro (Laínez)
7. S. Celso (Bobadilla)
8. S. Lucia del Gonfalone (Salmerón)
A. Piazza Altieri
B. Piazza del Pantheon
C. Campo dei Fiori
D. Banchi

FIGURE 6.2

Sites of early Jesuit preaching in Rome, identified on Bufalini's 1551 *Pianta*.

Master Ignatius preached in Spanish at S. Maria de Montserrato; the others preached in Italian: Master Favre at S. Lorenzo in Damaso, Master Jay . . . at S. Luigi [dei Francesi], Master Salmerón at S. Lucia [del Gonfalone], Master Simon [Rodrigues] at S. Angelo in Pescheria, and Master Bobadilla at a church near the Banchi, and Master Laínez at S. Salvatore in Lauro.[9]

Ignatius' use of Spanish in preaching points to one of his personal limitations: he was no linguist. Raised speaking Basque, he used Castellaño at the Spanish court. He did not study Latin seriously until after his conversion, when he was more than 30 years old. In seven years in France he apparently picked up enough French to get by, but his command of Italian remained, until the end of his life, unrefined and confused.

Linguistic limitations, however, never dampened Ignatius' zeal for preaching. Even in the busy years after he became Superior General of the Society, he continued to preach and teach catechism not only in churches but on street corners and in the commercial *piazze* of Rome. In depositions taken before Ignatius' beatification, eyewitnesses recalled learning their catechism on the streets from Ignatius and hearing him preach *viva voce* in Piazza Altieri in front of S. Maria della Strada, on a nearby street corner (*cantone dei Maddaleni,* "where the carts were hitched up"), at the Zecca Vecchia, in Piazza della Rotonda, and in Campo di Fiori. Lorenzo Bini's testimony adds a charming, human note: Ignatius, counselor to popes and princes, was ridiculed by his young listeners. They mocked his baldness, his limp, and most of all his curious pronunciation: "the kids threw apples at him, but he kept his composure with great patience, without becoming angry, and continued his preaching."[10] Such street preaching was not Ignatius' exclusive province: in the early Society, Jesuits preached not only in commercial *piazze* but

> *in hospitals, prisons, aboard ships in dock, in fortresses, on playing fields, in hospices and restaurants, in confraternities. . . . The Jesuits were not creating new institutions when engaged in preaching in sites like these but imbuing older practices in certain localities with a new zest and trying to introduce them into other localities.*[11]

TO A HAUNTED HOUSE

The house near Ponte Sisto, whose exact location is unknown, was a stop-gap; the lease probably expired on the feast of St. Remigius (October 1), the traditional Roman day for contract renewals. In the fall of 1538, mail to the fathers was addressed to them at the house of Antonio Frangipani near the Torre Melangolo. The house was located in Rioni Campitelli, equidistant from the Campidoglio and Palazzo S. Marco. The house, much rebuilt in the seventeenth century, still stands at Via dei Delfini 16 and was leased at very favorable terms because it had a reputation for being haunted by rowdy poltergeists.[12]

While living in that house, the foundations of the Society of Jesus were laid. The geopolitical situation had not improved, and the pilgrimage to the Holy Land was out of the question for the foreseeable future. Once the companions received their sentence of acquittal from the Governor of Rome, almost immediately they made a formal "oblation" (in Latin, *holocaustum*) of their lives and energies to the pope.[13] Although it is impossible to date precisely a 1538 meeting between the pope and the companions recounted in Bobadilla's *Autobiography*, the message of the meeting and the definition of the Jesuits' mission that emerged from it were consistent with the spirit of their oblation:

> *Later on in 1538, all [the companions] gathered at Rome in a rented house, in order to preach in the churches and* piazze, *and beg alms throughout the city. . . . Four of the companions were holding a disputation before the Supreme Pontiff Paul III, who gladly received them and listened to them, saying "The more frequent our meetings are, the more content I shall be." And one day he said to one of them "Why do you so avidly desire to go to Jerusalem? Italy is a good and true Jerusalem, if you wish to produce fruit in God's Church." They carried these words home to the other companions, and they began considering instituting a religious order; up to that time they had always had in their hearts and on their lips the fulfillment of their vow for the Jerusalem pilgrimage.*[14]

The companions, moreover, were receiving invitations from various quarters to engage in new apostolic works. News of their prior apostolic success in northern and central Italy and of their Roman works spread quickly. "We are being overrun [*infestados*] by a number of prelates who want us to go, if the Lord allows it, to engage in fruitful labor in their own lands."[15] As early as 1538, King John III and Emperor Charles V implored the companions to work in the burgeoning missions of the Portuguese and Spanish Indies.[16]

Having placed themselves at the pope's service, the dispersion of the small group was a foregone conclusion. Before that happened, however, important decisions had to be made. Would they formalize their commitment to one another and seek canonical approval as a religious order?

PREPARING
FOR THE DIASPORA

> *Lent [1539] was drawing to a close. The time was approaching for us to be scattered and parted from one another. We were eagerly anticipating this time so we could the sooner achieve our appointed goal on which we had set our minds and hearts. We therefore resolved to get together for a good long time before our dispersal and to discuss our vocation and our covenanted way of life. . . . Some of us were French, others Spanish, Savoyards, or Portuguese. . . . No one ought to wonder that a diversity of views would be found among us.*[17]

In some ways *where* and *how* that deliberation took place were as important as *what* was determined. Once they decided that they wanted to remain together, it became clear that an organizational structure based on vowed obedience would have to be created to complement the vows of poverty and chastity they had taken when they were ordained priests. For such a group of independent, highly-motivated men as the companions, shaping that model was bound to be a long and complicated task, and some voices in the group suggested that the discernment could be most easily undertaken in solitude:

> *Would it expedite our discernment if we all went away to some hermitage for thirty or forty days, giving ourselves over to meditation, fasting, and penance, so that God might listen to our desires and mercifully impress on our minds the answer to our question? Or should three or four undertake this enterprise in the name of all with the same intent? Or would it be better if none of us went to the hermitage but all remained in the city, devoting half of every day to this our one principal occupation and the rest of the time to our customary work of preaching and hearing confessions? The half devoted to our principal concern would be time less crowded with other concerns, more suitable for meditation, reflection, and prayer.*
>
> *After examining and discussing these possible courses of action, we decided that we would all stay in the city. The first reason (based on the characteristic tendency of people to make rash judgments) was this: we wanted to forestall rumor and scandal in the city and among the people, who would make judgments and think that we had fled, or undertaken something new, or were unstable and inconstant in carrying out what we had begun. The second reason was this: we did not want by our absence to lose the great results we saw from confessions, teaching, and other spiritual works. So great was the need that even if our number were quadrupled we could not have satisfied all who needed our service any more than we can do now.*[18]

The two reasons given for continuing the discernment and decision-making process in the city are, in fact, one: the companions were in no way willing to compromise their ministry of helping any and all who needed their spiritual and temporal assistance. Thus, they opted to carry out crucial discussions and interpersonal negotiations in a distracting urban setting. The deliberations continued from March through the end of June 1539. The famine and unusual cold reportedly lasted through late May that year. The house on Via dei Delfini was in all probability still crowded with those who flocked to the fathers for assistance.

THE FIRST DEPARTURES

Even before the deliberations were completed, the first diaspora had already begun: the pope sent Broët and Rodrigues to Siena, where they were charged with the reform of a decadent convent of Benedictine nuns. They also preached very successfully at the University of Siena and gave the Spiritual Exercises to a number of important persons.[19] A few days before the end of the deliberations, Laínez and Favre were sent to Parma, a city described as "worse than a bacchanalian forest: so many murders, robberies, and stonings have been committed here."[20] Their preaching and Spiritual Exercises there garnered them a number of important early vocations. Soon after, Codure was sent to preach in Velletri, Jay to Brescia and Bagnoreggio, and Bobadilla on a delicate papal mission to Ischia near Naples, where he worked–unsuccessfully–to reconcile Don Ascanio Colonna with his estranged wife Doña Juana of Aragon.[21]

Ignatius remained in Rome, where he drafted a *summa* or description of the Institute the companions hoped to found. The document, called the *Quinque Capitula* or "Five Chapters," was presented to the pope at Tivoli. On September 3, 1539, Paul III orally approved the sketch, although a full year was required to convince all the members of the Curia that the foundation of a new religious order was warranted and desirable. The Society of Jesus formally came into existence with the publication of the bull *Regimini militantis ecclesiae,* signed at Palazzo S. Marco and dated September 27, 1540.[22]

In 1539, Ignatius made an important catch: his first Italian recruit, Pietro Codacio, a priest from Lodi, who had been a chamberlain at the papal court for several years.[23] Through Codacio's connections at the Curia, Ignatius obtained a downtown base of operations, the small chapel of S. Maria della Strada ("St. Mary of the Street") located on the Via Papale at Piazza Altieri (modern Piazza del Gesù), one block from the papal palace of S. Marco. The chapel was also referred to in other contemporary documents as S. Maria dell'Urbe (St. Mary of the City) and as S. Maria Alteriorum on Bufalini's 1551 plan.

AN IMPORTANT
ITALIAN RECRUIT

FIGURE 6.3

The Approval of the Society of Jesus, Ignatius at work, and the dispersal of the Companions, Ribadeneyra's *Vita*.

A. *Paulus Tertius Pontifex Maximus, anno salutis 1540, Societatem Iesu confirmat.* L.4.2.c.17.   B. *Constitutiones ac regulam. S. Pater, scribit.* L.4.c.2.   C. *Filios suos ad prædicandum euangelium in uarias mundi plagas dimittit.* L.4.3

On November 18, 1540–less than two months after the first written approval of the Society–Codacio was named pastor of the rundown parish, whose parochial roster 20 years before had numbered only ten families.[24] Seven months later (in the bull *Sacrosanctae Romanae Ecclesiae,* dated June 24, 1541), Paul III accepted Codacio's resignation of the pastorate and assigned the benefice and properties of S. Maria della Strada to the superior general of the Society of Jesus in perpetuity. Codacio's brief pastorate was a holding action: the newly recognized Society had no superior general until Ignatius was elected in April 1541.[25]

"A CELEBRATED LOCATION"

Two important documents give testimony to Ignatius' motivation in obtaining the della Strada church and property. "De Origine Domus Professae Romanae" relates that after Ignatius had occasion to celebrate mass and perform other pastoral works at S. Maria della Strada,

> *seeing that the site was convenient for what he was planning, Father Ignatius obtained for our Society said church and a house along with a little piece of orchard that was there; Father Ignatius turned down the house and Church of S. Girolamo that had been offered to him, preferring to that [place] this site as more appropriate for what the Society was planning.*[26]

Orlandini's 1614 *Historiae Societatis Iesu prima pars* cites Juan de Polanco, Ignatius' personal secretary, as the source of a very important observation on the choice of the della Strada property: "Polanco tells that it [S. Maria della Strada] was preferred over the rest of the city by Blessed Father Ignatius himself, more because it was opportune for our uses because of its celebrated location, than because it was sufficiently spacious or comfortable."[27]

The oldest clear documentary evidence of the chapel of S. Maria della Strada is a record of the burial of Paulutio Astalli there in 1419. The twelfth-century *Liber Censuum* of Cencio Camerario lists a "S. Maria Hastariorum" in the Rione della Pigna; at the same time Astaldus de Astallis was a member of the college of cardinals. The anonymous fourteenth-century Catalogue of Torino lists a church of "S. Maria de Astara" staffed by one priest, while nearby S. Marco boasted a cardinal and 10 clerics and S. Maria Sopra Minerva and S. Maria in Aracoeli each had 50 friars. It is possible that "Hastariorum," "Astara," and "[della] Strada" are all corruptions of the family name "Astalli." Between 1419 and 1526, 12 members of the Astalli family were buried in what was certainly considered their family church and sepulchral chapel.[28]

From the time of the Jesuits' arrival, the chapel of S. Maria della Strada was inadequate for the large crowds who flocked to hear the Jesuits' preaching, make their confessions, assist at mass and devotions, and receive catechetical instruction. In 1547, Polanco gave an account of the difficulties to the provincial of Spain:

> *It is true that for the crowds of people, the church is hardly suitable: when we arrived, it was very rundown, and we considered its good location and the possibility of rebuilding it and expanding it more important than its present convenience. It is small and badly furnished, although before it was even worse; so much so that those who come to it and persevere must endure its defects with great patience.*[29]

TAKING OUT OPTIONS

Even before the Society was approved, Codacio, the "minister" responsible for the practical details of community life, began to take out options on properties near S. Maria della Strada. On August 19, 1540, he leased from Gian Pietro Caffarelli a small orchard that abutted the della Strada property. Early in 1541 the companions moved from the house on Via dei Delfini to a cramped and decrepit house across from the della Strada chapel. The house was rented from the Astalli for 30 scudi *per annum.*[30] Shortly thereafter Codacio bought another plot of land fronting on the Via Papale and Piazza Altieri. The bill of sale describes the property:

> *A certain portion of the terrain is unbuilt, and a portion is occupied with a certain lime burning kiln for the cooking of marble, and another small building . . . in the Rione della Pigna, in that place popularly called "Via Papalis" . . . the entire property is bounded on one side by the church called S. Maria della Strada, on another by the little house of Mariani de Altieri, on the other is the recently constructed public street that leads towards the Campidoglio; behind is the lot that had been leased from Master Fabrizio de Pellegrini by Master Pietro Codacio, and before it is the square called "Piazza Altieri."*[31]

The Bufalini plan of 1551 gives the general composition of the street grid at the time of Ignatius' arrival there; it also provides the only extant visual evidence of the size and orientation of the della Strada chapel.[32]

In 1542 Paul III gave over to the Society the titles, lands, goods, and buildings of three small chapels, Ss. Vincenzo ed Anastasio, S. Nicolò, and S. Andrea della Frate, that had been arrayed in a corona around S. Maria della Strada. The chapel of Ss. Vincenzo and Anastasio (located somewhere on what is modern Via del Plebiscito, most probably in the area presently occupied by the Chiesa del Gesù), and the chapel of S. Nicolò (in the area of the modern corner of Via Aracoeli and Via Botteghe Oscure) had already been demolished as part of Latino Manetti's extensive street-widening campaign prior to Charles V's visit in 1536. The S. Andrea buildings adjoining S. Maria della Strada were partially demolished and partially incorporated into the Jesuits' first construction, the Roman Casa Professa.[33]

CASA PROFESSA, 1543

Work on the Casa Professa began in 1543, and Ignatius and his companions moved in during September 1544. No early drawings of the house exist, although Ugo Pinard's 1555 bird's-eye-view map gives a schematic rendering of the block that contained the house and the della Strada chapel and its relationship to the papal residence at Palazzo S. Marco. Documents (including the receipts for its construction[34]) and the physical evidence garnered in the recent 1989–1990 restoration of the rooms of St. Ignatius testify to the poverty of the construction. The edifice was a simple structure: thick plastered walls haphazardly constructed of dressed and rough stone intermixed with brick; low beam and plank ceilings of unfinished oak and ash; floors of yellow, unglazed *mattoni* from the Val d'Inferno district near Torre Magliana. The residence originally housed 30 persons, but it was repeatedly expanded. By the time Ignatius died there in 1556, some 80 Jesuits lived in several connecting wings, floors, and in adjacent houses bought by the Society.[35]

Once their downtown headquarters had been established, Ignatius set his mind to replacing the inadequate della Strada chapel with a larger, nobler structure. Polanco, writing under commission of Ignatius, described the situation in 1548 to Antonio Araoz:

> I do not know whether Your Reverence knows that Master Pietro Codacio has, with the help of God, built us a sufficiently large house; I think that there are more than forty rooms that can be comfortably inhabited, and he has already drawn larger plans, and bought three nearby houses to expand into.
>
> As for the church, he has made truly sumptuous plans, which [despite] having a site and great hope, cannot yet be undertaken. As Your Reverence recalls from your experiences preaching there, the church is so uncomfortable that, as Master Salmeron used to say, those who continue to frequent it must be among the predestined. Because he does not know if we will live to enjoy the church according to Codacio's design, and because he sees the present great need to repair and furnish the [existing] church so that it allows the people who come from without to hear the word of God and to receive the holy sacraments, Our Father [Ignatius] has destined the first 200 or 300 ducats that God sends us to be used in this [repair] work, so that some people will not say (as has already been said) that we build a palace for ourselves and do not take care of the church. They are wrong who say this, since much has been spent since the beginning on the church and on the property purchases.[36]

DELAYS

Shortage of funds, the premature death of Codacio in December 1549, and an unfavorable decree from the *maestri delle strade* mandating a general

FIGURE 6.4

The S. Maria della Strada-Casa Professa neighborhood, detail from Bufalini's *Pianta*, 1551.

FIGURE 6.5 (UPPER RIGHT)

The S. Maria della Strada–Casa Professa neighborhood, detail from Ugo Pinard's *Pianta*, 1555.

FIGURE 6.6 (LOWER RIGHT)

Nanni di Baccio Bigio's sketch for a new church and Casa Professa, 1553.

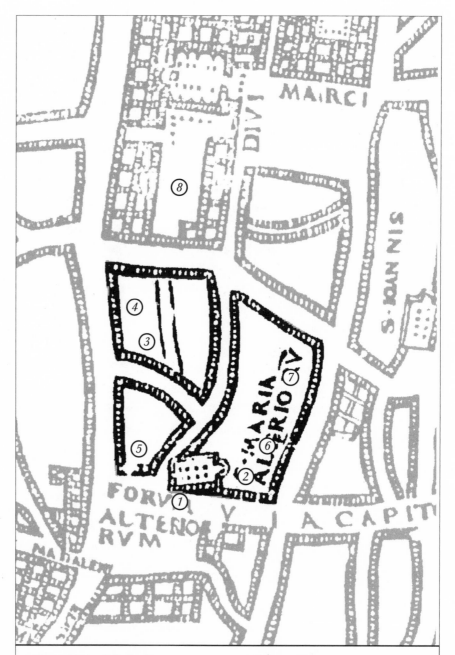

1. *Santa Maria della Strada*
2. *Chapels of S. Andrea, S. Nicolò,*
   (Site of Casa Professa construction, 1544)
3. *Palazzo Astalli*
   (Rented rooms, 1541-44)
4. *Chapel of Ss. Vincenzo ed Anastasio (?)*

5. *Palazzo Altieri*
6. *Palazzo Muti*
7. *Palazzo de'Delfini*

8. *Palazzo S. Marco (Paul III)*

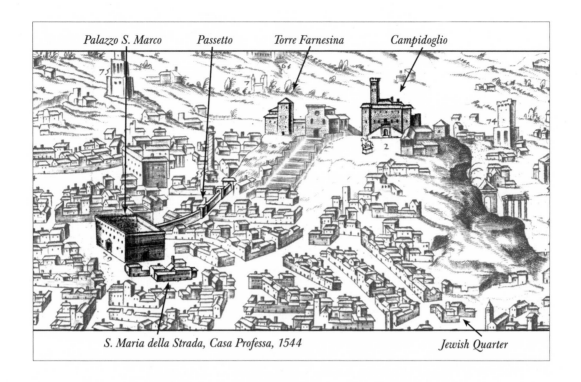

Palazzo S. Marco   Passetto   Torre Farnesina   Campidoglio

S. Maria della Strada, Casa Professa, 1544   Jewish Quarter

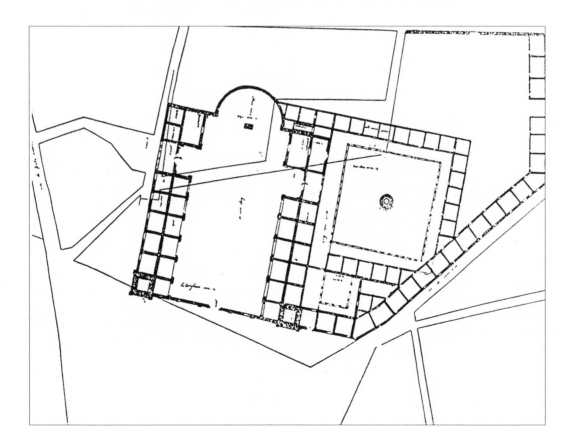

redesign of the entire area of Piazza Altieri stalled planning work on the new church through much of the 1550 Jubilee Year. With the arrival of Francisco Borja, *olim* Duke of Gandia and already *in pectore* member of the Society, political pressure was brought to bear on the *maestri*. Florentine architect Nanni di Baccio Bigio prepared a site plan for a new church and Casa Professa complex, and a cornerstone was laid on December 14, 1550. [37]

A NEW PLAN

A drawing found in the Cabinet des Estampes of the Bibliotèque Nationale, Paris, shows a plan for the Chiesa del Gesù and the new Casa Professa attributed to Nanni di Baccio Bigio and dated to 1553. It represents his second design for the complex.[38] Drawn under Ignatius' supervision 15 years before Vignola reworked it for the present church, the design already presents what would become the characteristic notes of Jesuit liturgical architecture: a large, single nave that served as an aula for preaching and a shallow sanctuary that stressed the visibility of sacramental activity. Moreover, the plan linked a large downtown residence to the fabric of the church.

Ignatius' attempts to buy enough property to build his church-residence complex were met with strong opposition from his neighbors, particularly Muzio and Lucrezia Muti, who had unsuccessfully tried to claim some of the S. Andrea property ceded to the Order for their chicken yard. Protracted legal actions forced redrawing plans for the complex, a task undertaken "solely for devotion, without any [financial] interest" by the aged Michelangelo in 1553-1554. A second cornerstone was laid in October 1554.[39]

Work had scarcely begun when Muti took the law into his own hands, threatening the bricklayers at swordpoint. Ignatius suspended all new building activities for the sake of peaceful relations with his neighbors, and, truth be told, because he lacked the resources to complete such an immense task.[40] Minor additions to the della Strada fabric were carried out, including a widening of the nave and the construction of a *penitenciaria,* a separate area for the hearing of confessions.[41]

From a carefully-chosen center in a small but strategically-located downtown church, Ignatius and his companions set about developing an extensive network of social, pastoral, and educational ministries to serve the diverse population of city of Rome. Aptly named for the streets on which they worked, the della Strada community took to the byways and street corners of the busy city in search of souls.

THE REFORM CONTEXT

The extraordinarily diverse downtown ministries of the early Society in Cinquecento Rome must be understood in the context of spiritual and social reform movements spearheaded by the lay confraternities and new religious orders. From the mid thirteenth through the early sixteenth centuries, the mendicants generally acted as animators and chaplains for the confraternities. In the second quarter of the Cinquecento, the leadership shifted to the new religious orders of the Catholic reform movement.[42]

ORATORIO DEL DIVINO AMORE, 1517

The best known Roman confraternity of the early Cinquecento was the Oratorio del Divino Amore, established at the church of S. Dorotea in Trastevere in 1517. The mixed group of clerics and laymen had its origins in the Genovese confraternity of the same name founded in 1497. The confraternity spread throughout Italy, and one of its Genovese founders, Ettore Vernazza, helped to establish the Roman offshoot.[43] The group had two distinct goals: the reform of the clergy, to be accomplished through prayer, and service to the destitute through charitable activities, particularly those performed at the hospital of S. Giacomo in Augusta under the patronage of St. Jerome. From as early as 1495, confraternities of S. Girolamo had been established in northern Italian cities to fund and administer hospitals for the "incurables," victims of the syphilis epidemic that spread over Europe at the close of the fifteenth century. In several cities the memberships of the confraternities of Divino Amore and S. Girolamo were coterminous.[44]

THEATINES REVISITED

In 1524, four of the leaders of the Roman Confraternity of Divino Amore, including the ferocious Neapolitan nobleman Gian Pietro Carafa and the saintly Gaetano Thiene, founded the first "reformed" congregation, the Order of Clerics Regular (or "Theatines"). The Theatines' spirituality was oddly schizophrenic: while insisting on charitable service to the urban poor in hospitals, they fled from psychic and physical noise of the city into an intensely cloistered life. That kind of ambiguity had led Ignatius, even before his ordination in Venice and a number of years before the foundation of the Society, to express his concern for the Theatines' future and politely yet resolutely to rebuff a 1553 offer of union with the Theatines.[45]

"COMPAGNIA DEGLI ORFANI"

While living in Venice, Ignatius had encountered well-organized initiatives and networks of assistance for the poverty-stricken and infirm.[46] In addition to hospitals for the syphilitic where he worked, he had direct contact with the dramatic pastoral work founded by Girolamo Emiliani in behalf of the orphans of that city. Emiliani's orphanage at the Ospedale degli Incurabili was a prototype for the orphanages conducted by his *Compagnia dei servi dei poveri* all over Italy. The founder's death in 1537 interrupted plans to open an orphanage in Rome.[47] In 1541, Ignatius was one of the Roman founders of the *Compagnia degli orfani,* a confraternity that administered separate orphanages for girls and boys. After Ignatius' death, the boys' orphanage was transferred to the Somaschi.[48] The precise extent of the Jesuits' involvement in the Roman orphanages is unclear, but there is no disputing the fact that these were the first of many such institutions—with their corresponding lay confraternities—that the Society helped to found throughout Europe, in India, and in Brazil.[49]

JEWISH NEIGHBORS

For almost three years Ignatius and his companions lived on the very edge of Rome's Jewish neighborhood. The house near Piazza Margana was on the fringe of what would become, in 1555, the Ghetto of Paul IV. Ignatius had been raised in the anti-Semitic atmosphere of *reconquista* Spain. All Jews who would not convert to Christianity had been expelled, and those who had converted were held in contempt. The *conversos* were called *marranos,* "swine"; the Inquisition often subjected them to interrogation and persecution.[50]

Given his upbringing, Ignatius' attitude towards the Jews was surprisingly tolerant and, indeed, sympathetic. His intense devotion to Christ seems to be the key to understanding his openness: that devotion was so personally focused that he said on a number of occasions that he wished he had been born Jewish, in order to share in physical kinship with Christ *secundum carnem*.[51] Among his first and closest companions was Diego Laínez, considered a "New Christian" because his great-grandfather was a Jewish convert to Catholicism. New Christians and recent Jewish converts were freely admitted into the Society and reached positions of responsibility: Ignatius named Gaspar Loate rector of the Jesuit's college in Genoa and Alfonso de Pisa and Giovanni Battista Eliano professors at the Collegio Romano. Laínez was elected general after Ignatius' death.[52]

MINISTRY TO THE JEWS

Ignatius himself actively preached and taught catechism to his Jewish neighbors in Rione Campitelli. He sought and obtained legal remedy for medieval legislation that impeded converts from Judaism to Christianity: until Paul III signed the bull *Cupientes iudaeos* (1542) that Ignatius promoted, Jewish converts were required to forfeit all property to the (papal) state and were excluded from full citizenship and the right to inherit goods and property. The new legislation had the result of increasing the number of catechumens not only in Rome but in other large cities of the papal states (including Bologna, Ferrara, Modena, Parma, and Reggio) where the Jesuits were working. Circular letters to the whole Society boasted of the numbers of conversions being made.[53]

The increased number of Jewish catechumens in Rome strained the Society's resources; potential converts were housed in the Jesuits' already tight quarters at the rented Astalli house near S. Maria della Strada. With the help of Margaret of Austria ("Madama," the illegitimate daughter of Charles V) and Girolama Orsini, both daughters-in-law of Pope Paul III, Ignatius established houses for male and female catechumens. In the bull *Illius qui dominici* of February 19, 1543, the pope approved the Jesuit's work with Jews, work, established a lay archconfraternity to run it, and granted it the church of S. Giovanni del Mercato at the foot of the Campidoglio. Ignatius served on the governing board of the work until 1548.[54]

PROSTITUTES

Prostitution had, of course, always existed in Rome; it was a significant service industry in a city whose population was predominantly male and largely transient or clerical.[55] Prostitution was more or less accepted in the fifteenth century. Alexander VI had added a footrace of courtesans to the *carnivale* festivities; the church of S. Salvatore (modern S. Stansilao dei Polacchi) between the Jesuits' house on Via dei Delfini and Piazza Altieri bore the epithet *in pensili,* "at the bordellos."[56]

The advent of syphilis and the changing moral tenor of Rome in the second and third decades of the Cinquecento led to numerous reform movements, most notably the Oratorio del Divino Amore's establishment of a *convento delle convertite* on the Via del Corso in 1520. As early as the thirteenth century, similar strictly cloistered convents, usually dedicated to St. Mary Magdalene, had been founded in Italy and elsewhere for *conversae,* women who wished to leave their life in the streets and embrace a rigorous religious life of penance.[57]

Not all prostitutes who wanted to regularize their lives were ready to become cloistered nuns: some were validly married, and others, although single, wanted to marry but were unable to do so for want of a dowry. It was to such as these that Ignatius addressed his energies in Rome with the 1543 founding of the Casa S. Marta and the Compagnia della Grazia.

CASA S. MARTA

Casa S. Marta was a marked departure from the severe monastic model of the convents of the *convertite*: its goal was the rehabilitation of former prostitutes and their reintegration into ordinary social life. The institution functioned as a "half–way house" for as many as 60 women at a time. Its residents, whose case histories were obtained through a surprisingly modern interview process, stayed at the house only until they had reorganized their lives. Some decided for the religious life, but many others were reconciled to their husbands or provided with a dowry so they could marry. The Roman house of S. Marta was not the first such "half-way house" but was certainly the most famous and copied exemplar of the period. Houses of St. Martha quickly sprang up under Jesuit auspices in Bologna, Florence, Pisa, Padua, Milan, Modena, Messina, Agrigento, Palermo, Trapani, and Valladolid.[58]

The house itself was one of the Society of Jesus' first constructions. During the building of the Casa Professa in Piazza Altieri, Pietro Codacio was pleased to find a number of finely carved ancient Roman marbles in the excavations. In spite of the large expenses and insufficient gifts to cover the cost of the building of the Casa Professa, Ignatius ordered Codacio to sell the antiquities and then applied the hundred ducats raised from the sale to the construction of the chapel and house of S. Marta.[59] Inspired by Ignatius' generosity and unusual commitment to the prostitutes, a number of important people began to support the enterprise. The confraternity organized to administer the work, the *Compagnia della Grazia,* was a veritable "Who's Who" of Cinquecento Rome: among its 170 founding members were 15 cardinals, seven bishops, several ambassadors to the papal court, and seven women, among them Constantia Farnese and Girolama Orsini (respectively the pope's daughter and daughter-in-law), Leonora Orosio de Astorga (wife of Charles V's ambassador to the papal court), and Vittoria Colonna. Although Margaret of Austria was not listed among the members, she was an early and generous supporter of the enterprise.[60]

The Jesuits' work with the prostitutes and, in particular, Ignatius' personal dedication to the work was the cause of no little scandal and gossip. Tongues wagged when Ignatius personally led women of bad reputation to the shelter.[61] In 1546 when the mistress of papal postmaster Matthia da San Cassiano entered the Casa S. Marta, the angry mailman began a smear campaign against the fathers, accusing them of keeping "two or three concubines each" among the residents of S. Marta. When rumors and accusations against the Jesuits reached the point that their integrity and apostolic effectiveness were being compromised, Ignatius demanded an official investigation, and all charges of misconduct against them were dismissed.[62] Criticism of the Society's advocacy of women occasioned misunderstanding and criticism in many different locales. At their missions in India, for example, strong Jesuit preaching against the sale of natives as slaves and concubines put them at odds with the local Portuguese authorities.[63]

Ignatius' sensitivity toward women is seen with particular clarity in his establishment of refuges for the daughters of prostitutes in Rome and elsewhere. The *Conservatorio delle Vergini Miserabili,* founded at the Church of S. Catarina dei Funari next to Ignatius' former residence on Via dei Delfini, was an attempt to rescue girls whose social and economic circumstances were likely to force them into a life of prostitution. The *Conservatorio*—literally, a place to conserve youthful virtue—housed girls from nine to 12 years old, taught them Christian doctrine and domestic skills, and provided them with dowries. The Roman conservatory was quickly emulated, and before Ignatius' death there were similar houses in Naples, Florence, Milan, Brescia, Parma, Bologna, Siena, and Venice. Brian Pullan's description of the

FIGURE 6.7 (RIGHT)
Rome,
Jesuit Social Minsitries.
Ignatius, another Jesuit, and lay collaborators outside the Conservatorio delle Vergini Miserabili. This Flemish engraving is anacronistic in showing Ignatius standing in front of the Della Porta facade of S. Caterina dei Funari, constructed in 1564, eight years after Ignatius' death.
From Ribadeneyra's *Vita.*

Publica Romæ pietatis opera instituit: coenobia mlie-
rum male nuptarum: virginum S. Catherinæ ad funa-
rios: puellarum SS. quatuor coronatorum: pueroru item
qui orbi parentibus per Vrbem vagi mendicant: Cathecume
norum: aliorumq̃ collegia magna oium admiratione, fructuq̃.

63

Jesuits' Casa delle Zitelle in Venice is applicable to this entire category of social work: "[the Jesuits] were not attempting mere hand-to-mouth charity by the temporary relief of physical needs: instead, they aimed at a take-over bid, at establishing an institution which would, in the interests of the soul, assume all the functions of a zealous and exacting parent."[64] It is tantalizing to speculate whether Ignatius' own personal history might have focused some of his social concern on the lot of young women: recent research indicates that before his conversion he may have fathered a daughter.[65]

OTHER WORKS

Ignatius was a formidable organizer: his work ranged from saving young girls from prostitution to the programing of systematic collections for the *poveri vergognosi*, members of the gentry fallen on hard times; from establishing homes for orphans to involvement with confraternities to foster Eucharistic devotion; from lobbying for the Jews to sending Jesuit recruits to work in hospices for the dying.[66] No work of charity was beyond the imagination of the nascent Society of Jesus.[67]

"GOD IN ALL THINGS"

What set the early Jesuits apart from their lay collaborators and from the other reformed congregations of the period was not their originality. Most of their works had been tried by others, sometimes with greater success. It was, rather, their breadth, their readiness to tackle all the needs of a complex urban milieu that distinguished the Jesuits. While groups like the Theatines, the Somaschi, the Barnabites, and later the Oratorians tended to focus in on one pious work to the exclusion of others, the Jesuit vision was one of great depth of field, "finding God in all things" and not only in accustomed works. Their willingness to enter into conversation with the urban environments they inhabited gave them an intimate knowledge of the social scene and a liberating ability to move back and forth across lines otherwise closed by prejudice, class distinctions, and fear. For them, the city was a vast proscenium on which they could improvise their *Opera Pietatis* with delight and virtuosity. At the center of the urban stage, in a vineyard at a crossroads, they acted out their commitment in variations ancient and new.

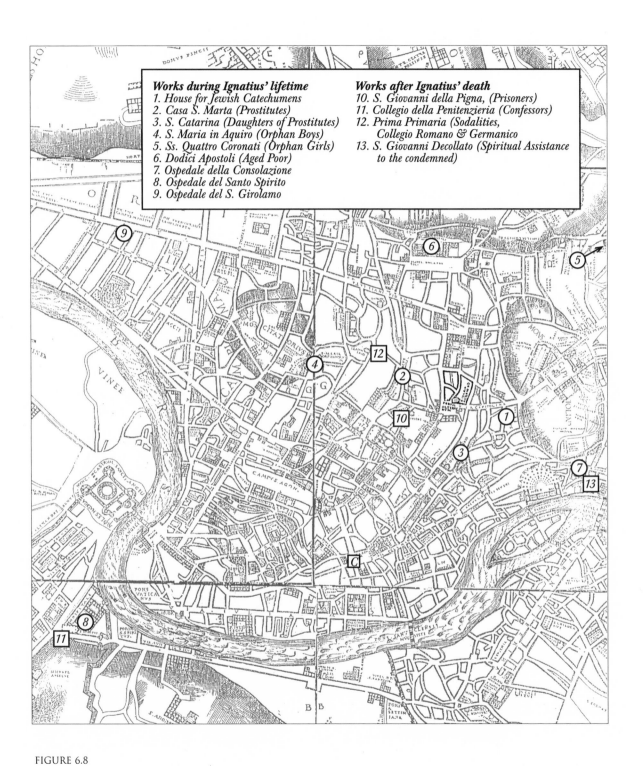

Works during Ignatius' lifetime
1. House for Jewish Catechumens
2. Casa S. Marta (Prostitutes)
3. S. Catarina (Daughters of Prostitutes)
4. S. Maria in Aquiro (Orphan Boys)
5. Ss. Quattro Coronati (Orphan Girls)
6. Dodici Apostoli (Aged Poor)
7. Ospedale della Consolazione
8. Ospedale del Santo Spirito
9. Ospedale del S. Girolamo

Works after Ignatius' death
10. S. Giovanni della Pigna, (Prisoners)
11. Collegio della Penitenzieria (Confessors)
12. Prima Primaria (Sodalities,
    Collegio Romano & Germanico
13. S. Giovanni Decollato (Spiritual Assistance
    to the condemned)

FIGURE 6.8
Rome
Jesuit Social and Pastoral Works,
overlaid on Bufalini's *Pianta*.

CHAPTER VII
"THE MORE UNIVERSAL, THE MORE DIVINE"

evelopment of any human organization shares much in common with the process of architectural design and realization. The case of the founder of a religious order who goes on to legislate its daily life is analogous to that of an architect who builds his or her own family house.[1] A rough sketch is thrown down on paper after a long discussion of the needs and desires of the family who will live in the structure. The sketch is reviewed, modified, and refined and must pass internal and external review: does it both suit the family's needs and fit into local zoning and building codes? Only then can the architect begin to prepare mechanical drawings. Sometimes there is major revision or rethinking during the design process, although the decision on the fundamental function of the building–this is a home and not a foundry, for example–informs the entire process. Changes occur throughout the construction phase: a light switch here, or another bathroom there?[2] Even after the family moves in, there is inevitable remodeling: a home is a dynamic reality, not just a shelter from the wind and rain.[3]

VISION
INFORMS MISSION

Although Ignatius Loyola was a prolific writer of Formulae, Constitutions, Declarations, and Rules and a prodigious builder of buildings, he never lost sight of the evangelical and apostolic vision that informed his mission. That mission of service began with his profound personal experience at Manresa when he encountered the Jesus "who went about in all the cities and villages teaching in their synagogues and preaching the gospel of the kingdom, healing every kind of infirmity" (Mt. 9. 35). That experience sustained Ignatius through the disasters and adventures of the 15 years that followed his conversion: a failed crusade, a painful return to school "so he could help souls," misunderstandings and accusations of heresy in Spain, France, and Italy, the discovery of companions who shared his vision, and the first dramatic apostolic and recruiting successes in northern Italy and Rome.

Until 1538, the image of Jerusalem and the idea of traditional missionary work among the "infidels" formed and informed the minds and hearts of Ignatius and his companions. They vowed to go to Jerusalem and work in literal imitation of Jesus as his missionary companions. With the move to Rome—thanks to the interference of geopolitical reality and their keen attention to the social realities surrounding them—the goal of the historical Jerusalem was transposed into work in the contemporary City of Man, wherever the pope might send them. The Jerusalem metaphor, then, no longer encapsulated or constrained the mission.[4]

The realities of the world that Ignatius had encountered in his travels and that the companions met each day in their diverse apostolic works made new demands, prompting a new form of religious life to evolve out of their missionary commitment. Their "oblation" to the pope and their readiness to go anywhere to undertake any mission given to them by the Holy See was nothing less than a "vow of mobility" that effectively removed the Society from the tradition of the monks and the "order-centric" obedience of the mendicants.[5] An early preparatory document, the *Constituciones circa missiones* (1544-1545), testifies to the radical unrootedness of the Jesuits:

> *Coming from diverse countries and provinces and knowing not which regions to go to or stay in, among the faithful or unbelievers, in order not to err in the way of the Lord, and because we were not sure where we could best serve and praise God our Lord through his divine grace, we made this promise or vow that His Holiness might distribute or send us for the greater glory of God our Lord, in accordance with our promise and intention to travel through the world, and if we did not find the desired spiritual fruit in one city or the other, to pass on to another and yet another, and so on and so forth, going about through cities and other particular places for the greater glory of God our Lord and the greater spiritual profit of souls.[6]*

In practice, this vow makes the Jesuit a cosmopolitan being at home in the world—anywhere in the world. The Jesuit, according to Ignatius himself, was to live "always with one foot raised, ready to hasten from one place to another, in conformity with our vocation and our Institute, that we follow in the Lord."[7] Jerónimo Nadal, who according to Ignatius himself "knows my mind and enjoys the same authority as myself,"[8] described the Jesuit mission of mobility in words that distantly echo the Franciscans' concept of the world as *spatiosi claustri amplitudo*: "There are missions, which are for the whole world, which is our house. Wherever there is need or greater utility for our missions, there is our house."[9]

ARTICULATING
THE MISSION

Articulation of that mission and the shaping of their general conceptual plan on paper was a task the first companions entrusted to Ignatius in 1539, even as some were beginning to disperse on papal missions of preaching and teaching in Italy and others were preparing to sail for Portuguese India. Three months of deliberation among the companions had laid down the general parameters for the "Institute." They would have a general superior, elected for life. They would vow special obedience to the pope "as regards the missions." They would teach the rudiments of the faith "to children and everyone else" for 40 days a year. Recruits to their company would usually make the Spiritual Exercises, go on pilgrimage, and "serve the poor in hospitals or elsewhere" for a total of three months.[10]

Among the decisions was an important determination regarding poverty and property:

> [We] may receive houses with a church attached but without any right to their property so that those who give their use may freely take them back if they so wish; furthermore, we shall have no right to claim them in court (in whatever way they may give them) against anyone whatever, even if they claim them unjustly.[11]

"QUINQUE CAPITULA"

At this earliest phase of its self-understanding, while the first Jesuits were still living in rented quarters, the Society saw itself following the primitive Franciscan model of *usus simplex* of property. They rejected the Dominicans' tenet that the professed community can own real property, buildings, or movable goods like furniture. Differing from the earliest Franciscan practice, however, Ignatius' sketch (which developed into the "Five Chapters" or *Quinque Capitula*) permitted acceptance of cash donations and sale of donated goods, both movable and immovable, "to buy necessities for themselves." That decision reflects the reality of living in a cash-based urban economy. Finally, the Jesuits shared with the mendicants an utter aversion to fixed revenues from benefices or stable goods that produced a regular income.[12]

The text of the 1539 *Quinque Capitula* or "Five Chapters," submitted to Paul III as a draft of the *Formula Instituti* or fundamental rule of the Society, is explicit on the motivation for these decisions.

> From experience we have learned that a life removed as far as possible from all contagion of avarice and as like as possible to evangelical poverty is more gratifying, more undefiled, and more suitable for the edification of our fellowmen. We likewise know that our Lord Jesus Christ will supply to His servants who are seeking only the kingdom of God what is necessary for food and clothing.

Therefore our members, one and all, should vow perpetual poverty, declaring that they cannot, either individually or in common, acquire any civil right to any stable goods or any produce or fixed income for the maintenance or use of the Society.

Rather let them be content to enjoy only the use of necessary things, with the owners permitting, and to receive the money and the value of things given them in order to buy necessities for themselves.[13]

The Five Chapters made one important exception to the rule against ownership and fixed revenues. In 1539 a number of talented young men had already enlisted in the as-yet-unrecognized company, and the question arose as to how to provide them with proper training for future apostolic labors. Looking back to his own experience, Ignatius remembered how the begging journeys of his student years distracted him from the work of obtaining an education so he could later "help souls." A provision, therefore, was made for the education of young men who wished to "serve as soldiers of God beneath the banner of the cross in our Society":

[We] may, however, acquire the civil right to stable goods and to fixed income in order to bring together some talented students and instruct them, especially in sacred letters, in the universities, that is, for the support of those students who desire to advance in the spirit and in letters and at length to be received into our Society after probation when the period of their studies has been finished.[14]

At this early stage, there was no consideration of founding educational institutions. Ignatius and his companions had studied at the University of Paris and had lived in "colleges," residential facilities or dormitories for matriculated students. A similar formation and living situation was envisioned for the early recruits of the Society.

DRAFTING
THE CONSTITUTIONS

Drafting the Society's foundational documents, in particular its *Constitutions*, occurred over almost 20 years. That process was extremely complicated.[15] Nevertheless, in order to understand the evolution and novelty of the Jesuit urban vision articulated in these documents, three strands of questions, three interwoven issues, must be examined in some detail. Those issues are, first, how the Society defined its mission in the world; second, how changing apostolic demands (particularly the opening of schools) changed the shape of that fundamental mission; and third, how poverty and property holding were reconciled. Part VII of the *Constitutions* is the flexible, durable fabric produced by interweaving the answers.

The world had changed radically in the 300 years that separated Ignatius from Francis and Dominic. As Ignatius learned in his travels throughout Europe, the Renaissance city was a complicated overlapping mosaic of social, linguistic, and ethnic groups—recall that only about a quarter of the Romans were natives;[16] each group, moreover, had particular pastoral needs and its own voice and dialect, whether linguistic or social. In order to converse with them, a highly articulate and extensive ministerial vocabulary had to be developed, one that could communicate with the pope one minute and the prostitutes who lived around the corner the next.

"PRINCIPLE AND FOUNDATION"

At Manresa, Ignatius discovered a basic truth that he would later formulate as the "Principle and Foundation" of the *Spiritual Exercises:*

> *Human beings are created to praise, reverence, and serve God our Lord, and by means of doing this to save their souls. The other things on the face of the earth are created for human beings, to help them in the pursuit of the end for which they are created. From this, it follows that we ought to use these things to the extent that they help us toward our end, and free ourselves from them to the extent that they hinder us from it. . . . We ought to desire and choose only that which is more conducive to the end for which we are created.*[17]

This credo is preeminently practical: use what one needs, do what one needs to do—and, conversely, do not use what one does not need, and do not do what one does not need to do—in order to serve God and save one's soul. This principle, summarized in the rhyming Latin *tantum quantum,* is a basic descriptor of how the Jesuit is to relate to the created world.

DISCERNMENT AS DIALECTIC

Of course, that principle requires figuring out—in Jesuit-speak, "discerning"—what assists the work at hand and what impedes it, a process both difficult and subtle. This process of Ignatian discernment is more than a mechanical prioritizing of pros and cons. It is, rather, a dialectic between practical experience and spiritual goods: practical experience always measured reflectively and prayerfully against the goal of the greater good and the service of God and neighbor.

Practical apostolic experience prayerfully reflected upon led the first companions to eliminate a number of the most hallowed elements of religious life from their Institute. For example, there were to be no distinctive habit, no fixed penances, and no mandatory choir.

> *One is not to impose on the companions under pain of mortal sin any fasts, disciplines, baring of feet or head, color of dress, type of food, penances, hairshirts, and other torments of the flesh. These, however, we do not prohibit because we condemn them, for we greatly praise and approve them in those who observe them; but only because we do not wish Ours either to be crushed by so many burdens together or to allege any excuse for not carrying out what we have set before ourselves.*[18]

Similarly, the reasons for dispensing with the obligation of choral recitation of the Divine Office and for mandating simplicity in liturgical celebrations are grounded in the needs of the apostolate:

> *All the members who are in holy orders, even though they can acquire no right to benefices and revenues, should nonetheless be obliged to recite the office according to the rite of the Church, but not in choir lest they be diverted from the works of charity to which we have fully dedicated ourselves. Hence too they should use neither organs nor singing in their Masses and other religious ceremonies; for these laudably enhance the divine worship of other clerics and religious and have been found to arouse and move souls, by bringing them into harmony with the hymns and rites, but we have experienced them to be a considerable hindrance to us, since according to the nature of our vocation, besides the other necessary duties, we must frequently be engaged a great part of the day and even of the night in comforting the sick both in body and in spirit.*[19]

Eminently practical in its layout, this new model of ministry put the demands of active service before the requirements of tradition.

While the early Jesuits always agreed upon the general goal of working "for the good of souls," the specification of the Society's ministries underwent an evolution that can be seen in a comparison of the texts of the *Formula of the Institute*. The *Formula* is the Society's most fundamental document, equivalent to the Rule of monastic orders. It was a document that was presented both to the Holy See for ratification and to applicants for their consideration. Based on the deliberations of 1539, the *Formula* underwent three distinct redactions: the 1539 *Quinque Capitula* presented to Paul III, a slightly revised edition in the 1540 bull of approval *Regimini militantis ecclesiae,* and the expanded version found in the 1550 bull of confirmation *Exposcit debitum.* (The words in *italics* are additions to the earlier texts, ~~strikethroughs~~ are significant deletions).

THE FORMULA
The *Formula* describes who the Jesuit is: "he is a member of a Society founded chiefly for this purpose":

1539 *Quinque Capitula:*

"to strive especially for the progress of souls in Christian life and doctrine and for the propagation of the faith by the ministry of the word, by spiritual exercises, by works of charity, and specifically by the education of children and unlettered persons in Christianity."

1540 *Regimini:*

"to strive especially for the progress of souls in Christian life and doctrine and for the propagation of the faith by the ministry of the word, by spiritual exercises and works of charity, and specifically by the education of children and unlettered persons in Christianity."

1550 *Exposcit:*

"to strive especially for the *defense* and propagation of the faith and for the progress of souls in Christian life and doctrine, *by means of public preaching, lectures, and any other ministration whatsoever* of the word *of God, and further by means of the* Spiritual Exercises, ~~and specifically~~ the education of children and unlettered persons in Christianity, *and the spiritual consolation of Christ's faithful through hearing confessions and administering the other sacraments. Moreover, he should show himself ready to reconcile the estranged, compassionately assist and serve those in prisons or hospitals, and indeed to perform any other works of charity, according to what will seem expedient for the glory of God and the common good.*"[20]

MINISTRIES OF THE WORD

The third version of the *Formula* shows clear evidence of evolution from the earlier drafts. *Exposcit* of 1550 includes public preaching, lectures and the hearing of confessions and the administration of other sacraments, as well as requiring a readiness on the part of the applicant to engage in any work of charity that "will seem expedient for the glory of God and the common good." The "defense" of the faith seems to have been added to the 1550 text in reference to the order's increased work in combating the Protestant Reformation in northern Europe. Such work was certainly not an explicit priority when the order was founded.[21]

The Society's vision and aims, as they emerge from these texts, are profoundly apostolic and evangelical: the Jesuit, in virtue of his vowed obedience to the Holy See and his superiors as regards his mission, is required to be *ready* to undertake a wide variety of different ministries, ministries whose exact scope would evolve as existential circumstances changed. Moreover, the insistence on the ministries of the word–preaching, teaching, and spiritual conversation holding pride of place–point to an understanding of the priesthood that is more prophetic than cultic. Even the corporal works of mercy, excellent in themselves, were seen as secondary to this fundamental work of communication and conversation: the Jesuit is "to show himself ready" to perform those works, but the imperative weight rests on "whatsoever ministry of the Word of God."[22]

The Society's outright refusal to assume parochial responsibilities underscored its commitment to those who were not ordinarily objects of the parish church's attention. Nadal wrote "The Society has the care of those souls for whom either there is nobody to care, or, if somebody ought to care, the care is negligent. This is the reason for the founding of the Society . . . its strength . . . its dignity in the Church."[23] Paradoxically, that emphasis often translated into a bipolar ministry aimed at the spiritual care of near-saints and the rescue of confirmed sinners. In 1548, Polanco noted that the Jesuits attracted two extremes: those "inordinately intent upon deepening their spiritual lives, and others whose lives up to that point had been notably bad."[24]

At about the same time Polanco was making this observation, the Society was embarking on a new apostolic endeavor that would, in the eyes of most, become its signature: the establishment of formal secondary- and university-level educational institutions.[25] Although not addressed to the extremes–adolescent males of the late Renaissance were no more saints nor hardened criminals than today's–the move into education was certainly in line with the Society's confirmed desire to minister to those for whom "care was negligent."

The first Jesuits had received at Paris the finest Catholic education Europe had to offer. Themselves well-educated men, they were committed

FIGURE 7.1 (RIGHT)
Ministries of the Word. Engraving shows Ignatius preaching while other Jesuits hear confessions, distribute Holy Communion, and teach catechism. Given that the engraving was made in Flanders more than 40 years after the demolition of S. Maria della Strada, it should not be construed as an accurate depiction of the first Jesuit church. From Ribadeneyra's *Vita*, 1609.

Sacramentorum, piarumq concionum vsũ Romæ
renouat, ac rationem pueris tradendi doctrinæ
christianæ rudimenta Romanis in templis,
ac plateis inducit.

to providing a thorough theological and humanistic preparation to those who joined them. The 1539 *Formula* provided for the establishment of residential *collegia* at major universities "to bring together some talented students and instruct them, especially in sacred letters."[26] In the Society's first four years, seven such colleges were founded at Paris, Louvain, Cologne, Padua, Alcalá, Valencia, and Coimbra. The Jesuits found that it was difficult to fund these small residences because benefactors (with the exception of King John III of Portugal) were hesitant to endow facilities for the exclusive training of members of a little-known and recently-founded order.[27]

"MODUS PARISIENSIS"

Although the Jesuits were committed to teaching catechism to children and the unlettered, perceived utility and external pressure rather than a deliberate, strategic decision occasioned their move into the classroom. The earliest documents were opposed to such undertakings: the *Constitutions* of 1541 are quite explicit that "no formal studies nor lectures" were to be held in the colleges of the Society.[28] The proscription was laid down when the Society was still tiny, and its overall membership was limited to 60. The founders feared that taking on teaching responsibilities would severely limit their mobility. However, because they were not always content with the progress their recruits were making or the methodology that was employed in the universities to which they were sent, the Jesuits sometimes held "in-house" courses and review sessions for their own seminarians or "scholastics," employing the *modus parisiensis*.[29]

As early as 1543, though, Jesuits began teaching a variety of subjects at a seminary for local boys at Goa, and the order assumed responsibility for the institution in 1548. At about the same time, the imperial court and the Catholic bishops of Germany put great pressure on the Jesuits to provide professors for theology faculties decimated by Reformation defections. In 1549 Ignatius reluctantly sent three of his best theologians, Claude Jay, Alfonso Salmerón, and Peter Canisius to lecture at the University of Ingolstadt.[30]

GANDÍA

In 1544, Francisco Borja arranged to have certain revenues transferred to the Jesuits in his small ducal city of Gandía for the training of their students. Since there was no university there, the Jesuits assumed responsibility for instructing their own students. In November 1545, at Borja's insistence, non-Jesuit students were admitted and received instruction alongside the scholastics. Among the Jesuits' first lay students was the duke's son Carlos. At Borja's request, Paul III chartered the school as a university.[31]

MESSINA

While Borja's powerful personality played a decisive role in the founding of the *collegium mixtum* at Gandía, civic need and the appeals of friends led to the establishment of the first Jesuit school designed specifically for lay students. The magistrates of the city of Messina joined forces with the

Viceroy Don Juan de Vega and his wife Doña Leonora Osorio, who had actively supported the foundation of the Casa S. Marta and other Roman works of the Society before their transfer to Sicily. They appealed directly to Ignatius:

> *This noble city has a great desire to have some very well educated and highly religious persons of your same Company who, through their teaching and evangelical works are most helpful to the Christian republic, that they might teach, preach, and bear that fruit they are accustomed to bear wherever they decide to dwell.*[32]

The city fathers asked for teachers of theology, the arts, grammar, rhetoric, and ethics. Ignatius sent an international group of some of his most promising men, including Nadal, Peter Canisius, André des Freux, and Cornelius Wischaven, and the enterprise began in the spring of 1548.

LAY STUDENTS

There is no single document that explains the motivations for this important shift in apostolic direction.[33] Ignatius apparently analyzed the situation and saw that the colleges for lay students would serve a variety of ends: they would make it easier to fund the order's formation efforts, while bringing quality Christian formation to the sons of all classes of urban dwellers. Colleges provided the Society with solid platforms for its urban ministries and raised the Society's profile within the cities where colleges were founded. Firmly grounded in the humanistic traditions of the Renaissance, the Jesuits believed in the moral power of education for the good of the city and for its reform. "If we see to the education of youth in letters and morality, then great help for the republic will follow, for good priests, good senators, and good citizens of every class come from these efforts."[34]

Moreover, education was understood as a work of charity in the fullest sense: "We accept for classes and literary studies everybody, poor and rich, free of charge and for charity's sake, without accepting any remuneration," Ignatius wrote in a circular letter to the whole Society. He insisted that there be "no distinction between rich and poor students."[35] Admission was based on ability alone; students from all classes studied together. The Jesuits' network of free schools for boys of all classes has been called Europe's first systematic attempt to provide education to a substantial portion of the urban population.[36] The Jesuits even had to ignore complaints from some of their benefactors who argued that providing a liberal education to the lower classes would deprive the city of artisans and craftsmen. Entering students, however, had to be able read and write, a condition that militated against boys from the poorest classes.[37]

FLOWERING OF COLLEGES

The decade that followed the opening of the Collegio S. Nicolò in

FIGURE 7.2

Annual Growth of Jesuit Colleges
and Houses, 1538-1556.

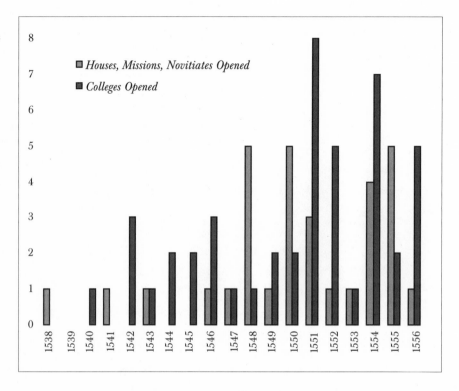

Messina saw a rapid, even extravagant flowering of Jesuit colleges across the European landscape. By the time Ignatius died in 1556, 46 colleges were open, and he had approved the foundation of at least eight more in Mexico City, Malta, Jerusalem, Constantinople, Cyprus, and several cities in Eastern Europe.[38] As the schema found in Figure 7.3 shows, Jesuit institutions were opened in almost every vigorous and important city in Catholic Europe.

The rapid opening of so many colleges strained Jesuit resources to the breaking point. Ignatius was forced to make rules—which he often broke— requiring a foundation sufficient to support 14 professors and scholastics before the foundation of a new college could take place.[39] Foundations meant fixed revenues, and colleges meant real estate holdings, two anathemas in Ignatius' view of poverty. The fact of the move into education, therefore, required a major rethinking of the issues of poverty and mobility, and a major reconfiguring of where and how most Jesuits would live.

TO THE BREAKING POINT

From the beginnings of the Order, there were tensions between the ideal of poverty and the economic realities that impinged on an apostolic enterprise like the Society of Jesus. The *Quinque Capitula* stated most explicitly that the Jesuits

FIGURE 7.3

Chronology of Foundations of the
Society of Jesus, 1538-1556.

CHRONOLOGY OF THE FOUNDATIONS
OF THE SOCIETY OF JESUS, 1538-1556

PH = Professed House, H = House or Residence,
C = College, M = Mission, N = freestanding Novitiate[40]

1538
ROME, PH

1540
PARIS, C

1541
LISBON, PH

1542
COIMBRA, C
LOUVAIN, C
PADUA, C

1543
GOA C, M

1544
COLOGNE, C
VALENCIA, C

1545
GANDÍA, C
VALLADOLID, C

1546
ALCALÁ, C
BARCELONA, C
BOLOGNA, C
COMORIN, M

1547
SALAMANCA, C
ZARAGOZA, H

1548
BASSEIN, M
COCHIN, M.
MESSINA, C
MOLUCCA, M
SAN TOMAS, M
SOCOTORA, M

1549
INGLOSTADT, H, C
ORMUZ, M
PALERMO, C

1550
BAHIA SALVADOR , M
BURGOS, C
ESPIRITO SANTO, M.
MESSINA, N
SAN VINCENTE, M
TIVOLI, H, C

1551
CHORÃO, M
EVORA, C
FERRARA, C
FLORENCE, C
MEDINA DEL CAMPO, C
OÑATE, C
PALERMO, N
PORTO SEGURO, M
ROME, C (ROMANO)
VENICE, C
VIENNA, C

1552
BUNGO, M
GUBBIO, C (†54)
MODENA, C
NAPLES, C
PERUGIA, C
ROME, C (GERMANICO)

1553
LISBON, C
MONREALE, C

1554
AMANAGUCHI, M
ARGENTA, C
COIMBRA, N
CÓRDOVA, C
CUENCA, H
GENOVA, C
LORETO, C
PLACENCIA, C
ROMA, VILLA
SYRACUSE, C
ZARAGOSA, C

1555
AVILA, H
GRANADA, H
MURCIA, C
SEPTIMANCA, N
SEVILLA, H
TOURNAI, H

1556
AMERIA, C
BILLOM C
BIVONA, C
MONREAL, C
PRAGUE, C
SAMANCA, N
SIENA, C

FIGURE 7.4

Cumulative Growth, Jesuit Colleges and Houses, 1538–1556.

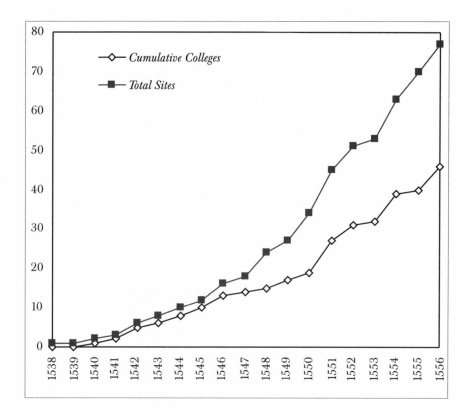

FIGURE 7.5

Jesuit Institutions by Type, 1556.

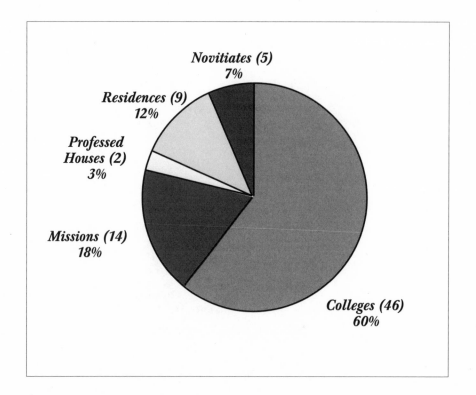

> *cannot, either individually or in common, acquire any civil right to any stable goods or any produce or fixed income for the maintenance or use of the Society.*
>
> *Rather let them be content to enjoy only the use of necessary things, with the owners permitting, and to receive the money and the value of things given them in order to buy necessities for themselves.*[41]

That same document, though, made an exception for an endowment to support Jesuit students in university studies.

The explicit ideal of the early Society was that the "professed" fathers (those who took a fourth vow of special obedience to the Pope "as regards the missions" in addition to their vows of poverty, chastity, and obedience) would live in "professed houses," apostolic centers that were to be supported only by alms. Professed Jesuits would receive neither remuneration nor stipends for their ministries. Their houses would not be supported by any kind of investments, foundations, benefices, or any other kind of regular, fixed income.[42]

THE POVERTY
OF THE PROFESSED

In April 1541, perhaps surprised by the unexpected costs of supporting their growing community and maintaining their decrepit church of S. Maria della Strada, the six original companions who gathered in Rome for the election of their first superior general mitigated somewhat the Society's first severe rulings on poverty. While maintaining a strict prohibition against the endowed support of the professed (i.e., for food and clothing), fixed revenues were permitted for secondary needs like the support of the cult in the church and for incidental expenses like postage, journeys, medicine, fuel, and books.[43]

The question of poverty, however, still rankled. When Ignatius set to writing the *Constitutions* in 1544, two issues preoccupied him: the missions of the Society and the poverty of the professed. Ignatius devoted 40 days of intense deliberation and fervent, often mystical prayer to the question of poverty. At the end of that period–detailed extraordinarily in his *Spiritual Diary* of 1544–1545[44]–he decided to put aside the 1541 decisions about fixed incomes. The numerous passages in the Constitutions pertaining to the absolute poverty of the professed and the professed houses reflect this decision and testify to Ignatius' fundamental belief that the professed houses were to be the usual residences of the Society.[45]

> *Poverty, as the strong wall of religious life, should be loved and preserved in its integrity as far as this is possible with God's grace. . . . In the houses or churches which the Society accepts to aid souls, it should not be licit to have any fixed revenue, even for the sacristy or building or anything else, in such a manner that any administration of it be in the control of the Society. But the Society, relying on God our Lord whom it serves with*

the aid of his divine grace, should trust that without its having fixed revenue, He will cause everything to be provided which can be expedient to his greater glory. . . . The professed should live on alms in the houses when they have not been sent away on missions.[46]

This admirable conceptual framework, however, was never to be realized. When Ignatius died in 1556, the Society had 73 active residences: 46 colleges, 14 overseas missions, five novitiates, and only nine residences. Of the residences, only two—Ignatius' residence in Rome and another in Lisbon—could be called professed houses according to the letter of the *Constitutions.*[47] The other seven residences were communities planning to form colleges, communities in transition, and the villa of the Collegio Romano.

The colleges, in a very brief span of years, became indispensable apostolic centers for the Jesuits: not only did they teach in the schools, but they used the facilities—especially the church which was considered an integral part of any college complex—as centers for preaching, counseling, and other pastoral ministries. So great was the impact of the colleges that Ignatius himself recognized that they had become the Society's normative institutions and residences. Polanco wrote to Borja in 1555:

Our Father's intention is, especially in the beginning, that colleges should be multiplied and not the residences. For it is necessary to have accommodations to receive and instruct many students, and that [our] workers will not want for a place to labor, without obliging the Society to have many houses that require much provision for those who live on alms.[48]

THE BLUEPRINT:
PART VII OF
THE CONSTITUTIONS

One of the first drafted and most important chapters of the Society's *Constitutions* is the seventh part, entitled "The distribution of the incorporated members in Christ's vineyard and their relation there with their fellowmen."[49] These 51 constitutions and explanatory declarations [603-654 in the standard text numbering[50]] lay out with precision and clarity answers to the crucial definitive questions—the who, what, when, where, and why—of the Jesuit mission.

Detailed and practical considerations—about *who* is to send and be sent, *what* is to be done, *when* works should be modified or abandoned, and *where* the Jesuits should focus their energies—are organized around two simple, typically Ignatian concepts: the greater glory and service of God and the more universal good.[51] Together, they form a single foundational criterion. For Ignatius, it was impossible and unthinkable to separate those concepts into two distinct criteria.

> *To proceed more successfully in this sending of subjects to one place or another, one should keep the greater service of God and the more universal good before his eyes as the norm to hold oneself on the right course. . . . The more universal the good is, the more it is divine. [622, a and d, emphasis added]*

MISSIONS FROM THE POPE

The Jesuits' decision to put themselves at the pope's disposition for missionary work was predicated on the belief that the pope as universal pastor of the Church has the most profound knowledge of the needs of the flock or, to use a favorite image of Ignatius, the "vineyard."[52] For churchmen of Ignatius' time, there was no neat distinction between Church and world: the two were considered as co-extensive. Although ultimate missioning authority rested in the pope's hands, for practical efficiency that power was ordinarily delegated to the Society's superior general. In practice, while the pope sometimes mandated that certain works be undertaken in certain specific locations, in all but the most extraordinary cases the choice of particular men for a given work was left to the discretion of the general or delegated by him to the local provincial.

GREATER GLORY, MORE UNIVERSAL GOOD

Once the principle of delegation was firmly established, Ignatius attempted to draw up guidelines for determining what "the greater service of God and the more universal good" meant at any given moment or in a situation where a choice had to be made among several valid options. The methodology Ignatius proposed was the same one that he laid out for making an "election" or choice of a way of life "in a time of tranquility" in the *Spiritual Exercises*. In the absence of certain knowledge obtained by spiritual illumination or deeply experienced "consolation or desolation,"

> *I consider first the end for which human beings are born, namely, to praise of God our Lord and to save their souls; then, desiring this, as the means I elect a life or state of life within the limits of the Church, in order to be helped in the service of my Lord and the salvation of my soul.[53]*

PRACTICAL METHODOLOGY

When applied to the question of the choice and management of undertakings, this methodology is eminently practical and thoroughly unro-

123

mantic; it proposes a careful weighing of a large number of factors: apostolic needs, levels of commitment appropriate to meet those needs, physical factors of manpower, location, and available resources, a balancing of chances for success against personal and corporate dangers.

"THE MULTIPLIER EFFECT"

The most notable linguistic feature of Part VII is the constant *ostinato* of comparative adjectives and adverbs. The underlying criterion of the *greater* service of God and the *more* universal good grounds all choices in what the modern social sciences call "the multiplier effect." All decisions—whom to send, where they are to work, what they are to do, what norms they are to follow—are subordinated to the unrelenting demand of the *magis,* the greater service, the more universal good. That criterion makes hard demands and imposes the responsibility to measure hierarchically-arranged values against one another. At the same time, Ignatius acknowledged that any one existential situation can and usually does differ from the next and can require that hierarchically-arranged values be reordered according to the concrete needs of a time and place. The norms he proposed function *ceteris paribus,* "when other considerations are equal." Given that other considerations are rarely equal, that liberating qualifier leaves superiors room to diverge from past decisions in any given situation.

The text of Part VII [622, 623] (given in full in Appendix B, pp. 195 ff.) proposes an interlocking series of criteria for judging apostolic importance of works and choosing a place to work.[54] The norms are shot through with sturdy realism that always aims at maximizing impact. Work that will last is to be chosen over transitory "hit and run" ministry. Work that reaches large numbers of people is generally to be chosen over work that is focused on individuals, unless, of course, the individuals are in positions of influence and can make the effects spread more widely. "Great nations such as the Indies, important cities, and universities which are generally attended by numerous persons who by being aided themselves can become laborers for the help of others" are deemed ideal target locations. The schema developed in Figure 7.6 shows how Ignatius related location and needs, norms, the shaping and siting of works as sketched out in sections [622] and [623].

"IMPORTANT CITIES, GREAT UNIVERSITIES"

What emerges from these norms is a clear-cut "preferential option" for urban settings for Jesuit works in the developed world. The multiplier effect clearly mandates the choice of "important cities, and great universities, which are being attended by numerous persons who by being aided themselves can become laborers for the help of others" [622e]. Cities and major universities, located perforce in an urban setting,[55] are the chosen arenas for the multiform ministries sketched out in the *Formula* and fleshed out in the programs of the *Constitutions*. The urban setting provided the greatest diver-

FIGURE 7.6 (RIGHT)
The Mission.

THE MISSION

"The Greater Glory of God and the More Universal Good"

RESPONSIBLE FOR MISSIONING

POPE

↓

SUPERIOR GENERAL

NORMS FOR CHOOSING A SITE
[622a–f]

*[622 a] The greater service of God,
the more universal good:
Where there is greater need,
lack of workers, misery and
weakness of inhabitants,
peril of damnation*

*[622 b] Where greater fruit can be
reaped by the Society's usual means*

*[622 c] Where there is greater
indebtedness (benefactors);
where there are houses, colleges*

*[622 d,e] Where persons can be reached
who can cause the good to spread
(princes, prelates, scholars)*

[622 f] Where there is greater opposition

NORMS OF IMPORTANCE
[623 a–f]

*[623 a] The greater divine honor,
the greater universal good*

*[623 b] Works of mercy:
spiritual works > corporal works
greater perfection > lesser perfection*

*[623 c] Urgency
more pressing > less pressing*

[623 d] Availability of other ministers

*[623 e] Moral safety for ministers
relative speed in dispatching work*

*[623 f] Impact on more people
preaching, teaching > work with
individuals*

*[623 g] Durability
long range effects > short term*

TARGET LOCATIONS
[622 e]

"Preference ought to be shown to the aid which is given to
great nations such as the Indies,
or to important cities
or to universities,
*which are generally attended by numerous persons who by being aided
themselves can become laborers for the help of others."*

sity of possibility "where the greater fruit will probably be reaped through the means that the Society uses" [622 a,b]. The city's critical mass of population, wealth, and apostolic needs and opportunities provided possibilities for spiritual, social, and pastoral ministries, public preaching and private conversations, the long-range social impact of work with those who have power to effect systemic change, and the promise of reforming a world by educating its youth.

Composed after almost a decade of ministerial experience, the *Constitutions'* Part VII sketched a blueprint for the Jesuit mission. The ideal Jesuit was conceived of as a man on the move, one sent by his superiors to labor in the vineyard. Nadal's commentary on the Introduction to Part VII summarizes this missionary attitude:

> *"When they are dispersed to any part of Christ's vineyard." This dispersion of the professed and coadjutors will indeed take place in the founding of professed houses, and also of the colleges and houses of probation, in important cities as well as in large and populated towns. But we must always look and strive for that great goal of the Society, which is not only that Ours live in our houses and from them come to the aid of the city or town or even the nearby countryside, but that the professed and coadjutors be engaged in journeys that are undertaken by a commission either from the supreme pontiff or from our superiors.*[56]

The practical reality that confronted the first Jesuits was different from the early ideal of constant movement; it became clear that the Society needed bases of operation. The same Nadal who waxed eloquent about the road-as-house admitted the need for fixed dwellings:

> *The houses of the Society should be like a garrison from which the troops go out to make raids and sorties against the enemy and then to return. So, too, from the houses of the Society some will go out here and there to battle against vices and demons, others will return and rest for a while, as Christ our Lord said. They retreat to regain strength and others will take their place.*[57]

While the professed house was envisioned in the documents as the typical residence of the Society, in fact "they are few because the professed are few."[58] The overwhelming majority of Jesuits lived in colleges, which "exist for the acquisition of learning, [while] the houses [exist] that those who have acquired it may put it in practice" [289].

In the last section of Part VII ("Ways in which the houses and colleges can help their fellowmen" [636-654]), Ignatius reiterates the essential program of urban ministries in an order different from that laid out in the various editions of the *Formula*. In addition to helping their fellow citizens by prayer and good example [637-638], masses, other divine services, the administration of the sacraments, especially the hearing of confessions, sermons, lectures, the teaching of Christian doctrine (in the Society's churches, other churches, and in public places), spiritual conversations, the Spiritual Exercises, and the corporal works of mercy ("both by their personal work and by getting others to do it") are listed as the chief apostolic works [640-651], and "can be done in the colleges and their churches . . . according to the opportunity that exists and the superior's design"[652]. This reordering is not a reprioritization of ministries but rather reflects pastoral praxis and relative frequency of each various activity.[59]

Ignatius found his vineyard not on the terraced slopes of the Pincio but at the busy corner of Piazza Altieri, in downtown locations all over Europe, and ultimately in crowded cities all over the globe. At crossroads in the heart of the vineyard, the word was to be proclaimed unremittingly, "for the greater glory of God and the more universal good."

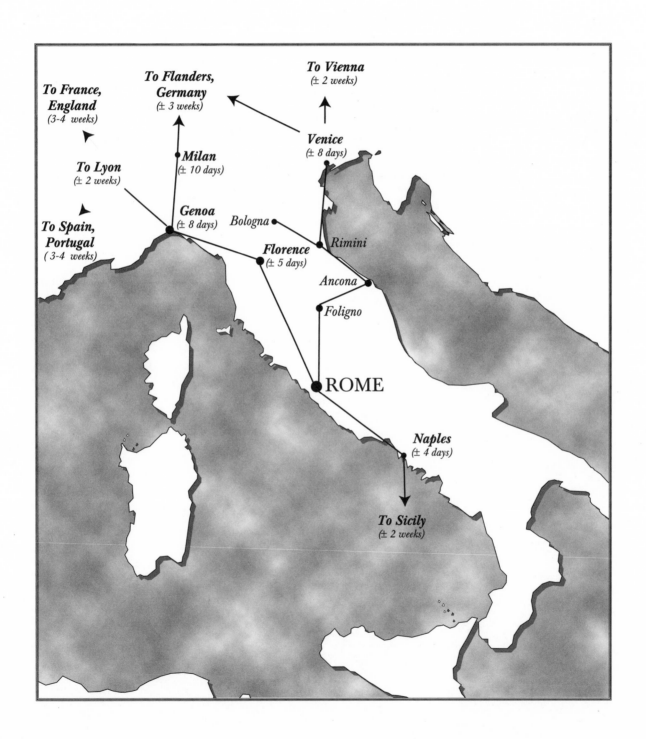

CHAPTER VIII
GOD IN THE DETAILS

In the 1540s as in the 1990s, the Italian post could try the patience of a saint. In Ignatius' time, it took weeks, months, and sometimes even years to exchange news and information. Although fast and very expensive "pony express" service was available, ordinary mail moved across Europe at a leisurely pace. In good conditions, a letter from Rome could reach northern Italy in about a week; Sicily, Lyons, or Vienna in about two weeks; Paris, Brussels, or Barcelona in three weeks; London, central Spain, and Portugal in about a month. It took almost three years for news of Javier's death off the shores of China to reach Ignatius in Rome.[1] If, for Ignatius, the post was a particular purgatory, it was also his most frequently used and useful tool for shaping and governing his nascent society and contributing to the union of minds and hearts of its members.

Rome was one of Europe's most important postal centers. As administrative center of the Catholic Church, it served as a kind of belvedere of Europe. Princes needed to stay in touch with the Holy See, their cardinals, and ambassadors. In spite of the Reformation there was still a rich traffic in benefices administered by the papal *Dataria,* which ranked requests according to the date received. Moreover, for much of the sixteenth century, Rome served as a hub for the Spanish empire, linking Naples and Sicily to the Iberian peninsula, Flanders, and Germany.[2]

COMMUNICATION IN DIASPORA

From its inception, the Jesuit community was destined for dispersion. In view of this diaspora, frequent communication among members and between members and headquarters was not only valued but mandated. Part VIII of the *Constitutions,* following immediately on the mission section, is entitled "Helps toward uniting the distant members with their head and among themselves." The first and most important section is

FIGURE 8.1 (LEFT)
Postal network emanating from Rome,
16th century.

Chapter 1, entitled "Aids toward the union of hearts."

> *The more difficult it is for the members of this congregation to be united with their head and among themselves, since they are so scattered among the faithful and unbelievers in diverse regions of the world, the more ought means to be sought for that union. For the Society cannot be preserved, or governed, or consequently, attain the end it seeks for the greater glory of God unless its members are united among themselves and with their head. [655]*

It was deemed very important that the general and provincial superiors could be easily reached and accessible at least by reliable postal service:

> *That the location may be favorable for communication between the head and his members, it can be a great help for the general to reside for the most part in Rome, where communications with all regions can more easily be maintained. Similarly, for the greater part of the time the provincials should be in places where they can communicate with their subjects and the superior general, as far as they find this possible in our Lord. [668]*

For Ignatius, the physical centrality of Rome as a convenient headquarters site complemented its ideological importance as center of the papacy. In 1547, he commissioned Polanco to write a circular newsletter to the communities in Portugal reporting on works at the Roman Casa Professa. In that letter, Polanco developed a somewhat overwrought yet ultimately telling metaphor for the centrality of Rome to the Jesuit vision:

> *I know that everyone there wants to know about what Our Lord is doing for those who are in Rome, the city that is in one respect the head, and in another the stomach of all Christendom. For this Society it seems to be both the one and the other: and, if one could add a third element, it is the heart of the Society. It is like the head in that from here the Society is directed and moved, and like the stomach in that from here are dispensed and distributed to all its members that which maintains their well being and their fruitful progress. So too one can call it the heart, in as much as it is the [vital] principle of the other members, and also because it seems to be the seat of life of the entire body of the Society. Without the connection to Rome, no matter how much the Society were to increase in numbers, things would surely go badly for its preservation. For this reason, those who know the importance of this house in Rome most reasonably want to know what is going on here in it.[3]*

If Rome was head, heart, and stomach of Christendom, it was also a nerve center for information gathering, diffusion, and communication.

Ignatius created a detailed, comprehensive "nervous system" for the Society through the requirement of frequent and detailed letter writing.

> Another very special help will be found in the exchange of letters between the subjects and the superiors, through which they learn about one another frequently and hear the news and reports which come from the various regions. The superiors, especially the general and the provincials, will take charge of this, by providing an arrangement through which each region can learn from the others whatever promotes mutual consolation and edification in the Lord. [673]

Complicated schedules were established requiring weekly, monthly, and quarterly letters to be exchanged up and down the hierarchical structure of the Society. Newsy "letters of edification" were to be sent to other regions and to major benefactors. Problems, scandals, and confidential matters were to be treated on separate sheets called *hijuelas*.[4]

6.815 LETTERS

Ignatius was the most prolific letter writer of the sixteenth century: only royal and papal courts produced more paper flow than his small office on Via Aracoeli. Dominique Bertrand's statistical analysis of the correspondence places the letters and instructions of Ignatius in context with the correspondence of some of the leading humanistic and religious figures of his age:[5]

WRITER	PERIOD OF MAJOR PRODUCTION	LETTERS WRITTEN	TOTAL CORRESPONDENCE
Erasmus	1519-1536	1,980	3,145
Luther	1520-1546	3,141	4,337
Ignatius	**1548-1556**	**6,815**	**9,178**
Calvin	1548-1564	1,247	4,271
Catherine de Medici	1561-1588	6,381	n.a.
Peter Canisius	1548-1571	1,414	2,420
Teresa of Avila	1576-1582	457	470

The secular reader approaches the correspondence of a saint with a certain reluctance; one expects—even dreads—being overwhelmed with spiritual platitudes and other-worldly speculation. In 8,500 pages of the 12-volume Monumenta Historica Series *Letters and Instructions of St. Ignatius*, piety is decidedly secondary to praxis. The letters of Ignatius are preeminently practical and only very rarely hortatory: while 72.5 percent of the letters are addressed to Jesuits, only about five percent can be classified as spiritual instruction.[6] The vast majority are the works of an administrator

FIGURE 8.2
Property agreement with
Lorenzo Astalli, signed and
sealed by Ignatius, 1552.

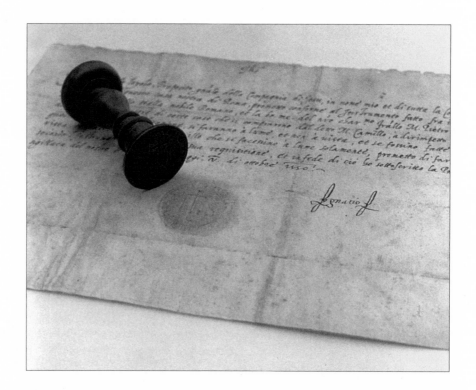

who finds God in the details and who seeks to help his correspondents
discern that elusive presence in the ordinary business of life.

Because little of the corpus has ever been translated from the equally
tortured Spanish, Italian, and Latin originals, most Jesuits know only one of
Ignatius' almost 7,000 letters: an atypically stern admonition on obedience,
which used to be read monthly to all in the refectory.[7] The rest of the letters,
however, reveal an Ignatius few people have encountered: a man of restless
curiosity, of flexible and ready intellect, capable of anger, great compassion,
and deliberate change.

RANGE AND SCOPE

From his carefully chosen central headquarters, he chides Javier for not
sending detailed geographical and climatological reports from the Orient,
and begs the King of Spain for money.[8] He patiently instructs a new teacher
how to correct homework themes, and gives tips to a brother in the kitchen
on how best to scour pots and pans.[9] He writes to the superior in Ferrara
about a hermaphrodite, and sternly insists that Spanish novices sleep
alone.[10] He hires a Neapolitan agent to buy wine for the community in
Rome "until Father Salmerón learns to negotiate, which will happen no time
soon."[11] He gives reasoned arguments for admitting converted Jews and
Moors into the Society in Spain and Portugal, and writes joyfully from his
sick bed of "two of ours, placed among the roll of martyrs, killed preaching

the gospel."[12] He is able to discourse at length on where best to invest and exchange money (Naples), and how to smuggle money (in bags of sugar) from Spain into Italy to avoid paying import duties.[13] He carries on a lively correspondence with a number of women, simple and famous, and writes exquisite letters of condolence to the bereaved which echo both his deep faith and his courtly training.[14]

A NON-TRADITIONAL
TESTAMENT

In the last six months of his life, he writes a long series of letters to Venice negotiating the purchase of a printing press for the Collegio Romano, and even sends back type fonts because they are too hard to read.[15] His last ten letters deal with the printing press, personnel problems and negotiations for deferred payment for property recently purchased in Naples, the Society's obligation to pray for its benefactors, a prohibition of singing choral office in

FIGURE 8.3

Overall relationship of relevant
letters and references in the
total Ignatian correspondence.

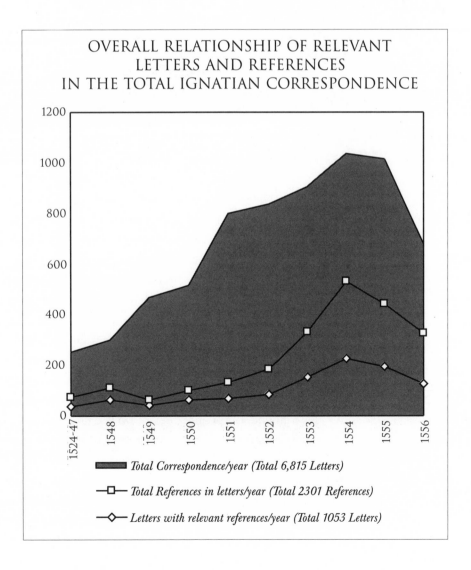

OVERALL RELATIONSHIP OF RELEVANT
LETTERS AND REFERENCES
IN THE TOTAL IGNATIAN CORRESPONDENCE

■ *Total Correspondence/year (Total 6,815 Letters)*

—□— *Total References in letters/year (Total 2301 References)*

—◇— *Letters with relevant references/year (Total 1053 Letters)*

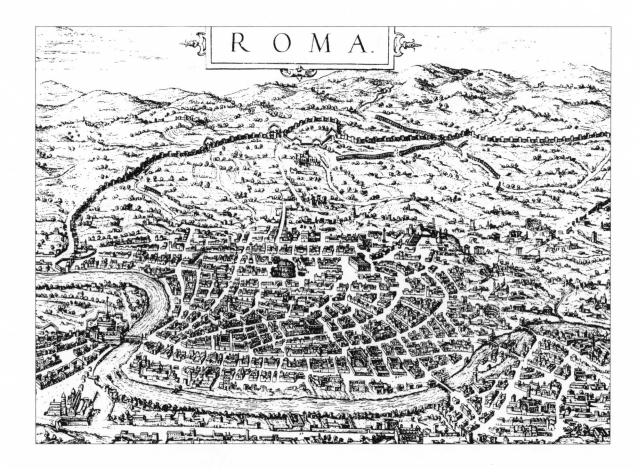

FIGURE 8.4
Rome
from Braun's *Civitates orbis terrarum,* ca. 1575.

the Society's churches, a receipt of a property deed for a new college, an introduction for a traveler, and an appeal to Philip II for assistance in regularizing the Society's legal status and residence in Louvain.[16] While they would hardly be considered a traditional "spiritual testament," these last, ordinary letters testify to Ignatius' ability to find God in all things, howsoever mundane.

Given Ignatius' practicality, finding letters on contracts, finances, and property transactions among his last writings is not too surprising. What is startling is how frequently these and related topics appear in the corpus of Ignatius' wide-ranging correspondence. As the database compiled for this study shows (found in Appendix A, pp. 175 ff.), 1,053 or 15.45 percent of the 6,815 extant letters of Ignatius made some reference to property transactions, strategic planning for obtaining property or buildings, building and construction, finances for building and construction, urban ministry or manpower requirements. Since many of the letters deal with more than one of these relevant categories, the overall number of entries or references in this database is quite large: 2301 instances where Ignatius discusses siting and

ROMA.

DOMVS AC PIETATIS OPERA QVÆ S.P. IGNATIVS ROMÆ FACIENDA CVRAVIT, QVÆQ. SOCIETAS SVÆ CVRÆ COMMISSA HABET.
A. *Domus Patrum Profeſſorum* B *Collegium Romanum.* C *Colleg. Pœnitentieria.* D *Nouitiatus.* E *Orphanorum atque orphanarum domicilia.* G *Catechumeni.* H *S. Marthæ, tunc mulierum pænitentium perfugium* I *S. Catherina de Funarys, Virginum in lubrico verſantium portus.* K *Coll. Germanicum.* L *Anglicanum.* M *Seminary Romani.* N *Maronitarum.*

FIGURE 8.5

Roma Ignaziana
Galle/Mallery reworking (ca. 1610) of the 1575 Braun plan of Rome, showing Jesuit buildings and "opera pietatis"–works of mercy–in large scale, Ribadeneyra's *Vita*.

strategy issues relevant to the order's urban mission (see Fig. 8.3, p. 133).[17] The evidence of this large sample confirms the intuition that emerged from the chance discovery of an engraving known as the "Roma Ignaziana": Ignatius deliberately and strategically opted for downtown sitings of his most important works, both in Rome and elsewhere. The engraving, a reworked map of Rome printed at the time of Ignatius' beatification in 1609, shows Jesuit schools and apostolic centers radiating in a corona around the order's mother church, the Chiesa del Gesù. In a much less elegant yet even more convincing form, the data base establishes direct evidence of Ignatius' strategic decision to target downtown locations for the Society's works and residences.

Three major classifications dominate in the database sample: strategy, property transactions, and finances. The strategy category is composed of two elements: a very few letters written to potential benefactors and a vast majority written to Jesuits instructing them how to negotiate, what kind of terms to seek, whom to contact, etc. In general, the rubric "strategy" implies Ignatius' preliminary instructions and inquiries. In all there are approximately 625 "strategic" references. The property transaction category (577

FIGURE 8.6

Incidence of finance, property transaction, and strategy references in Ignatian correspondence.

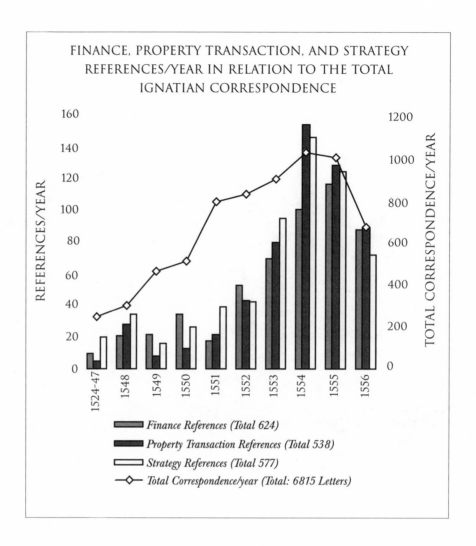

FINANCE, PROPERTY TRANSACTION, AND STRATEGY REFERENCES/YEAR IN RELATION TO THE TOTAL IGNATIAN CORRESPONDENCE

Finance References (Total 624)
Property Transaction References (Total 538)
Strategy References (Total 577)
Total Correspondence/year (Total: 6815 Letters)

references) includes letters that can be divided into two complementary classifications: those letters dealing with the personal and legal transactions of buying or selling property (456), and letters focusing on building and construction (121). The finances category (538 references) is likewise divisible into two parts: general financing of transactions (389), and the particularly difficult problem of funding the Roman houses and institutions (149).[18]

"COMMODO LUOGO"

The Jesuits were founded not to acquire real estate, but to save souls. Ministry, particularly in the urban context, was their project, the *proposito* frequently referred to in the letters of Ignatius. Finding a convenient, central location where that project could be realized, what Ignatius called the *commodo luogo*, was a major concern from the beginnings of the Society. For Ignatius, the idea of commodity had little to do with physical comfort: rather, it denoted aptness and convenience for the needs of the ministry.

There is a clear correlation between Ignatius' writings on ministry in the

FIGURE 8.7
Financial references to Rome
and other sites.

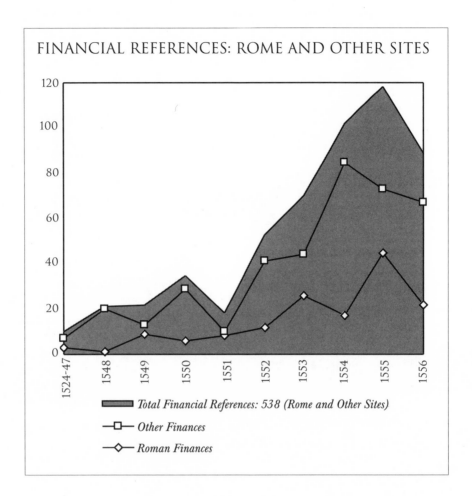

FINANCIAL REFERENCES: ROME AND OTHER SITES

Total Financial References: 538 (Rome and Other Sites)
—□— *Other Finances*
—◇— *Roman Finances*

letters and the foundation of new houses: as the ministries expanded, so did the number of centers and residences founded to house them. There is a similar correlation between his writings on ministry and references to negotiations to find the *commodo luogo* in which those ministries could be performed. Just any site would not do; each site had to be appropriate, and conveniently located, for the works it was to shelter.[19]

The Society's headquarters location in Rome was not chosen because of the size and comfort of its buildings but because the site itself was conveniently located as a center for diverse urban ministries. *Mutatis mutandis,* the same principle was employed when the Jesuits settled in other cities throughout Europe and in the Spanish and Portuguese colonies.

The ministerial *proposito* for a residence or professed house required certain "commodities": a church unencumbered by parish obligations where the Jesuits could preach, teach, and celebrate the sacraments; a convenient location that was easily accessible to large numbers of citizens; and a residence for the fathers. Proximity to the local court was a decided advantage.

FIGURE 8.8

Roma Ignaziana
highlighting the major Jesuit
works in Rome arrayed around
the Gesù-Casa Professa complex.

As to the location of the residence, whichever is chosen, there they [the local superiors] should consider which would be most expedient: from here [Rome] presupposing the equal service of God that is to be hoped for, it seems that three things should be considered. First, with all things being equal, to settle in that location where, with the passage of time, you think it would be useful to establish some works; secondly, where there might be found greater readiness and openness toward the service of God after the manner of our Institute; thirdly, where the good accomplished might receive good repute, such that those who govern would hear of the work of the Society for divine service. If there were a ready opportunity, it would be good to see to it that the residence was near the court.[20]

When the Marchesa of Cordova offered a pleasant rural site for a professed house in her city, her Jesuit son Father Antonio de Cordova was ordered to report on the location.

The site is pleasant, healthful, and quiet, and has good facilities for the house of the professed and for the Exercises; but if it is too far removed,

> *then it could not serve the principal [works] of the professed Society,*
> *namely, hearing confessions and preaching. That is to be considered. You*
> *should consult [with other fathers], and Father Ignatius would like to*
> *hear from them before he gives his opinion.*[21]

"MODO DE PROCEDER"

With the rapid explosion of Jesuit colleges that began in 1551, policies and guidelines had to be issued for those founding new works.[22] Ignatius and Polanco composed a series of instructional documents that were referred to as *nuestro modo de proceder,* "our way of proceeding." Those documents were given to new superiors sent out to found colleges and were also provided to superiors already in place. The *modo de proceder* type documents were written for several specific purposes. The most general were written to assist those sent to a new city in laying foundations for future works, particularly colleges. The first and most frequently copied of such documents is *EpistIgn* 3, 1899 (dated June 13, 1551), which is reproduced in full in Appendix C, pp. 199 ff.[23]

> *It seems that there are three things that needs must be required: first, that*
> *those of the Society should be sustained and developed in spirit, number,*
> *and learning; second, that they be mindful of the edification and spiritu-*
> *al development of the city; and finally, that the temporal affairs of the*
> *new college are established and developed such that in the first and sec-*
> *ond instances, the Lord may be served ever the more.*[24]

The second and third sections of these documents are particularly interesting: they clearly lay out concrete strategies for developing the urban mission on both spiritual and practical levels.

"EDIFICATION"

The "edification" of the city was understood in the full sense of that rich word: the Jesuits were concerned not only with giving a stirring moral example but literally with the "building up" of the Church through the Society's usual ministries of teaching, preaching, conversation, and the corporal works of mercy.

STRATEGY

In order to accomplish their overlapping spiritual, social, and educational missions, those sent to various cities were given specific political and strategic directives. They were told to cooperate actively with the local rulers of Church and state and to pay special attention to the rulers' preferred charities. In financial matters, "in order to better maintain appropriate spiritual authority, see to it that temporal matters are negotiated with the ruler and with others by friends, and not by you yourselves. Thus, you will avoid any evil accusations of cupidity."[25]

FIGURE 8.9
Prague
Jesuit church and Collegium
Clementinum at the
Charles Bridge,
19th century engraving by H.
W. Brewer.

SITING

Finally, the important question of siting was addressed:

> *Take special care that you obtain a good and sufficiently large site, or one*
> *that can be enlarged with time, large enough for house and church, and*
> if possible, not too far removed from the conversation of the city;
> *and having bought that, it will be a good beginning for all that follows.*
> *[Emphasis added]* [26]

The Jesuits followed this final counsel with a vengeance. Downtown properties were avidly sought, haggled over, and often purchased at great expense in major cities all over Europe. In Naples, long negotiations led to the purchase of a "convenient and salubrious site at the very umbilicus of the city."[27] Similar boasts were made for the siting of colleges at Perugia, Florence, and Ferrara.[28] In Prague, the Jesuits obtained two hectares of property near the strategic Charles Bridge, and in Vienna the King of the Romans negotiated the gift of a rundown monastery one long block from the Cathedral

> *with a very beautiful and extremely large church in which well attended and fruitful assemblies are anticipated, as well as being useful for the exercise of the Society's other ministries. It was located in the densest part of the city, practically in the center of the city, and thus it is most convenient for [attracting] the maximum confluence of young scholars.*[29]

In Armerina, a church "a little off the beaten track" *(un poco fora di mano)* was accepted "because the city is not too big, and those who wish or have dedication to come there for sermons, catechism, or classes will accept that little exercise with patience."[30] This interjection stands out precisely because it is a most decided exception to the usual rule of central siting.

"TANTUM QUANTUM"

When the health of Jesuits was jeopardized, Ignatius applied his *tantum quantum* rule. In Modena, the community founded in 1553 was first located in an unhealthy neighborhood and within a short period of time became "a hospital full of sick people." The ongoing difficulties there brought an uncharacteristically ironic response from Ignatius:

> *Concerning the site, although the saints lived in caves etc., and if it were for the greater divine service they still could live in them, . . . however, given also that this house has no classroom space, it seems that it is impossible to work there, and since you must work, it seems necessary to attempt to obtain another house, even if you have to beg and negotiate with many people.*[31]

Because of continuing illnesses, Ignatius ordered the Modena Jesuits to leave their "cave suited for wild beasts."[32] The community finally resettled in a house with a garden near the city walls, "since the city is small . . . [and] the distance is tolerable."[33] Such was Ignatius' preoccupation with the health of his subjects that the *Constitutions'* final paragraph is a declaration on the need to guard against the *mal aria* of Renaissance cities: "it is expedient that attention should be given to having houses and colleges in healthy locations with pure air and not in those characterized by the opposite." [827]

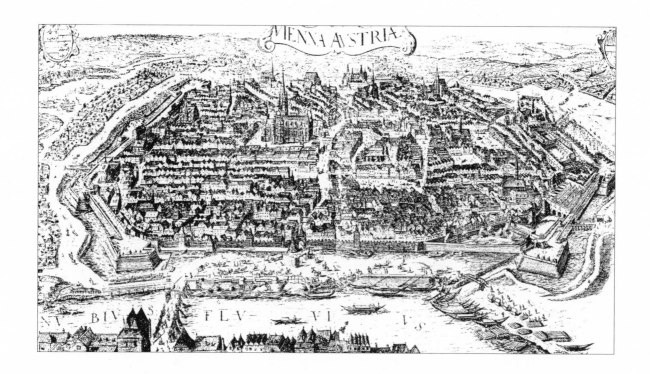

FIGURE 8.10 (ABOVE)
Vienna
engraving from Braun's *Civitates*,
ca. 1575.

FIGURE 8.11 (RIGHT)
Vienna
detail, showing site of Jesuit
church and college.

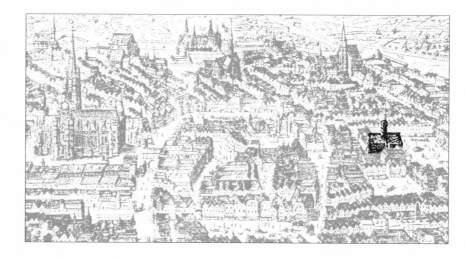

WHICH TOWN?

Ignatius was concerned not only with the siting of buildings in strategic parts of town but also with the choice of which towns the Jesuits should choose as their "vineyards." As the idea of the Jesuit college caught on, Ignatius was flooded with requests from all over Europe. The first big surge of eight college foundations in 1551 caused such a manpower and financial drain on the young Society that Ignatius was forced to reevaluate his criteria for allowing new foundations. A policy made in 1553 required the appellant city or its ruler to guarantee the gift of land, buildings, and a sufficient financial foundation to support 14 Jesuit professors and students before a new college could be opened.[34]

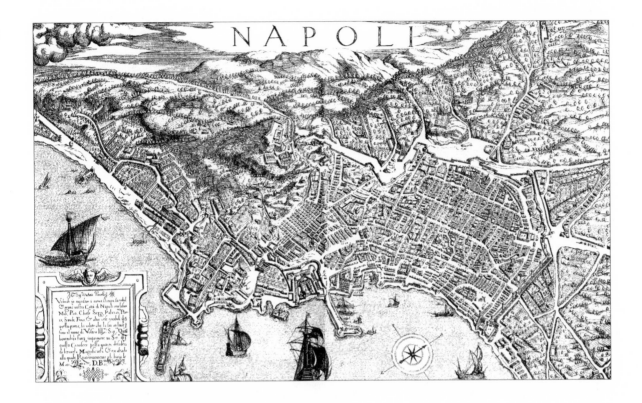

FIGURE 8.12 (ABOVE)

Naples
engraving by Donate Bertelli,
ca. 1585.

FIGURE 8.13 (RIGHT)

Naples
detail, showing showing site of
Jesuit church and college.

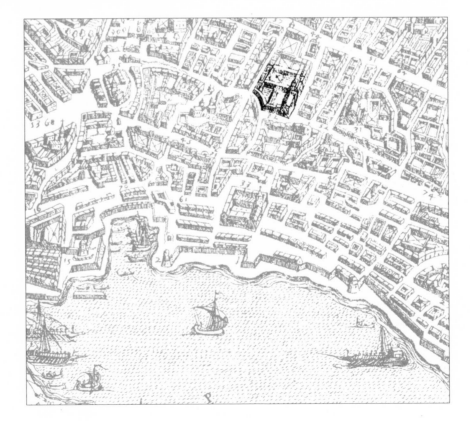

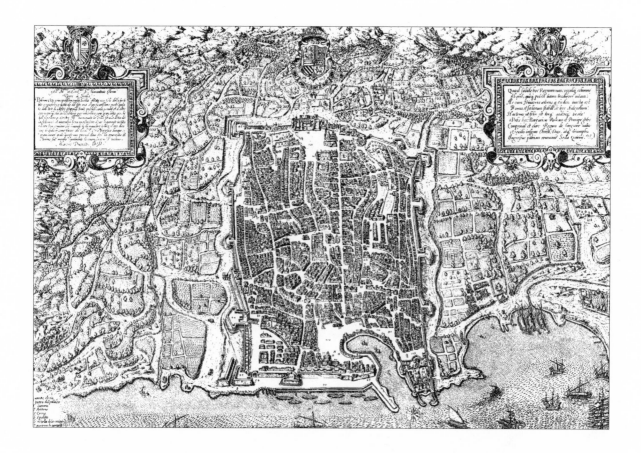

FIGURE 8.14 (ABOVE)
Palermo
engraving by Orazio Majocchi
ca. 1580.

FIGURE 8.15 (RIGHT)
Palermo
detail, showing the site of the
Jesuit church and college.

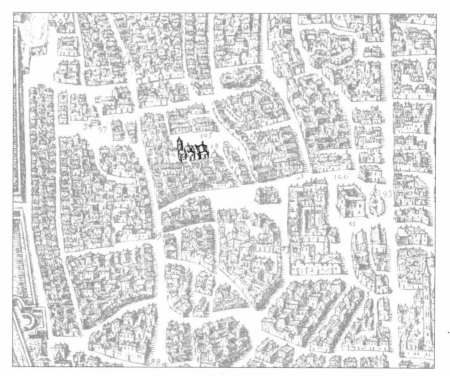

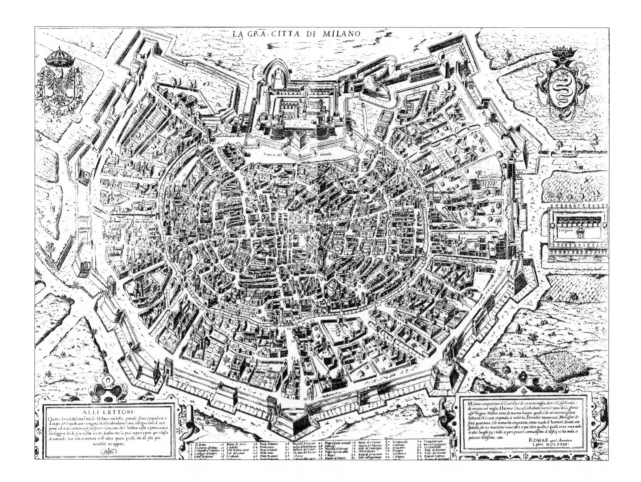

FIGURE 8.16 (ABOVE)

Milan
engraving by Antonio Lafréry,
1573.

FIGURE 8.17 (RIGHT)

Milan
detail, showing site of Jesuit
church and college.

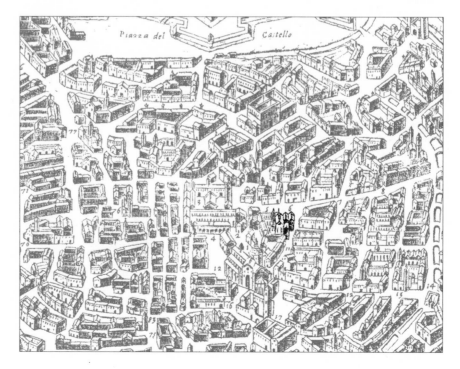

FIGURE 8.18
Lisbon
engraving from Braun's
Civitates,
ca. 1575.

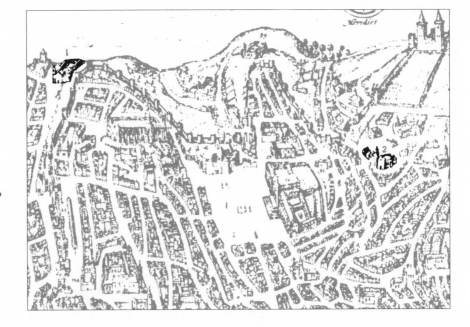

FIGURE 8.19
Lisbon
detail, showing the sites of the
Jesuit church and professed
house of S. Roch (upper left),
and the first college of S. Antão
o velho.

FIGURE 8.20
Coimbra
showing the site of the Jesuit
college, engraving from Braun's
Civitates, ca. 1575.

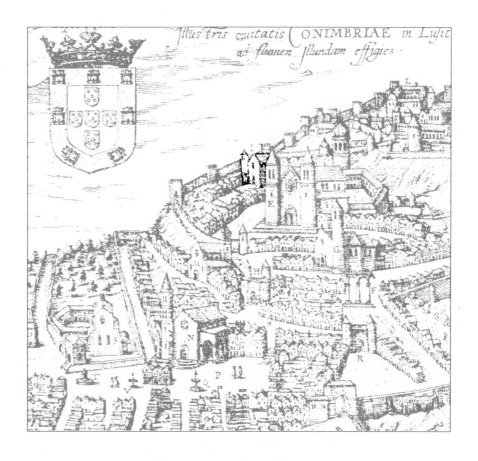

FIGURE 8.21
Aquila
engraving by Jacopo Lauroca,
showing site of Jesuit college,
1600.

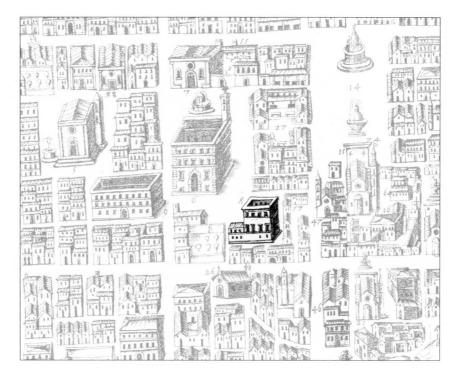

In a number of cases, Ignatius had to decide between two simultaneous offers. He always opted for the larger population center. The criterion of the more universal good led him to choose densely populated Naples over Parma, and the university city of Granada over San Lucar.[35] The *collegietto* of Gubbio in the Umbrian hills was closed in 1554 after two years' existence to free up manpower for a new college in Genoa.[36]

You should know that our Society has no great desire for these collegietti *. . . . Moreover, I tell you truly that we are considering eliminating those that already exist, if they are not provided with church, house, and sufficient incomes. These [same benefits] are being offered to us in diverse and important places in Italy, Sicily, Spain, and Portugal, and the Society cannot accept them for want of manpower. Indeed, we find that some of those [small colleges] we have are a bad bargain, when they [the citizens] think it enough to provide us with food to live on, while the other colleges could serve the common good in matters of great importance.[37]*

FLORENCE

Nowhere is Ignatius' dedication to great and important cities better demonstrated than in his ten-year, 76-letter correspondence about establishing a Jesuit college in Florence. Indeed, the Florence correspondence is a kind of concert of Ignatius' entire strategic orchestra, a toccata and fugue in which all his many and varied voices are heard.

ELEONORA AND DIEGO

At the center of the Florentine maelstrom was the erratic, neurotic Grand Duchess of Tuscany. Eleonora of Toledo, herself the daughter of Charles V's Viceroy to Naples and kin to the Dukes of Alba, married Cosimo II Medici in 1539. Beautiful, haughty, and addicted to gambling–her non-Jesuit moral theologian reassured her that loosing 2,000 ducats in a single night was not a grave matter–Eleonora was, oddly, drawn to the Society. She once said that were she a man, she would give 20,000 ducats to become a Jesuit.[38] More particularly, she was deeply, even obsessively attached to one of her Jesuit spiritual advisors, Diego Laínez. Much of the correspondence is a kind of tug-of-war between the Duchess and Ignatius over Laínez's absences from Cosimo and Eleonora's court.[39]

Laínez had been sent to Florence in 1547 to smooth over a diplomatic *faux pas* committed by young Father Juan de Polanco. Polanco had preached rather too strenuously to the court on the need for simplicity, reminding the Grand Duchess that extravagant clothing, delicacies, and palaces derive "from the sweat of the poor . . . God gives you much, that it might be well used and not wasted."[40] Ignatius' reproach was terse, and reflects a solid pragmatism when it came to the importance of image and damage control:

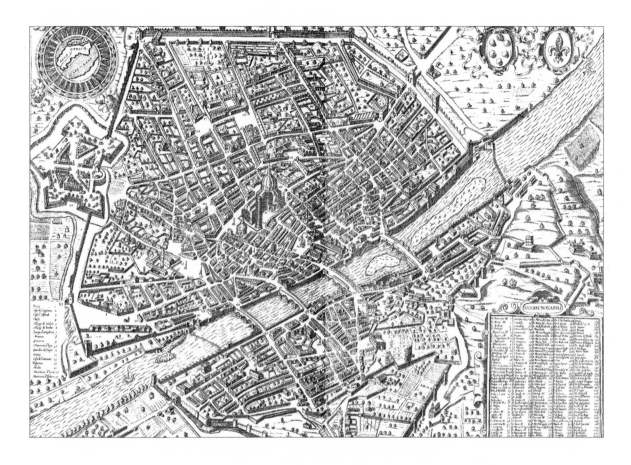

FIGURE 8.22
Florence
engraving by Matteo Florimi,
ca. 1598.

We [already] have a reputation among some persons who do not trouble to find out the truth, especially here in Rome, that we would like to rule the world. This . . . [as well as the recent scandalous accusations of the Papal Post Master against the Jesuits and the Casa S. Marta] contributes to undoing our work for the greater service of God our Lord.[41]

Shortly thereafter, Polanco was called to Rome to become Ignatius' secretary, and Laínez was sent to Florence to begin negotiations for the foundation of a new college.

Laínez carried out his frustrating diplomatic mission with great finesse, attempting to convince the vacillating and easily distracted royals of the need for a Jesuit college in Florence. Between fishing and hunting trips, Cosimo and Eleonora half-heartedly offered the Jesuits sites in Prato and Pisa.[42] Ignatius himself sent a number of detailed memoranda to his men on the scene instructing them on how "not to get on the Duchess' nerves," on proper Spanish court etiquette, and even on how to tease her with accounts of the Infanta Juana's generosity to the Society.[43]

Most notably, though, Ignatius spelled out his reasons for wanting to locate his college in downtown Florence rather than in the less important cities of Pisa and Prato. His reasoning is fully consonant with the "preferential option" for urban ministry sketched out in the *Formula of the Institute* and in the *Constitutions:*

> *The arguments that you must present to her excellency the Duchess for establishing that the college be located at Florence rather than at Pisa:*
>
> *First, Because a house has already been offered in Florence.*
>
> *Second, Because it will be of greater public advantage for the city of Florence; since thus its younger sons who cannot be sent afar can be taught by Ours [the Jesuits] in humanities, and thus will be better prepared to go later to Pisa, where advanced courses are taught to those already prepared and more capable.*
>
> *Third, Because it is very important that the children of Florence, from their early years, should be taught Christian doctrine and good morals together with their letters, and receive that good seed which with maturity will produce fruits of great virtue, as we see already in Messina, Palermo, and other places where, using this same method in our colleges, admirable fruit is borne even in the tender years of the citizens' sons.*
>
> *Fourth, Because there is a greater number of poor people in Florence who, not being able to pay teachers nor go to Pisa, will have the convenience of studying in Florence at least the fundamentals of Latin and Greek.*
>
> *Fifth, Because in Florence, there will be greater opportunity to aid the populace with confessions and preaching.*
>
> *Sixth, Because being closer to the rulers in Florence than in Pisa, they will better understand the proceedings of the college.*[44]

The Jesuit rationale of urban ministry is clearly laid out in these six points. All classes of people are to be served, from the scions of the royal family to the poor who cannot afford to send their children for costly private instruction. Although the primary motivation for the new foundation is educational, the Society's ordinary ministries of the Word figure importantly in the equation of greater service to greater numbers and, hence, the "greater service of God." Finally, the document stresses cooperation with local authorities for the "edification" of the city.

After 76 letters and ten years of diplomatic struggle, Ignatius got exactly what he wanted: the downtown church of S. Giovannino next to the Medici Palace, in the shadow of the Medici family church of S. Lorenzo, one block from the Duomo, with enough land to build a college and residence.[45]

The old pattern of the centrifugal mendicant sitings had been broken. The Jesuits intentionally gravitated to the center, not the edge of the urban fabric. At Siena, the church of S. Vergilio less than 100 meters from the Piazza del Campo became the Jesuit headquarters; in Ferrara, their college

FIGURE 8.23
Florence,
detail, showing site of Jesuit
church and college.

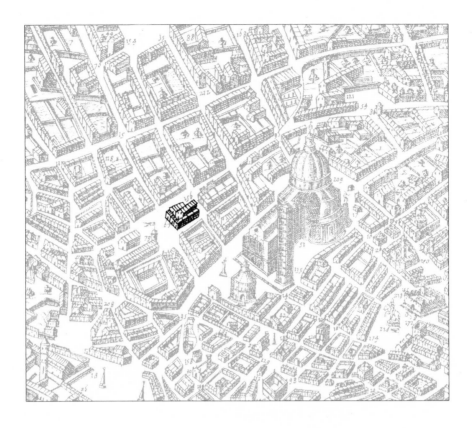

rose on the main *piazza* of the city, "next to His Excellency the Duke."[46] In Naples, Lisbon, Palermo, Messina, Prague, and Milan,[47] as in Rome and many other cities, the Jesuits obtained significant downtown properties and churches physically close to the centers of political and social life.

CLERICAL OPPOSITION

Local parochial clergy and mendicant communities did not always welcome such acquisitions. Sometimes even the hierarchy opposed the Jesuits' entry into a city or region. The popularity of Jesuit preachers threatened local pastors: they feared losing their congregations—and collections—to the eloquent newcomers. Long-established mendicant communities saw their urban support eroded by the aggressive urban ministry of the new order.

The most thoroughly documented case of united opposition to the Jesuits was the long and bitter struggle in Spain between the Jesuits and the Augustinian canons, the local diocesan clergy, and the Archbishop of Zaragosa.[48] When the Society opened a downtown house as the first step toward founding a college, the canons joined forces with the local pastors and persuaded the archbishop to excommunicate the Jesuits for infringing on local ministerial prerogatives. The canons, marching behind a black-veiled crucifix, paraded around the Jesuits' property singing psalms of malediction. The clergy organized youthful demonstrators, who carried placards showing "an *iniguista* together with a demon" and threw stones at the Jesuits' house.[49] In response the Jesuits mobilized powerful friends, including members of the Borja clan and the Regent of Spain, the Infanta Juana, who eventually forced the local ordinary and clergy to accept the Jesuits' presence.

RULE OF THE "CANNAE"

The principle most often invoked against the Jesuits was the mendicants' rule of the *cannae*. As medieval cities grew, Franciscan and Dominican foundations that had been built near medieval gates were absorbed into the central fabric of the city; the Augustinian canons continued to hold important collegiate churches in downtown neighborhoods. When the Jesuits were looking for properties, they often found that their religious neighbors attempted to block their entry into desirable central neighborhoods.

Ignatius wrote almost 40 letters addressing the issue of the mendicant rule of the *cannae*. He defended the numerous exemptions to preach, to teach, and to build that had been granted to the Society in various papal bulls and sometimes forwarded notarized copies of the bulls to local officials. He argued that the colleges, being endowed, did not work to the disadvantage of the local mendicant communities and that Jesuit churches did not take up collections.[50] Because of ongoing squabbles, particularly in Spain, the Society eventually obtained direct relief in two papal bulls, *Etsi ex debito* (Pius IV, April 13, 1561) and *Salvatoris Domini* (Gregory XIII, October 30, 1576).[51] Those documents gave the Society perpetual and irrevocable permission to build anywhere in the world and freed the order, at least in theory, from any obstruction from mendicants or interference from the local hierarchy. In practice, however, the struggles, excommunications, and misunderstandings continued, even into nineteenth-century San Francisco.

Ignatius readily acknowledged that "one needs to have strong shoulders of patience and long endurance"[52] to haggle over real estate or prevail in zoning battles. For him, though, the most trying property transaction or the most difficult confrontation was more than a challenge or an obstacle: it was a potential moment of grace. Writing to his troubled brethren in Zaragosa when the successful resolution of their difficulties was still only to be imagined, Ignatius spent for their encouragement some of the "treasure of hopes" that underwrote all his property transactions and personal dealings:

> *As experience teaches us, where there is much contradiction, there is much fruit. Thus, the Society is better founded and it seems that it should be a splendid and distinguished spiritual edifice, for such deep foundations have been built on contradictions. This is what it means to trust in what God our Lord will do.*[53]

Ignatius, mystic and master of the particular, read patterns of what he perceived as God's providence in the details, professing that the major income he needed was faith and hope.[54] The large number of strategic decisions and property transactions chronicled in his correspondence testifies to how prodigally he spent those resources.

CHAPTER IX
LANDMARKING

On July 31, 1556, Ignatius died at the Casa Professa on Via Aracoeli. His company that numbered ten companions in one house in 1538 had grown to 1,000 members in 74 houses on three continents. In 1579 there were 5,165 members in 200 houses; in 1600, 8,500 in 350 houses. When the Society celebrated its centennial in 1640, the order had grown to 15,683 members in 868 houses.[1]

Such explosive growth, of course, generated a constellation of crises and difficulties, both personal and practical. Entrance criteria were frequently called into question, and Rome was forced to keep a vigilant eye on finances and new foundations.

As general, Ignatius usually reserved to himself important decisions on property purchases and construction. The Society's structure is extremely centralized, and the general's role is more that of monarch than moderator. Ignatius demanded that detailed reports be sent to him on transactions and that drawings of new buildings be submitted to him for approval. While he sometimes allowed a trusted local superior to exercise a "local option" and even gave some local superiors blank sheets of paper with his signature on them for use as needed, as the Society became more diffuse he tended to rely on direct communication through letters and on sending personal delegates or "commissars" like Nadal or Borja to study and resolve difficulties *in situ*.[2]

After Ignatius' death, his policies were codified into the Society's law. At the first general congregation in 1558, his *Constitutions* were approved, and Diego Laínez was elected second superior general. Among the canons or directives of that congregation, one dealt directly with the question of building.

FIGURE 9.1 (LEFT)

*Horoscopium Catholicum
Societ. Iesu*
from Athanasius Kircher's *Ars
Magnae Lucis et Umbrae,* 1648,
showing the distribution of
Jesuit houses throughout the
world 108 years after the
Society's foundation.

What sort of buildings ours should be. . . . As far as it is in our power, we should impose norms for the buildings belonging to our houses and colleges, so that besides other appropriate developments they may not become at some point palaces befitting the nobility; they must be sound buildings, sturdy, and well built [sana, utilia, et fortia], *suited to be our residences and the place from which we can discharge our duties; they must be such, however, as to demonstrate that we are mindful of poverty—buildings that are not luxurious, therefore, or too fancy. On the other hand, nothing was said about church buildings, and the entire matter appeared to call for further consideration.*[3]

In this decree, a typically Jesuit triad of practicality, healthfulness, and strength replaced the Vitruvian canons of firmness, commodity, and delight, at least in so far as the Jesuits' own residences and workplaces were concerned.

CHURCH AS FULCRUM

The deliberate exclusion of churches from these rules was practical as well as ideological: beautiful and comfortable churches attract large crowds. Ignatius himself spared no expense on his attempts to make S. Maria della Strada more commodious and delightful, and had engaged two renowned architects to draw plans for a new church for the site. From the very beginning, the urban church was conceived as the fulcrum and foundation of the Society's mission.

"MODO NOSTRO"

From 1558 until his death in 1575, Jesuit architect Giovanni Tristano served as the general's official *consiliarius aedilicius,* a combination architectural overseer and building superintendent for the entire Society. The *consiliarius* reviewed all plans, site selections, and negotiations and insured that all buildings conformed to what the Jesuits were wont to call *modo nostro.*[4] That *modo,* summarized in the *utilia, sana, et fortia* decree of the first general congregation, was further institutionalized when another of Ignatius' practices was enacted into the Society's law in the second general congregation (1565). That congregation decreed that drawings and construction plans, *forma ac modus,* for all new building had to be sent to Rome for review and approval before buildings could be erected.[5]

In 1564, Pius IV (Medici, 1559–1565) ceded the Palazzo S. Marco to the Venetian Ambassador and focused all his energies on the development of the Borgo Pio near the Vatican. That shift marked the end of a papal concentration on the renewed downtown that dated back to the Palazzo's construction by Paul II in the mid fifteenth century. Four years later the great era of Jesuit construction began.

THE JESUIT POLE

Italian urban historians Enrico Guidoni and Angela Marino describe the creation of a "Jesuit Pole" in Rome:

In 1568 the Church of the Gesù was begun; in 1583 the Collegio Romano. Giving a new thrust to the entire central area of Rome at the foot of the Campidoglio, these two edifices conditioned and transformed the relationships between the city's religious buildings, creating, in modern terms, a "third pole" that, levering against the renovated fulcrum of the Capitol, tended to relegate towards the periphery the traditional religious points of reference, the Vatican and the Lateran. Every other initiative of the new orders–from S. Andrea della Valle, to the Oratorians, to S. Carlo–would in fact be subordinated to the central Jesuit presence, notably reinforced with the construction of the church of S. Ignazio.

In the last decades of the Cinquecento and the first decades of the Seicento, first in Rome and then in all the other Catholic capitals, we see the Jesuit college and church constituting new centers of attraction, and centers of urban growth within the urban organism. These are quickly surrounded by a series of churches or secondary institutions, always bound to the Society, which form a corona around the principal edifices, invariably located, wheresoever it is possible, in the city center.

This central siting, cold-bloodedly planned and pursued, invariably collided with the interests of other orders and other urban religious institutions. The older mendicant and reformed orders found themselves in a position of clear-cut inferiority; the new orders (Oratorians, Theatines, etc.) had to compete with the Jesuits to occupy the best positions at the urban centers.[6]

ROMAN PARADIGM

In the highly centralized Society of Jesus, the strategy of the Society's diffusion in Rome became more or less paradigmatic for other installations. Beginning with a small church and a piece of property for a residence in the center of town, a base of operations was founded at S. Maria della Strada, the site of the present Church of the Gesù. As ministries multiplied and the community increased in size, both church and residence were enlarged and ultimately replaced by larger, more noble structures erected for the Society by important patrons.[7]

CHIESA DEL GESÙ

Although the building of a large downtown church was Ignatius' first priority, the Gesù, the Church of the Holy Name of Jesus, was not realized until after his death. Twice he tried to build a new church, but both attempts were thwarted by insufficient funds and neighborhood opposition.

Work on the new Church did not actually begin until 1568. Some 12 years after Ignatius' death, Francisco Borja, elected third superior general of the order in 1565, combined diplomacy, political pressure, and enough ready cash to buy out the Altieri, Astalli, and Muti families that had stubbornly blocked the project. His major benefactor was Cardinal Alessandro Farnese, grandson of Pope Paul III. Farnese's court architect Vignola reworked the 1550 plan of Nanni di Baccio Bigio. The Cardinal himself took an active role in the design of the Church, insisting that the nave be vaulted

FIGURE 9.2
Chiesa del Gesù and the first
Casa Professa, ca. 1580
As the church neared comple-
tion, the community lived in a
variety of buildings on and
around the original della
Strada property.

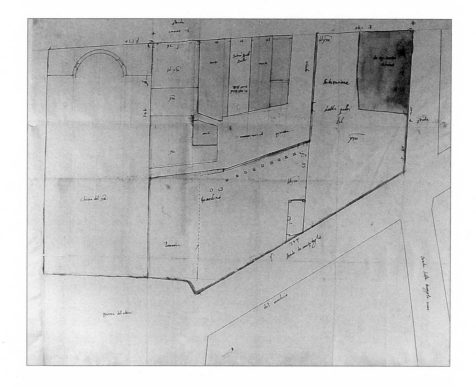

CASA PROFESSA

FIGURE 9.3 (RIGHT)
Chiesa del Gesù and the "new"
Casa Professa, 1604.
Detail of a portrait engraving of
Cardinal Robert Bellarmine by
Francisco Villamena.
This earliest known view of the
Casa Professa (begun in 1598)
clearly shows that the east and
south wings were still under
construction.

rather than roofed and that the facade be oriented squarely onto the piazza
that fronted the Via Papale.[8] After the laying of the cornerstone, Farnese
considered various designs for the facade prepared by Vignola, Galeazzo
Alessi, and Giacomo della Porta. He chose della Porta's plan, which was
nearly completed for the Holy Year 1575. Thus, after the laying of three
cornerstones and the approval of five separate building permits, the Chiesa
del Gesù, oriented to face the processional flow of the Via Papale, finally arose
on the site chosen by Ignatius almost 30 years before.[9]

Neighborhood opposition to the Jesuits' plans to expand the Casa
Professa continued throughout the last years of the Cinquecento, always led
by an increasingly cantankerous Muti and his heirs.[10] Because of serious
structural damage to the Casa Professa caused by the flood of December 24,
1598, Claudio Aquaviva, the fifth general, appealed again to the Farnese family. Cardinal Odoardo Farnese, the nephew of Cardinal Alessandro, paid for
the replacement of the original residence. The new Casa Professa designed
by Jesuit Giovanni de Rosis encompassed the entire block bounded by the
Church, Via degli Astalli, Via S. Marco, and Via Aracoeli, a perimeter of
more than 300 meters. Built with rooms for 145 residents, it served as the
Jesuits' General Curia or headquarters from the time of its construction until
the suppression of the Society in 1773 and again from the restoration of the
Society in 1814 until the Risorgimento (1873).[11]

The last piece of property for the Casa Professa, located on the south-east corner where Via degli Astalli meets Via S. Marco, was not obtained until 1618. As late as 1612 General Aquaviva had to deal with complaints from the Venetian ambassador (in residence at Palazzo S. Marco), who lamented that the new Casa Professa was "squeezing the street."[12]

Both in terms of historical importance and sheer volume, the Collegio Romano–S. Ignazio complex rivals its nearby neighbor the Casa Professa-il Gesù. Ignatius himself founded the college, a seminary for Jesuit students of all nations. In early 1551, a "free school of grammar, humanities, and Christian Doctrine" opened in rented rooms at the Campidoglio end of Via Aracoeli. Quickly outgrowing these limited quarters, the college was soon relocated on Via del Gesù near the apse of the Church of S. Stefano del Cacco, and in 1552, students from the Jesuits' newly founded collegio Germanico began to take their lessons there as well. The course of studies included Latin, Greek, Hebrew, and the liberal arts. The College's public "disputations," demonstrations of the academic and linguistic prowess of faculty and students, held in local churches, became a popular entertainment for the Roman intelligentsia. Philosophy and theology were soon added to the curriculum, and in 1556 Paul IV gave the Collegio the authority to confer academic degrees.[13]

In 1557, the collegio was again moved to larger quarters, this time in Palazzo Salviati, near the site of the present Piazza Collegio Romano. In 1560, Pius IV persuaded the Marchesa Vittoria della Tolfa, widow of Principe Camillo Orsini and herself sister of the late Paul IV, to donate her palazzo and adjoining property to the Society of Jesus. Located on the site of the present Church of S. Ignazio, the site was described in a contemporary document as

> *very lovely, and located in a very convenient part of Rome: nearby to the east is Monte Quirinale, to the west the Pantheon, to the south the Arch of Camillus and to the north, the Portico of Antonino Pio where there is the orphanage [directed by the Jesuits]. The site is ample, although not yet organized in the most desirable form.*[14]

The organization of that conveniently located site occupied Jesuit architects, builders, and patrons of the Society for the next century. Brother Giovanni Tristano designed and oversaw the construction of the Church of the Annunziata on the site between the years 1561 and 1567. Skeptical Roman neighbors were impressed not only by the grace of the small church, but by the fact that it was constructed entirely by the labor of Jesuit lay brothers and students[15].

The admission of lay students and non-Jesuit seminarians strained the facilities of the Collegio to the breaking point.[16] Jesuit Giuseppe Valeriani designed a new facility, whose immense facade–the largest in Rome until the building of the Maderno facade of S. Pietro– and major classrooms more than doubled the space available to the College.[17] In 1581 Pope Gregory XIII (Buoncompagni, 1572–1585) expropriated an entire neighborhood and then paid the equivalent of 4,116 kilos of refined silver on construction of the edifice.[18] The grateful Jesuits named him "founder" of the College.

"TEMPUS GREGORIANUM"

Gregory's faith in the Society matched his lavishness in building for it. He entrusted the Jesuits with the English College, the Church of S. Stefano Rotondo, and S. Apollinare with the Palazzo d'Estouteville near Piazza Navona as a seat for the German College. During the early stages of construction of the Collegio Romano, he ordered that fired-brick walls replace simple rubble walls that were rising on the site, a construction detail that Cardinal Odoardo Farnese would later insist upon in the building of the Casa Professa. The quality and expense of this "Jesuit" brickwork was commented on by architect Vincenzo Giustiani in his *Discourse on Architecture*:

FIGURE 9.4
The "Jesuit Pole"
detail from Maggi's 1625 plan of Rome showing the Collegio Romano and Gesù complexes.

> *This way is not generally used because it is of more than middling expense, even though it turns out to be beautiful and long lasting, since it resists the influence of both air and fire, and for that reason, the Jesuit fathers are accustomed to using it more than others, as men who exquisitely observe the beginnings, the progress, and the end of all their actions.*[19]

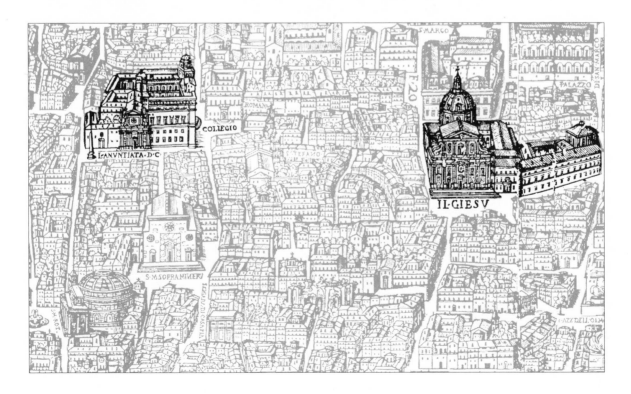

Gregory XIII inaugurated the complex in 1584, amid loud applause for the dawning golden age, a "tempus Gregorianum."[20]

Tristano's small church of S. Annunziata was quickly outgrown. By the beginning of the 17th century the Collegio had more than 2,000 students, and it lacked a space adequate for its liturgical and ceremonial functions. Encouraged by the canonizations of Ignatius and Francisco Javier in 1622, the Jesuits appealed to Gregory XV (Ludovisi, 1621–1623) to help them with the construction of an ample and decorous church on the site of the oldest residence buildings donated to the Collegio by the Marchesa della Tolfa. The pope's nephew Cardinal Ludovico Ludovisi and other members of the Ludovisi family endowed the construction, and in 1626 the cornerstone of the new church was laid. Orazio Grassi, professor of mathematics at the Collegio Romano and opponent of Galileo, designed the church and the last portion of the residence complex. When Grassi was transferred to Savona, the direction of the works was passed to Jesuit Antonio Sasso, whose alteration of Grassi's design was to cause a long, ultimately futile dispute that blocked the construction of the cupola. The Dominicans of S. Maria Sopra Minerva complained because the cupola would rob light from their library. Grassi lamented because Sasso's heightening of the facade destroyed the proportions of the structure. Bernini, Borromini, Algardi, and Girolamo Rainaldi all gave written opinions, and Grassi proposed a number of alternatives. In the end, lack of funds for further construction resolved the ques-

FIGURE 9.5

"Gregory XIII founds colleges and seminaries within and beyond Europe"
Anonymous, c. 1655, from the "porteria" of the Collegio Romano Complex.
The painting shows foundation of colleges in Japan, Loreto, and Vilnius.

tion, and in 1685 Andrea Pozzo's masterful fictive cupola, a canvas some 17 meters in diameter, was installed.[21] Construction of the church continued fitfully for almost a century, and the structure was finally consecrated in 1722.

OTHER PROJECTS

Jesuit Bernardo Molli's work at the Collegio Germanico, Bernini's jewel-like S. Andrea in Quirinale built as the chapel for the Jesuit novitiate, and Alexander VII's grandiose design for Piazza Collegio Romano and widening of the corridor from Piazza del Gesù to Piazza Venezia (a work unfortunately undone by Clement X's construction of the long wing of his family's Palazzo Altieri) marked the culmination of a century of Jesuit urban construction and impact.[22]

Cold-blooded or not, the Jesuits understood the urban equation. By the time Ignatius and Javier were canonized, those Jesuits marching in procession before the saints' banner could call downtown Rome their own.

Shaping, siting, and sheltering the missions of the Society of Jesus consumed a major part of Ignatius' energy for the last 16 years of his life. Paradoxically, even as his Society grew exponentially and extended itself over the globe, Ignatius' physical world shrank to the circumscribed area of four tiny rooms in the heart of downtown Rome. Ignatius the pilgrim who dreamed of missionary work became an administrator, a legislator, the shaper of an urban missionary band that would change the social and educational face of Catholic Europe. While Ignatius labored quietly, his companions worked mightily to stem the Protestant tides in the lands of the Reformation, and to bring their own particular brand of adaptable and pluriform ministry to the New Worlds that Spanish and Portuguese colonization had opened.

Four outstanding traits in Ignatius' personality help to explain the Society's rapid expansion and—what some consider disproportionate—influence on the Church and Catholic culture: Ignatius was imaginative, practical, flexible, and fearless.

IMAGINATIVE

Born into a rigidly-structured, all but self-enclosed society, Iñigo Lopez de Loyola was nevertheless able to see beyond the medieval valley where he was raised. Although his dry and businesslike writings rarely reveal it, the man who created the Spiritual Exercises implicitly trusted the revelatory power of imagination. His actions bear ample testimony to that trust. Unfettered by the kind of conservatism of imagination that often paralyzed—and still paralyzes—the Church, Ignatius, because he trusted his experience, was able to invent a new model of religious presence that took the best of the tradition, looked at it with entirely new eyes, and then adapted it to meet the needs of a rapidly changing world.

PRACTICAL

Modern commentators often focus on Ignatius' mystical experiences at Manresa and La Storta but ignore his immense practicality. Ignatius was able to translate what he understood to be a direct experience of God and a personal call to service into a concrete blueprint, the Spiritual Exercises, which helps those who follow them to experience what Ignatius himself had experienced. No less imaginative was his construction of a practical institution, the Society of Jesus, which for 450 years has supported his vision of service.

FLEXIBLE

Ignatius the mystic was, at the same time, Ignatius the hard-nosed businessman; while his soul often soared, his feet never left the ground. He knew that human beings are neither angels nor demons and must be addressed *where* they are, both metaphorically and physically, if their hearts are to be turned to God. For this reason he became a master negotiator, master letter-writer, master builder. He placed his companions in the midst of the City of Man so that they would be able to lead its citizens more easily toward the City of God. That is why he abandoned cloister, habit, and choir and struggled to build downtown residences, schools, social centers, and churches.

Karl Rahner, a Jesuit of the twentieth century, understood what Ignatius had discovered in the sixteenth:

> One does not enter a temple, a shrine that encloses the holy and cuts it off from a godless and secular world that remains outside. In the free breadth of a divine world one erects a landmark, a sign of the fact that this entire world belongs to God, a sign precisely of the fact that God is adored, experienced, and accepted everywhere as the one who, through grace, has set all things free to attain to him, and a sign that this adoration takes place not in Jerusalem alone but everywhere in spirit and truth.[23]

The romantic dream of the mission to Jerusalem gave way to the reality Ignatius and his companions encountered in their travels and their apostolic works in human cities. They had set out following a dream that offered the comfort of ancient landmarks. When that dream proved impracticable, they did not abandon dreaming. Rather, they were creative enough to reshape that dream, and daring enough to begin building new landmarks in the cities where they lived.

As poor but gifted builders have always done, the Jesuits built their landmarks with whatever materials were ready to hand: brick, mortar, and ancient marbles; the needs of the prostitute, the student, the Jew, and the orphan; the generosity of the committed and the sinful; the longing of citizens for a shoulder to cry on and a teacher to show them the way; the living memory and history of the Church. Their edifices, although not always elegant, were "sound, sturdy, and well built." Built as they were on "so many contradictions," they had to be in order to stand.

A number of factors set the first Jesuits apart from the other reform movements in the late Renaissance Church. The Society, from its very beginning, was an organization international in both membership and outlook. The mixture of nationalities and experiences, like the many different kinds of wood in a fine violin, gave the Society flexibility, strength, and many diverse voices. Those resonant voices were trained to enter into conversation, into harmony with the symphony of cultures they encountered.[24]

Moreover, their avowed design as a *missionary* order disposed the first Jesuits to extend that conversation to those normally excluded from public discourse by prejudice, class distinction, or perceived cultural inferiority. Their ministries of the Word were broadcast across the entire social spectrum. They preached to prostitutes and to daughters of popes and they engaged the best artists to decorate their churches. They counseled princes and catechized street urchins. At home in the City of Man, but at the same time on pilgrimage toward the City of God, the first Jesuits were eager to take that conversation anywhere and to adapt it to any idiom.[25]

FEARLESS

Finally, there was a quality of fearlessness about Ignatius and his companions that makes them immensely attractive. They were ready to go anywhere and do anything to communicate the message they had received and desired so urgently to share. That fearlessness conferred a rare freedom to be all things for all people, to use all legitimate means "like the spoils of Egypt," to move anywhere or to settle on a street corner as the circumstances demanded.

Circumstances change. With changing circumstances over the past 450 years, Jesuits have acquired and lost more real estate than almost any other corporation in the West. The Society's suppression in 1773 effectively destroyed an empire, a world-wide educational and service-oriented partnership. As Daurin Alden points out, "by the mid seventeenth century, the Society enjoyed exclusive control of higher education in Italy, Poland, and Portugal, and administered more academies than any other entity in Spain, France, the Spanish Netherlands, or the Catholic-controlled regions of the Germanies and Hungary."[26] In the two centuries before the suppression, Jesuit colleges, parishes, retreat houses, houses of formation, and missions had amassed significant acreage, constructed important buildings, and administered large patrimonies across the globe. While the political, social, and religious causes of the suppression are well outside the scope of this study, there can be no doubt that those rich resources attracted the attention, envy, and avarice of the Society's many foes.[27]

After the Society's restoration in 1814, many of those institutions—and the prime sites they occupied—were never regained. Former Jesuit colleges and residences became secular academies, state archives, or apartment houses. New properites that Jesuits acquired were often farther removed from expensive town centers. Natural disasters continued to take their tolls. The 1906 San Francisco earthquake and fire leveled the hard-won St. Ignatius College and caused its relocation to a hilltop in the midst of cemeteries. The new site proved to be the approximate geographic center of the city and county of San Francisco, for which the University was renamed in 1930 on the seventy-fifth anniversary of its foundation.

In the United States, colleges founded downtown in the late nineteenth and early twentieth centuries tended to migrate in the second quarter of the twentieth century to more spacious campuses on the urban edge. Mass transit, the developing automobile-centered commuter culture, and the separate incorporation of high schools as distinct from colleges and universities led to the shift. In most cases, urban sprawl has engulfed the newer campuses, and brought them back into the mainstream of urban life.[28]

In the final quarter of the twentieth century, as Jesuits rearticulate their mission as "the service of faith and the promotion of justice," the "inner city" again looms large on the Jesuit apostolic horizon as pastoral centers like Proyecto Pastoral at Dolores Mission Parish, Los Angeles, the Jesuit Urban Center, Boston, and Holy Name Center, Camden, have been established to address the pressing needs of the urban poor. Middle schools modeled after New York City's Nativity School have sprung up in Milwaukee, Boston, Baltimore, New York, and Omaha and others are being planned in San

Francisco and St. Petersburg, Florida. As part of the mid-century urban renewal of New York City, Fordham University erected a campus at Lincoln Center, and in the 1990s Loyola Chicago dedicated a Water Tower Campus in the heart of the city. Other universities are experimenting with extension and "distance learning" programs to serve the increasingly diverse and diffused urban scene. Even with the advent of virtual reality and the Internet, though, Jesuits and their colleagues know that the Society's fundamental ministry of conversation with the world best takes place around lovingly created landmarks.

Some 439 years after the death of Ignatius, the 1995 thirty-fourth general congregation of the Society of Jesus reaffirmed the Society's age-old commitment to dialogue with human culture as lived out in our contemporary urbanized world. In a document entitled "Our Mission and Culture," 233 Jesuit delegates from every continent and nearly every race and tongue drafted a statement both traditional and challenging, a telling gloss on the Jesuit proverb that introduced this work:

> *"Ignatius loved the great cities"; they were where this transformation of the human community was taking place, and he wanted Jesuits to be involved in the process. The "city" can be for us the symbol of our current efforts to bring fulfillment to human culture. That the project, in its present form, is seriously flawed no one doubts; that we are more skeptical now than we were even thirty years ago is true; that there have been massive dislocations and inequalities is clear to all; that the totalitarian experiments of this century have been brutal and almost demonic in intensity none will dispute; that it seems sometimes to resemble the Babel and Babylon of the Gospel is all too evident. But our aim is the confused but inescapable attempt to cooperate in the creation of that community which, according to the Book of Revelation, God will bring about—and God will bring it about—in the form of the holy city, the radiant New Jerusalem: "By its light shall the nations walk; and the kings of the earth shall bring their glory into it, and its gates shall never be shut by day—and there shall be no night there. They shall bring into it the glory and the honor of the nations" (Rev. 21:24-26). Until that day arrives, our vocation is to work in the all-too-human city where there is poverty of body and spirit, domination and control, manipulation of mind and heart; and to serve the Lord there until he returns to bring to perfection the world in which he died.[29]*

Ignatius lived out his last 12 years in four little rooms on Via Aracoeli where his windows opened to the four points of the compass. Looking out his study window to the south he could see the City Hall on the Campidoglio and the Jewish ghetto. One block to the east lay Palazzo S. Marco, the favorite home of his friend and benefactor Pope Paul III. Out his chapel windows to the north and west, the city of Rome, alive, growing, beautiful, and very needy.

The old man felt very much at home.

It is May 1555, and Ignatius, as usual, is strapped for cash. His archenemy Gian Pietro Carafa has recently been elected pope, and large gifts promised to the floundering Collegio Romano have dried up. In a few months, the Theatine pontiff, rabidly anti-Spanish, will order the Casa Professa searched for Spanish arms.[30] The poorly-endowed college at Gubbio—one of 40 already in operation—has to be closed because of the manpower crunch. The excommunication of the Jesuits in Zaragosa is still in force, and Ignatius is negotiating with the Infanta Juana of Spain, who wants to become a Jesuit. In Spain, Jesuits are preaching on board ships before they depart for the New World. There is talk of founding a college in Mexico City. Ignatius' health is poor but stable.

At the end of a detailed report on the precarious finances of the Roman houses, Ignatius wrote to Francisco Borja: "Patience. Because of the treasure of hopes we have, everything is as nothing. God who gives the hopes will not confound them."[31]

Ignatius Loyola prodigally spent his treasure of hopes to build something new, a landmark on the landscape of the Catholic tradition. Wise builder that he was, he knew that where that landmark is placed makes all the difference.

FIGURE 9.6 (LEFT)
Rome
Facade of the Chiesa del Gesù
in its urban context.

DOMVS AC PIETATIS OPERA QVÆ S.P. IGNATIVS ROMÆ FACIENDA CVRAVIT. QVÆQ. SOCIETAS SVÆ CVRÆ COMMISSA HABET.
A. *Domus Patrum Professorum* B *Collegium Romanum.* C. *Colleg. Pænitentieria.* D. *Nouitiatus.* E. *Orphanorum atque orphanarum domicilia.* G. *Catechumeni.* H. *S. Marthe, tum* *mulierum pænitentium perfugium* I *S. Catherina de Funarijs, Virginum in lubrico versantium portas.* K. *Coll. Germanicum.* L. *Anglicanum.* M. *Seminary Romani.* N. *Maronitarum.*

AFTERWORD

On a muggy July morning in 1987 at the Jesuit Historical Institute Library on the flank of the Gianicolo in Rome, a book fell open to the right page, an image presented itself, and the cornerstone of the present work all but audibly slid into place. The book was a reprint of a collection of engravings from around the time of Ignatius' beatification in 1609. The image was a copper plate engraving called the "Roma Ignaziana" (left).

The map, a much reworked version of an earlier rendering of the Renaissance city, shows an immense Chiesa del Gesù dominating the center of the city, surrounded by a corona of out-of-scale buildings housing Jesuit social, pastoral, and educational works. A celebration of triumphalistic hagiography and Jesuit chauvinism, without a doubt. But there is more: an articulated relationship of parts to a center and a harmonic relationship of that center to the city center. The map suggested that the siting of the Gesù complex at the center of Rome was not accidental but deliberate. It raised questions about social history, theology, and Jesuit urban strategy that this book now attempts to address.

That summer day I was researching how and where St. Ignatius Loyola lived in Rome, in preparation for a larger project, the restoration of the rooms at the Gesù where he lived for the last 12 years of his life and where he died in 1556. Encouraged by Fathers Jack O'Callaghan, John Padberg, and my local Jesuit superiors in California, I had presented a sketch for the restoration to Father Peter Hans Kolvenbach, superior general of the Society of Jesus, in January 1987. His immediate interest and constant support gave me courage to undertake a four-year project in which archival research jumbled together with international and ecclesiastical diplomacy, fresco restoration, electrical rewiring, exhibition design, and fundraising. Hectic indeed, but I can recommend no better way to do one's thesis research.

The restoration project in Rome and the shaping of the ideas in this book lived in strange, mostly silent symbiosis for almost three years. One was inconceivable without the other, although the constraints of negotiating with government ministries and keeping fifty Italian workers more or less on schedule and within budget often forced me to give precedence to the practical over the theoretical. Still, a kind of preconscious interaction akin to Ignatius' paradox of contemplation in the midst of action informed both the project and this book. The ideas shaped the restoration, and the restoration—as well as working daily for two years in Ignatius' own rooms in the heart of Rome—formed the human framework that supported the growth of the ideas.

Early in 1990, as the physical work of the restoration was nearing completion, I was given a rare opportunity, to prepare the exhibition for the Biblioteca Apostolica Vaticana as part of the "Ignatian Year" celebration of the 500th anniversary of St. Ignatius' birth and the 450th anniversary of the foundation of the Society of Jesus. The Prefect of the Library, Reverend Leonard E. Boyle of the Order of Preachers, became my mentor, guide, and friend. His expert professional staff treated the project with great interest and me with great kindness. The 140-piece exhibit entitled "Saint, Site, and Sacred Strategy: Ignatius, Rome, and Jesuit Urbanism," ran from October 1990 to September 1991 in the Salone Sistino of the BAV. Preparation for the exhibit helped me to break much ground for this present book. Many of this book's illustrations, as well as many of its ideas, were first published in the exhibition catalogue.

In Rome, the staff of Archivum Romanum Societatis Iesu and the Jesuit Historical Institute library were most helpful. The Jesuit community at Via degli Astalli was most welcoming. Evonne Levy of the American Academy offered much constructive collaboration and advice, especially for the development of the BAV exhibit. Fathers Jack O'Callaghan, Eugen Hillengass, Johannes Gunter Gerhartz, and Eugenio Bruno of the General Curia and Tommaso Ambrosetti and Carlo di Filippi of the Italian Province of the Society of Jesus were constant and faithful supporters of my different projects. Friends like Beatrice and Marcello Sacchetti, Luigi Turolla, Maurizio de Luca, Gianni Ciani, and Pio Hilbert kept me going with many kindnesses. Rosanna and Bill Montalbano shared their family and home with me, as well as their editorial acumen.

In California, the Jesuits of my province have encouraged me for more than 20 years. Superiors like Tom McCormick, Carlos Sevilla, Paul Belcher, Jack Clark, and John Privett have given me freedom for creativity; Jesuit friends like Peter Togni, Kevin Ballard, Tom Rochford, Don Doll, Walter Deye, Tom Powers, Peter Pabst, and members of various Jesuit communities have patiently coped with my ramblings. My dad, Frank Lucas, and my sister and brother-in-law, Justine and Dennis Barnard, and their kids have always been there for me, offering everything from consolation to computer support, both long distance and near at hand.

At the Graduate Theological Union, Berkeley, the library staff and registrars Betty Over and Sharon Gay Smith were always helpful. John O'Malley of the Weston Jesuit School of Theology generously allowed me to mine his manuscript version of *The First Jesuits*. My doctoral director, John Baldovin, S.J., was a patient and attentive task-master. I am grateful for both his academic rigor and his persistent encouragement.

At the University of San Francisco, Dean Stanley Nel and Father Rector Edward Stackpoole, S.J., gave moral and financial support that helped bring this project into print. Liza Locsin Enriquez; Nancy Campagna; Ed Schmidt, S.J.; Peter Togni, S.J.; Martin Palmer, S.J.; John Pinelli; Beth Bachtold; Roland Navas; Marina Greco; Amy Fox; Joe Stevano; Rita George; and the staff of Gleeson Library provided invaluable help in the final phases of preparing the manuscript. Designer Elizabeth O'Keefe, the Queen of QuarkXpress, collaborated with me on the design of this book, tweaked it into shape, and produced its maps. I am most grateful for her hard work and transcontinental good humor.

At Loyola Press, the courtesy and attention of Publisher Father George Lane, S.J., Acquisitions Editor Jeremy Langford and Production Manager Anne Marie Mastandrea was surpassed only by the graciousness of my eagle-eyed and most enthusiastic editor, Ruth McGugan who insisted that this book be beautiful as well as good.

Great teachers are those who teach us to wonder about the wonders that are always before our eyes. Spiro Kostof taught me how to look at cities; William Bangert, S.J., taught me to love the history of the Society of Jesus; Leonard Boyle, O.P., taught me to treasure the cultural patrimony of the Church.

This book is for them.

Thomas M. Lucas, S.J.
University of San Francisco

APPENDIX A
DATABASE: RELEVANT LETTERS OF IGNATIUS LOYOLA

The following database was assembled as a research tool for the present study. It attempts to classify the letters of Ignatius according to fifteen categories that touch on the major issues of mission, planning, property acquisition, and means of obtaining desired properties, sites, etc.

The letters are chronologically arranged in the series *Sancti Ignatii Epistolae et Instructiones* (Monumenta Historica Societatis Iesu), 12 vols. Madrid, 1903-11. In the database, the years 1524-1547 are taken together because of the very small number of letters, and then each year is considered separately. Letters are identified according to the consecutive numbering in the MHSI Volumes. For the reader's convenience, the following tables show the breakdown of letters according to years and according to volumes in the MHSI series.

YEAR	LETTERS	TOTAL LETTERS
1524-1547	1-235	251
1548	236-525	301
1549	529-989	466
1550	990-1499	514
1551	1500-2301	802
1552	2302-3134	837
1553	3135-4027	907
1554	4028-5058	1037
1555	5059-6065	1014
1556	6066-6742	679
no date		7

VOLUME	LETTERS	YEARS
Vol 1:	1-258	1524-1548
Vol 2:	259-1136	1548-1550
Vol 3:	1137-2225	1550-1551
Vol 4:	2226-3306	1551-1553
Vol 5:	3307-3946	1553
Vol 6:	3947-4461	1553-1554
Vol 7:	4462-4924	1554
Vol 8:	4925-5341	1554-1555
Vol 9:	5342-5824	1555
Vol 10:	5825-6215	1555-1556
Vol 11:	6216-6600	1556
Vol 12:	6601-6742	1556
Vol 12:	Appendices	varia

Because of a number of double letters (indicated *"bis"* in the MHSI volumes) and some letters that were discovered after the individual volumes were already printed (these are included in the appendices of Vol. 12), the number of letters per year does not always correspond exactly with the consecutive numeration.

In the database, there are 15 categories. They include:

STRAT.: Strategy. Usually preliminary instructions to Jesuits on how to negotiate with local authorities or benefactors to obtain property, funding, or support. Ignatius addressed a few of these strategic letters directly to important benefactors.

PROP. TRANS.: Property Transaction. Includes legal negotiations, financial arrangements, deeds, and instructions relevant to buying and selling of property and construction.

GEN. FIN.: General Finances. Letters about money matters which deal with transactions and foundations of Jesuit works.

ROME FIN.: Roman Finances. Letters about funding of Jesuit works in Rome.

MINIST.: Ministry. Letters dealing with Jesuit urban missions and apostolic work in cities.

BLDG/CONST.: Building and Construction.

DELLA STRADA: Letters dealing with Jesuits' house in Rome and their apostolic work which was directed from it.

COM. LUOGO: "Commodo Luogo," Convenient Siting. Letters in which Ignatius argues about finding sites appropriate to the works of the Society.

MODO PROC.: "Modo de Proceder," the Jesuits' "way of proceeding." Instructions sent out for organization, financing, and foundation of new works.

LOCAL OPT.: Local Option. Letters in which Ignatius either grants or denies permission for the local superior to make property transactions, building, etc.

MEND. RULE: Mendicant Rule. Correspondence dealing with the controversies between the Jesuits and the mendicants over siting within 140 cannae of already established mendicant foundations.

CASA PROF.: Professed House. These letters lay out the evolution of Ignatius' conception of the professed house vs. the college.

CURA ANIMA.: "Cura Animarum," care of souls, or, more concretely, parish responsibilities. This category includes letters which discuss the Jesuits' refusal to accept churches that entail normal parochial responsibilities.

NOVIT.: Novitiates. Letters which discuss the establishment or running of free-standing novitiates.

MANPOWER: Letters about the manpower shortages Ignatius had to face. In this category are also the "rule of 14" letters sent out to local benefactors requiring that the Society's new colleges be sufficiently endowed to support 14 Jesuits.

LETTERS, 1524-1547

LETTER NUMBER	STRAT.	PROP. TRANS	GEN. FIN.	ROME FIN.	MINIST.	BLDG/ CONST.	DELLA STRADA	COM. LUOGO	MODO PROC.	LOCAL OPT.	MEND. RULE	CASA PROF.	CURA ANIMA	NOVIT	MAN-POWER
TOTAL 1524-47	20	3	7	3	22	2	5	4	2	1	0	2	0	2	2
18					1										
31					1					1					
33					1										
38	1		1												
40					1										
41					1										
61					1										
62			1		1	1	1								
70	1	1	1		1										
71	1		1												
76		1		1	1	1	1	1							
85					1										
91					1										1
98	1			1	1		1	1							1
101	1														
109	1		1												
111					1										
119	1			1	1		1								
121	1														
123					1				1						
128	1														
130	1							1							
136					1										
147					1										
150	1	1			1										
152	1														
154	1														
155	1														
164	1														
183	1				1										
185					1										
186			1												
194											1				
204	1				1							1		1	
208	1				1		1	1				1		1	
224	1														
235	1		1												

LETTERS, 1548

LETTER NUMBER	STRAT.	PROP. TRANS	GEN. FIN.	ROME FIN.	MINIST.	BLDG/ CONST.	DELLA STRADA	COM. LUOGO	MODO PROC.	LOCAL OPT.	MEND. RULE	CASA PROF.	CURA ANIMA	NOVIT	MAN- POWER
TOTAL 1548	35	25	20	1	15	3	3	3	1	0	2	0	0	0	2
236	1	1	1		1		1								
239	1		1												
242					1										
245	1		1			1		1							
257	1				1										
267				1											
274	1		1												
280	1														
281	1				1										
287					1										
290	1	1	1												
294	1														1
297			1												
307	1														
313	1	1													
314					1										
316	1		1												
317	1	1													
320		1													
323		1													
324	1														1
325	1														
334					1										
345	1	1			1										
360					1										
366					1		1	1	1						
367					1										
372	1		1												
375			1												
395		1													
397	1														
401		1													
408	1	1													
409	1		1												
413	1		1												
418	1														
427		1													
428		1													
431		1													
434	1	1													
437		1													
439		1													
456		1													
460		1													
461			1												
467	1														
472					1										
475	1	1	1		1			1							
480	1		1												
481	1		1												
483	1														
484	1														
489	1														
490		1	1												
491		1	1												
494		1	1												
497	1	1				1					1				
507	1								1						
508		1	1												
520						1	1								

LETTERS, 1549

LETTER NUMBER	STRAT.	PROP. TRANS	GEN. FIN.	ROME FIN.	MINIST.	BLDG/ CONST.	DELLA STRADA	COM. LUOGO	MODO PROC.	LOCAL OPT.	MEND. RULE	CASA PROF.	CURA ANIMA	NOVIT.	MAN-POWER
TOTAL 1549	16	4	13	9	9	4	4	0	0	3	1	0	1	1	0
533	1		1												
534	1	1									1				
551	1														
575					1										
650			1												
652					1										
661			1												
664	1														
667	1				1		1						1		
679				1			1								
684					1										
692			1	1											
702	1	1	1												
709	1														
739					1										
744				1		1	1								
755			1												
760	1													1	
768	1	1								1					
775					1										
779					1										
798	1														
803		1				1									
844	1														
856					1										
858					1										
889	1														
895	1		1												
908			1												
925			1												
927			1												
959				1		1	1								
960				1											
968	1		1												
978			1	1											
980	1									1					
986			1							1					
987	1					1									
993				1											
998				1											
1000				1											

LETTERS, 1550

LETTER NUMBER	STRAT.	PROP. TRANS	GEN. FIN.	ROME FIN.	MINIST.	BLDG/ CONST.	DELLA STRADA	COM. LUOGO	MODO PROC.	LOCAL OPT.	MEND. RULE	CASA PROF.	CURA ANIMA	NOVIT	MAN-POWER
TOTAL 1550	27	8	29	6	8	5	6	0	1	2	1	0	2	5	0
1004		1			1	1	1								
1010	1					1					1				
1019			1							1					
1027			1												
1020			1												
1028					1		1								
1030	1										1			1	
1032	1			1			1								
1044			1		1										
1047	1			1											
1056			1												
1057	1				1										
1062			1												
1072			1												
1075	1		1												
1096	1								1						
1107														1	
1109			1												
1115			1												
1115			1												
1116			1												
1119	1														
1122			1												
1123														1	
1125					1										
1126			1												
1134			1												
1153			1												
1166			1												
1168			1												
1170			1	1											
1179	1														
1184														1	
1185			1												
1187					1										
1190			1												
1191					1										
1206	1														
1207	1														
1224		1													
1229	1		1												
1250			1												
1274	1														
1277	1		1												
1330			1												
1338		1													
1346		1													
1358	1													1	
1367	1														
1389			1												
1392			1												
1406	1		1												
1426		1													
1408	1														
1443	1														
1473			1												
1475	1	1													
1483	1			1		1	1								
1484	1			1		1	1								
1485	1	1		1	1	1	1								
1497	1	1													
1507	1														
1508	1												1		
1512	1												1		

LETTERS, 1551

LETTER NUMBER	STRAT.	PROP. TRANS	GEN. FIN.	ROME FIN.	MINIST.	BLDG/ CONST.	DELLA STRADA	COM. LUOGO	MODO PROC.	LOCAL OPT.	MEND. RULE	CASA PROF.	CURA ANIMA	NOVIT	MAN-POWER
TOTAL 1551	40	12	10	8	10	10	8	9	11	1	0	1	0	0	0
1528		1						1							
1566									1						
1637	1														
1671		1													
1702	1														
1709	1														
1729	1														
1731		1													
1735		1	1		1			1							
1736									1						
1743						1									
1755	1		1					1							
1756	1			1		1	1								
1765				1	1	1	1					1			
1770	1					1		1							
1800			1												
1809						1									
1818	1														
1848	1								1						
1854									1						
1858		1	1			1	1	1							
1873				1		1	1								
1884				1											
1899	1	1	1		1	1		1	1						
1924				1		1	1								
1925			1												
1928			1						1						
1941									1						
1964				1		1	1								
1965				1											
1970	1	1			1			1							
1984	1	1			1			1							
1985	1				1										
1987	1														
2007	1														
2010	1														
2020	1	1								1					
2037				1			1								
2046	1		1					1							
2047	1				1										
2061	1				1										
2070	1														
2078	1				1										
2085	1														
2093	1														
2114			1					1							
2124		1													
2142	1														
2143	1														
2157	1														
2162	1														
2166	1														
2167	1														
2186	1														
2188	1														
2189	1														
2193	1														
2200		1													
2206	1														
2208									1						
2210	1														
2220	1														
2223		1													
2226	1		1		1				1						
2227	1								1						
2228	1								1						

LETTERS, 1552

LETTER NUMBER	STRAT.	PROP. TRANS	GEN. FIN.	ROME FIN.	MINIST.	BLDG/ CONST.	DELLA STRADA	COM. LUOGO	MODO PROC.	LOCAL OPT.	MEND. RULE	CASA PROF.	CURA ANIMA	NOVIT	MAN-POWER
TOTAL 1552	43	36	41	12	15	8	9	6	5	0	6	1	0	2	0
2307	1			1	1		1								
2309	1	1	1								1				
2311	1	1	1								1				
2320	1	1	1								1				
2313	1			1											
2335	1														
2360	1		1		1				1					1	
2379			1												
2386	1	1			1		1	1						1	
2402	1	1	1												
2403	1		1									1			
2411		1													
2426		1													
2429	1														
2441		1													
2443	1	1	1												
2447				1											
2449				1											
2459	1			1	1				1						
2466	1		1												
2469		1													
2477		1	1												
2483	1			1	1		1								
2487					1										
2490	1		1												
2502		1	1												
2517	1		1												
2518	1		1												
2521	1	1	1						1						
2528	1														
2538	1	1	1			1									
2541			1												
2577		1	1												
2590	1	1							1						
2621	1	1				1									
2625	1	1				1					1				
2626	1					1					1				
2633	1		1			1					1				
2649		1													
2650				1		1	1								
2675		1													
2686	1		1												
2709		1							1						
2715	1		1												
2751	1	1	1												
2755			1		1										
2781	1		1												
2793					1		1								
2764		1													
2795		1	1												
2808	1	1	1												
2812	1														
2829				1			1								
2830				1		1	1								
2843				1		1	1								
2831				1											
2890		1		1											
2875	1	1	1												
2861	1	1	1		1				1						
2944			1		1										
2948	1	1													
2956	1		1												
2959		1	1												
2970			1												
2973			1								1				
2974	1	1									1				
2975	1				1						1				
2984		1													
3000	1		1		1										
3029	1														
3048	1		1						1						
3059		1													
3064				1			1								
3087				1											
3088				1											
3089		1	1												
3090			1												
3091			1												
3094			1												
3107			1												
3110		1													
3111	1	1													
3119	1														
3134			1												

LETTERS, 1553

LETTER NUMBER	STRAT.	PROP. TRANS	GEN. FIN.	ROME FIN.	MINIST.	BLDG/ CONST.	DELLA STRADA	COM. LUOGO	MODO PROC.	LOCAL OPT.	MEND. RULE	CASA PROF.	CURA ANIMA	NOVIT	MAN- POWER
TOTAL 1553	96	75	44	26	18	6	10	38	2	7	0	3	3	0	2
3137		1						1							
3147		1						1							
3168			1												
3170				1											
3187		1	1												
3195				1											
3204				1											
3206				1											
3267	1			1				1							
3282				1											
3306	1			1											
3307			1												
3315	1	1	1												
3316	1	1	1												
3337			1												
3339	1														
3341		1	1												
3357		1			1										
3362			1												
3364			1												
3367			1												
3368	1				1										
3369					1										
3375	1	1	1						1						
3383		1													
3398		1								1					
3399			1												
3408		1								1					
3427	1	1													
3429	1														
3431	1														
3436	1														
3439			1												
3441	1														
3442			1												
3447			1												
3455	1	1	1					1		1					
3466					1										
3468			1												
3475		1	1												
3477		1						1							
3500	1	1						1							
3508	1		1		1			1	1						
3515				1											
3529	1	1			1										
3541	1	1						1							
3546	1														
3549	1	1													
3554	1	1	1		1										
3563	1														
3571	1	1													
3574		1	1	1											
3579	1	1		1											
3589	1														
3591	1	1						1							
3602				1											
3614	1														
3626	1							1							
3632	1														
3633	1	1						1							
3636		1		1	1	1	1								
3638						1	1								
3641			1												
3646		1				1							1		
3656	1														
3659	1	1													

LETTERS, 1553 (*continued*)

LETTER NUMBER	STRAT.	PROP. TRANS	GEN. FIN.	ROME FIN.	MINIST.	BLDG/ CONST.	DELLA STRADA	COM. LUOGO	MODO PROC.	LOCAL OPT.	MEND. RULE	CASA PROF.	CURA ANIMA	NOVIT	MAN-POWER
3663	1	1	1												
3665			1												
3666				1				1							
3667	1	1													
3675													1		
3681	1		1					1							
3685	1														
3689	1	1													
3690	1							1							
3693	1							1			1				
3694	1														
3699	1														
3700	1														
3701	1		1					1							
3705				1							1				
3714	1	1													
3721	1	1			1			1							
3723	1		1												
3726	1	1				1	1								
3728	1	1	1			1		1			1				
3733	1	1						1							
3734	1	1	1												
3735	1	1													
3739	1	1													
3744			1												
3745	1	1		1			1								
3750	1	1	1					1							
3751		1			1			1							
3755								1							
3758	1		1												
3761	1	1						1							
3770	1														
3776				1											
3783	1	1													
3784	1	1	1	1											
3798	1		1					1							
3800	1	1	1	1				1							
3804	1	1	1		1			1							
3805	1	1						1						1	
3806	1	1						1							
3807	1	1	1					1							
3814	1	1													
3815		1													
3816	1	1		1			1								
3817	1	1						1							
3818		1													
3827	1	1													
3834								1							
3837	1	1					1								
3838	1	1					1								
3839	1			1			1								
3840	1														
3841		1													
3842	1														
3843	1	1													
3849	1	1					1	1							
3851				1											
3857	1	1	1												
3861	1	1	1					1							
3863	1	1						1			1				
3864	1							1							
3871	1														
3877	1														
3883				1											
3884		1		1	1		1	1							
3887	1					1									
3893	1	1		1											
3897	1			1											
3898	1			1											
3899		1						1							
3901		1						1							
3914		1			1								1		

LETTERS, 1553 (*continued*)

LETTER NUMBER	STRAT.	PROP. TRANS	GEN. FIN.	ROME FIN.	MINIST.	BLDG/ CONST.	DELLA STRADA	COM. LUOGO	MODO PROC.	LOCAL OPT.	MEND. RULE	CASA PROF.	CURA ANIMA	NOVIT	MAN-POWER
3927	1														
3939	1	1	1												
3940	1	1	1												
3957					1										
3971	1	1													
3973	1	1	1												1
3978					1										
3985	1														
3986	1	1						1							
3992	1		1												1
3997	1				1							1			
4019	1	1				1									
4022	1	1											1		

LETTERS, 1554

LETTER NUMBER	STRAT.	PROP. TRANS	GEN. FIN.	ROME FIN.	MINIST.	BLDG/ CONST.	DELLA STRADA	COM. LUOGO	MODO PROC.	LOCAL OPT.	MEND. RULE	CASA PROF.	CURA ANIMA	NOVIT	MAN-POWER
TOTAL 1554	148	127	85	17	23	32	15	23	2	14	8	5	3	7	18
4028	1		1		1							1		1	1
4032	1														1
4033	1														
4043	1														1
4050		1				1									
4055	1					1				1		1			
4061		1	1												
4064	1	1	1												1
4074	1														1
4080						1								1	
4084	1														
4088	1	1						1							
4093	1														
4110	1	1	1												
4113	1														
4121	1														1
4124		1	1		1										
4125		1	1												
4131	1	1			1			1							
4132	1	1						1			1				
4144		1					1								
4145	1														
4149			1	1											
4152	1	1			1										
4155	1	1	1												
4156	1	1													
4162		1	1												
4167		1	1					1		1					
4168		2								1					
4169	1	1	1												
4178	1														1
4179	1	2	1												
4186			1												
4191	1	1													
4194	1		1												
4195	1		1												
4196	1		1								1				
4208	1		1										1		
4209	1		1												
4223	1	1					1	1							1
4226		1									1				
4227	1	1													
4234		1	1												
4245	1	1	1												1
4246	1					1	1								

LETTERS, 1554 (*continued*)

LETTER NUMBER	STRAT.	PROP. TRANS	GEN. FIN.	ROME FIN.	MINIST.	BLDG/ CONST.	DELLA STRADA	COM. LUOGO	MODO PROC.	LOCAL OPT.	MEND. RULE	CASA PROF.	CURA ANIMA	NOVIT	MAN-POWER
4248	1														
4251	1		1							1					
4252	1	1						1							
4254	1	1						1		1					
4256	1	1			1										
4257					1										
4258	1														
4259	1	1						1							
4265							1								
4267	1	1	1												
4269						1									
4270	1	1									1				
4274	1	1	1												
4295					1										
4309	1				1				1						1
4314	1	1						1			1				
4318	1														
4334	1	1	1												
4339	1												1	1	
4342		1	1			1	1								
4345	1	1													
4546	1														1
4349	1	1													
4355		1	1												
4356	1	1	1												1
4359	1														
4368	1	1													
4372		1													
4376	1	1											1		
4398	1														
4399	1														
4400	1	1													
4401	1	1	1												
4409		1													
4415	1														1
4418					1		1								
4421	1														
4423	1					1					1				
4425	1	1													
4426		1	1												
4427	1	1									1				
4429				1											
4436	1														
4441	1														
4443	1	1	1			1					1				
4445	1	1						1							
4453		1	1			1	1	1							
4455	1	1	1					1							
4465	1	1													
4473		1													
4474		1													
4476	1														
4478	1	1													
4480	1				1										1
4487	1	1						1			1				
4500	1	1	1												
4512	1														
4518				1											
4524	1		1			1									
4525		1													
4529				1				1							
4531				1				1							
4538		2													
4547	1													1	
4549						1	1								
4550			1	1											
4551						1									
4553	1				1	1					1				
4555		1	1	1											
4558			1												

LETTERS, 1554 (*continued*)

LETTER NUMBER	STRAT.	PROP. TRANS	GEN. FIN.	ROME FIN.	MINIST.	BLDG/ CONST.	DELLA STRADA	COM. LUOGO	MODO PROC.	LOCAL OPT.	MEND. RULE	CASA PROF.	CURA ANIMA	NOVIT	MAN-POWER
4562	1														
4567			1		1										
4571		1													
4584	1														
4586	1		1												
4597		1	1												
4598				1											
4499		1													
4603		1	1					1							
4604		1													
4611		1										1			
4615	1		1	1											
4617	1	1	1		1	1	1	1							
4624				1											
4626			1			1	1								
4627	1	1	1												
4628	1	1	1												
4638		1	1			1									
4653						1									
4657	1					1					1				
4658		1						1							
4660	1	1													
4665	1	1	1												
4668	1				1										
4669	1	1			1						1				
4670	1	1	1												
4680	1														
4682	1	1			1			1							
4697		1				1		1							
4700		1	1												
4708		1													
4710	1	1												1	
4711	1	1	1												
4712		1	1												
4718	1	1													
4716	1	1													
4739	1	1	1												
4744		1	1												
4746		1	1			1									
4747	1	1													
4748		1	1												
4752	1	1	1												
4761	1	1													
4763	1	1	1												
4767				1											
4770	1	1													
4771	1	1	1												
4772		1	1												
4776		1	1												
4777	1	1													
4790	1	1													
4794	1	1	1		1					1		1			
4796	1	1				1									
4798	1	1													
4799															
4806	1				1	1			1						
4811	1		1		1										
4825		1	1												
4828	1					1					1				
4832	1		1												
4833	1										1				
4835	1		1	1											
4836		1	1			1									
4839		1				1	1								
4841	1													1	
4842				1											
4855		1													
4856				1			1								
4857		1				1									
4858				1		1	1								

LETTERS, 1554 (*continued*)

LETTER NUMBER	STRAT.	PROP. TRANS	GEN. FIN.	ROME FIN.	MINIST.	BLDG/ CONST.	DELLA STRADA	COM. LUOGO	MODO PROC.	LOCAL OPT.	MEND. RULE	CASA PROF.	CURA ANIMA	NOVIT	MAN- POWER
4860	1														
4861	1	1				1									
4867	1	1	1			1									
4874	1														
4875	1	1													
4884	1														
4890	1					1	1								
4894	1							1							
4898	1	1													
4903		1													
4904	1	1	1					1							
4916	1	1						1					1		
4918						1									
4949	1	1									1				
4921	1	1						1			1				
4923			1												
4932	1		1					1							
4934	1					1									
4936	1		1												
4955	1	1													
4958				1											
4960		1													
4961	1	1													
4971	1														
4972	1														
4980	1	1													
4985	1		1												
4988	1		1												
4990	1		1												1
4995	1		1												
4996	1	1	1												1
5006	1														1
5011				1											
5012	1	1	1					1							
5021				1											
5027			1												
5028	1														1
5042	1	1	1												
5043			1		1	1									
5044	1	1													
5052	1	1													
5058	1		1											1	

LETTERS, 1555

LETTER NUMBER	STRAT.	PROP. TRANS	GEN. FIN.	ROME FIN.	MINIST.	BLDG/ CONST.	DELLA STRADA	COM. LUOGO	MODO PROC.	LOCAL OPT.	MEND. RULE	CASA PROF.	CURA ANIMA	NOVIT	MAN- POWER
TOTAL 1555	126	99	73	45	10	31	8	15	0	12	15	7	1	3	7
5060		1	1												
5063	1														
5064				1			1								
5065	1	1	1			1								1	
5071		1	1			1									
5076				1			1								
5078	1	1	1									1			
5079				1		1	1								
5080	1							1							
5086	1	1	1												
5090	1														
5091	1														
5092	1														
5095	1					1									
5079		1						1							

LETTERS, 1555 (*continued*)

LETTER NUMBER	STRAT.	PROP. TRANS	GEN. FIN.	ROME FIN.	MINIST.	BLDG/ CONST.	DELLA STRADA	COM. LUOGO	MODO PROC.	LOCAL OPT.	MEND. RULE	CASA PROF.	CURA ANIMA	NOVIT	MAN-POWER
5102			1												
5104	1														
5108		1	1												
5109		1	1												
5122	1			1											
5123	1			1											
5131	1														
5138			1												
5143			1												
5145	1	1	1												
5146	1														
5147	1														
5148	1														
5161		1													
5167	1														
5171	1	1	1												
5176	1		1												
5177				1			1								
5178	1		1												
5179				1											
5180				1											
5183	1														1
5186				1								1			
5190		1													
5193	1	1	1												
5198	1	1	1			1						1			
5204				1											
5209	1					1									
5219		1	1												
5222	1	1						1							
5224	1		1												
5225	1	1	1												1
5229	1	1				1									
5238	1		1												
5239		1		1											
5245	1	1	1			1					1				
5248	1		1												
5250	1	1	1												
5253		1										1			
5258	1	1			1										
5277	1	1			1	1					1	1			
5289		1	1	1											
5293	1	1	1		1			1							
5303						1									
5307	1			1		1									
5309	1	1	1												
5311		1	1												
5323						1									
5325	1	1	1												
5326	1				1										
5327	1	1			1										
5339	1	1	1												
5350	1														
5368	1	1													
5388	1	1		1		1									
5389	1	1													
5392	1	1			1										
5395	1	1	1												1
5396	1	1	1							1					
5399	1		1	1						1		1		1	1
5405	1		1												
5405	1		1												
5411	1	1	1	1											
5413	1														
5415	1	1						1					1		
5422	1		1	1										1	
5430	1		1												
5433	1	1	1							1					
5436			1												
5447				1											

LETTERS, 1555 (*continued*)

LETTER NUMBER	STRAT.	PROP. TRANS	GEN. FIN.	ROME FIN.	MINIST.	BLDG/ CONST.	DELLA STRADA	COM. LUOGO	MODO PROC.	LOCAL OPT.	MEND. RULE	CASA PROF.	CURA ANIMA	NOVIT	MAN-POWER
5448	1	1	1												
5451	1		1												
5452	1					1									
5453	1	1	1			1									
5457	1		1												
5460			1												
5461		1						1							
5466	1	1		1		1									
5477	1	1	1					1							
5487	1	1									1				
5495		1				1									
5497	1														
5501	1			1											
5502	1			1											
5503	1			1											
5507	1			1											
5514	1	1						1			1				
5526	1			1											
5532	1	1									1				
5545	1		1			1									
5550	1	1									1				
5551	1	1									1				
5554	1	1						1			1				
5559				1											
5560	1		1	1											1
5573		1		1											
5576						1									
5585	1														1
5602	1							1							
5606	1							1			1				
5607	1				1										
5608	1														
5610		1	1												
5619						1									
5628	1	1													
5631						1									
5632	1							1							
5634	1	1									1				
5636		1													
5643	1	1									1				
5645						1									
5650	1		1												
5653	1	1				1									
5656	1	1				1						1			
5661	1	1													
5663	1														
5671		1													
5672	1			1	1	1	1								
5673	1				1	1	1								
5674	1	1	1					1							
5689	1	1	1												
5692	1	1													
5702		1	1												
5706		1		1											
5716			1												
5727	1			1											
5729	1			1											
5730						1									
5733		1	1	1											
5744	1	1										1			
5745	1			1											
5746	1			1											
5747		1	1	1											
5750				1											
5751				1											
5752				1											
5759		1													
5763				1											
5778				1											
5789		1													
5790				1											

LETTERS, 1555 (*continued*)

LETTER NUMBER	STRAT.	PROP. TRANS	GEN. FIN.	ROME FIN.	MINIST.	BLDG/ CONST.	DELLA STRADA	COM. LUOGO	MODO PROC.	LOCAL OPT.	MEND. RULE	CASA PROF.	CURA ANIMA	NOVIT	MAN-POWER
5793				1											
5834	1	1													
5852	1	1													
5853	1		1												
5854	1	1	1					1							
5866	1	1	1								1				
5870			1	1											
5876		1	1												
5886		1	1	1											
5888			1			1	1								
5891		1													
5892	1		1												
5896		1	1												
5901	1	1													
5902	1		1												
5904		1	1								1				
5910	1	1				1									
5925	1	1										1			
5926	1	1													
5934	1														
5935	1														
5937	1										1				
5947	1	1									1				
5948	1	1									1				
5949	1	1									1				
5950	1	1									1				
5955	1	1	1												
5957						1									
5963		1				1	1								
5965			1												
5968		1	1												
5969		1									1				
5975		1	1												
5976	1	1						1			1				
5982		1													
5984	1		1												
5985	1	1				1					1				
5992		1	1												1
5998		1	1								1				
6000	1		1												

LETTERS, 1556

LETTER NUMBER	STRAT.	PROP. TRANS	GEN. FIN.	ROME FIN.	MINIST.	BLDG/ CONST.	DELLA STRADA	COM. LUOGO	MODO PROC.	LOCAL OPT.	MEND. RULE	CASA PROF.	CURA ANIMA	NOVIT	MAN-POWER
TOTAL 1556	73	70	67	22	19	20	8	17	9	2	5	0	0	2	13
6073		1				1									
6078	1					1									
6080						1	1								
6094					1	1	1								
6099	1					1			1						
6100	1										1				
6115	1	1	1		1										
6116	1	1	1												
6118			1												
6136	1	1	1												
6140	1	1			1										
6142		1		1											
6152						1	1								
6159		1				1	1								
6163		1	1												
6168	1	1													1
6169			1												

LETTERS, 1556 (*continued*)

LETTER NUMBER	STRAT.	PROP. TRANS	GEN. FIN.	ROME FIN.	MINIST.	BLDG/ CONST.	DELLA STRADA	COM. LUOGO	MODO PROC.	LOCAL OPT.	MEND. RULE	CASA PROF.	CURA ANIMA	NOVIT	MAN-POWER
6172	1			1											
6173						1	1								
6175	1	1	1								1				
6180	1		1												
6186	1	1									1				
6196				1		1	1								
6199						1	1								
6205	1		1		1				1						
6209	1		1	1											
6216		1									1				
6225		1													
6227		1	1												
6228							1	1							
6224	1		1												
6249		1	1												
6250		1	1												
6256		1	1	1	1										
6257		1													
6258	1		1												
6260	1	1	1												1
6261	1	1	1												
6266		1	1												
6267		1								1					
6268		1													
6271		1	1												
6274	1														1
6283			1												
6305	1														
6313	1	1	1												
6315		1	1												
6329	1	1	1								1				
6331			1	1											
6334		1													
6335	1	1	1												1
6336		1													
6339	1	1	1												
6344		1	1	1											
6352		1	1												
6364	1	1													1
6365	1	1	1												
6368	1	1	1		1										
6374	1				1				1						
6376	1		1												
6381		1							1						
6382			1												
6387		1	1												
6389		1	1	1											
6394	1			1											
6401	1		1	1											
6404	1		1			1									
6423	1														
6450	1	1	1		1				1	1					
6452	1	1	1		1				1	1					
6455		1	1	1			1		1						
6459			1												
6464		1	1												
6469	1	1					1		1						
6472	1	1	1						1						
6483	1														
6492	1			1											
6495		1	1	1											
6499	1		1												1
6523		1		1											
6526	1	1							1						
6534	1	1	1						1						1
6537				1											1
6540	1														1
6544	1	1													
6547	1	1							1						
6565	1		1			1			1						
6571	1		1												
6573	1	1	1						1						1

APPENDIX B
CONSTITUTIONS
OF THE SOCIETY OF JESUS,   [622, 623]

(*ConstEng*, pp. 274-76)

[622, a]–D. To proceed more successfully in this sending of subjects to one place or another, one should keep the greater service of God and the more universal good before his eyes as the norm to hold oneself on the right course. It appears that in the vineyard of the Lord, which is so extensive, the following procedure of selection ought to be used. When other considerations are equal (and this should be understood in everything that follows), that part of the vineyard ought to be chosen which has greater need, because of the lack of other workers or because of the misery and weakness of one's fellowmen in it and the danger of their eternal condemnation.

[b]. Consideration should also be given to where the greater fruit will probably be reaped through the means which the Society uses. This case would arise, for example, where one sees the door more widely open and a better disposition among the people along with compliancy favorable to their progress. This disposition consists in the people's greater devotion and desire (which can be judged in part by the insistence they show), or in the condition and quality of the persons who are more capable of making progress and of preserving the fruit produced, to the glory of God our Savior.

[c]. In places where our indebtedness is greater, for example, where there is a house or college of the Society or where there are members of it who study and are the recipients of charitable deeds from those people, and when it is granted that the other considerations pertaining to spiritual progress are equal, it would be more fitting to have some laborers there, and for that reason to prefer these places to others, in conformity with perfect charity.

[d]. The more universal the good is, the more is it divine. Therefore preference ought to be given to those persons and places which, through their own improvement, become a cause which can spread the good accomplished to many others who are under their influence or take guidance from them.

[e]. For that reason, the spiritual aid which is given to important and public persons ought to be regarded as more important, since it is a more universal good. This is true whether these persons are laymen such as princes, lords, magistrates, or ministers of justice, or whether they are clerics such as prelates. The same also holds true of the spiritual aid which is given to persons distinguished for learning and authority, because of that reason of its being the more universal good. For that same reason, too, preference ought to be shown to the aid which is given to the great nations such as the Indies, or to important cities, or to universities, which are generally attended by numerous persons who by being aided themselves can become laborers for the help of others.

[f]. Similarly, the Society ought to labor more intensely in those places where the enemy of Christ our Lord has sown cockle [Matt. 13:24-30], and especially where he has spread bad opinion about the Society or stirred up ill will against it so as to impede the fruit which the Society could produce. This is especially to be observed if the place is an important one of which account should be taken, by sending there, if possible, persons such that by their life and learning they may undo the evil opinion founded on false reports.

[623, a]—E. For better success in the choice of undertaking for which the superior sends his subjects, the same norm should be kept in view, namely, that of considering the greater divine honor and the greater universal good. This consideration can supply completely just reasons for sending a subject to one place rather than to another. To touch upon some motives which can exist in favor of one place or another, we mention these.

[b]. First of all, the members of the Society may occupy themselves in undertakings directed toward benefits for the soul and also in those directed toward benefits for the body through the practice of mercy and charity. Similarly, they may help some persons in matters pertaining to their greater perfection or to their lesser perfection; and finally, in regard to things which are of themselves of more good, or of less good. In all these cases, if both things cannot be done simultaneously and the other considerations are equal, the spiritual goods ought to be preferred to the bodily, the matters of greater perfection to those of less, and the things more good to those less good.

[c]. Likewise, when there are some things in the service of God our Lord which are more urgent, and others which are less pressing and can better suffer postponement of the remedy, even though they are of equal impor-

tance, the first ought to be preferred to the second.

[d]. Similarly too, when there are some things which are especially incumbent upon the Society or it is seen that there are no others to attend to them, and other things in regard to which others do have care and a method of providing for them, in choosing missions there is reason to prefer the first to the second.

[e]. Likewise also, among the pious works of equal importance, urgency, and need, when some are safer for the one who cares for them and others are more dangerous; and when some are easier and more quickly dispatched and others are more difficult and finished only in a longer time, the first should be similarly preferred over the second.

[f]. When everything mentioned above is equal and when there are some occupations which are of more universal good and extend to the aid of more of our fellowmen, such as preaching or lecturing, and others which are concerned more with individuals, such as hearing confessions or giving Exercises; and when further it is impossible to accomplish both sets of occupations simultaneously, preference should be given to the first set, unless there should be some circumstances through which it would be judged that to take up the second set would be more expedient.

[g]. Similarly too, when there are some spiritual works which continue longer and are of more lasting value, such as certain pious foundations for the aid of our fellowmen, and other works less durable which give help on a few occasions and only for a short while, then it is certain that the first ought to be preferred to the second. Hence it is also certain that the superior of the Society ought to employ his subjects more in the first type rather than in the second, since that is a greater service to God and a greater good for our fellowmen.

APPENDIX C
"MODO DE PROCEDER" LETTER

(*EpistIgn.* III, 1899, pp. 542-550)

IHS.

AN INSTRUCTION ON THE MODE OF PROCEEDING
sent to Ferrara, and in about the same tenor to Florence, Naples, and Modena,
with some modifications. [addressed to Jean Pelletier].

Three things should be aimed at . . . One is the preservation and increase of the members of the Society in spirit, learning, and numbers. The second is the edification and spiritual advancement of the city. The third is the consolidation and increase of the new college's temporalities so as to provide for the better service of the Lord in the first and second areas.

Part One:

The first part, regarding the members of the Society, provides the foundation for the others. For the better they themselves are, the more suitable will they also be for acceptance by God as instruments for the edification of externs and the permanence of the foundation.

1. Therefore all should strive to have a right intention, seeking exclusively "not the things that are their own but the things that are Jesus Christ's" [Phil. 2:21]. They should endeavor to conceive great resolves and desires to be true and faithful servants of God and to render a good account of themselves in whatever responsibilities they are given, with a genuine abnegation of their own will and judgment and a total submission of themselves to

God's government of them by means of holy obedience, whether they are employed in high or lowly tasks. They should pray as fervently as they can to obtain this grace from the Giver of every good. Moreover, the one in charge should from time to time remind them of these things.

2. So far as possible, the order and method of the college here [in Rome] should be followed, particularly in the matter of weekly confession and Communion, the daily examination of conscience and hearing of mass in the house, the practice of obedience, and not conversing with externs except according to the regulation of the rector, who will decide how much each man may be entrusted with for edifying others without danger to himself.

3. Within the house they should practice preaching daily during dinner and supper, a different man on each day of the week, with no, or at most an hour's, preparation for these sermons in the refectory. In addition, sometimes during the week they should practice preaching in the vernacular or in Latin, being assigned a topic to speak on *extempore;* there should be sermons in Greek also, making use of the "tones" [short stock sermons devised for exercising the gamut of "tones"–expository, threatening, consoling, etc.], though this latter may be varied according to the capacity of the student.

4. Each one should strive to advance in learning and assist the others, studying and teaching what is assigned him by the rector. Care must be taken that the lessons are accomodated to the students, and that all the students get a thorough grounding in grammar along with training in composition, with careful corrections by the masters. They should engage in disputations and conferences.

5. They should strive by means of academic and spiritual conversations to draw others to the way of perfection. With their younger pupils, however, this should be done only with the greatest tact; and not even older students may be received [into the Society] without their parents' approval. If it is deemed proper to receive an older student into the house (when he has made this decision for himself) or to send him to Rome or some other place, this may be done. However, discretion and the anointing of the Holy Spirit will point out the best course; or, for greater security in cases of doubt, they should write to the provincial or to Rome.

6. For these purposes, it will be useful to have some of the more advanced students carefully compose Latin discourses on the Christian virtues and deliver them publicly in the presence of all every week or every other week on Sundays and feast days. They should invite young men and others, especially those who seem suitable for religious life, to hear these talks. This will be a good way to dispose those whom the Lord may call for taking the path of perfection; at the least it will make a good impression and

give edification, and those in the house will obtain progress in literary practice and in the virtues.

Part Two:

Regarding the second aspect, that of working for the edification and spiritual profit of the city (over and above helping outsiders by means of prayer):

1. The first means is by providing an educations in Latin and Greek to all comers, according to their ability, by giving class lectures and having the students practice disputation and composition.

2. By taking care to teach Christian doctrine to the children every Sunday or on a weekday; and on another day having them memorize some little bit according to the program of the Roman College or however they deem best. This will be done in the house or in their own church or in any suitable nearby place that they think most appropriate. This practice could well produce more spiritual benefit than preaching.

3. By seeing to it that the pupils form good habits through having them hear mass daily if possible, attend the sermons given on feast days, go to confession once a month, and cease blaspheming, swearing, and using indecent language.

4. Thought should be given to whether it would be good to have preaching on Sundays and feast days, or only have one of the men teach catechism classes in the church or in the public place while some of the men practice preaching in the monasteries.

5. Thought should be given to the advisability of lectures on Holy Scripture or scholastic theology for priests–for example, on the sacraments or a manual of conscience cases–if not at the beginning at least later.

6. They should give special attention to heresies, and be properly armed against heretics. They should know by heart the topics of controversy and try to engage with these so as to uncover and cure their infections; or, if this is not possible, to impugn their wrong teaching–skillfully, however, and not antagonizing these persons but lovingly attempting to rescue them.

7. They should strive to draw people to the sacraments of penance and Communion, and be prepared for administering these.

8. Through spiritual conversation all of them can assist those they deal with, particularly when they find them so disposed as to give hope of good results. The Exercises of the First Week could be given to large numbers, but the remaining Weeks only to those who show themselves suited for the state of perfection and are dispoed to the be genuinely helped by devoting themselves totally to the Exercises.

9. Where there is time, they should take care to assist prisoners, visiting the jails if possible and having one of the men preach there urging them to go to confession and turn to God, and hearing their confessions when this is called for and can be done without detriment to tasks that are more obligatory and pleasing to God.

10. They should also remember the hospitals—if, as I say, they occasionally have time left over—striving to console and spiritually assist the poor as far as they can. Here also occasional exhortations will be profitable, unless an examination of all the circumstances indicates otherwise.

11. In general they should try to be aware of the pious works in the city where they reside, and do what they can to further them either by their own efforts or through others. Morevoer, they should show diligence and charity in starting new works that do not exist.

12. But while numerous means of helping the neighbor and numerous pious works are suggested, discretion will also guide them in which alternatives to embrace when they cannot undertake them all, as they keep their eyes always on the greater service of God, the common good, and the Society's good reputation together with the special interests of the college and the characteristic concerns of the Society.

Part Three:

The third part consists in striving skillfully to consolidate and increase the temporal goods of the new college. For this, over and above the sacrifices and prayers which should be offered by all in the house for this intention insofar as it is for God's glory, the observance of the points mentioned in the first and second aspects will be more effective than any other means on our part. But in regard to a few means special to this third aspect the following will be helpful:

1. They should work to maintain and increase the good will of the cardinal and of the municipality, complying with their wishes wherever this is possible according to God and serving them in the pious works in which they particularly wish to employ them, where this offers no prejudice to God's greater service. They should have a care for their own good reputation and authority with these persons, and speak so as to convince them of the Society's intentions to expand its work even though it ordinarily begins in a lowly way so that it may later grow rather than diminish.

2. They should also strive to win the good will of private citizens and benefactors and converse with them about spiritual matters. Special help given to such persons would be quite suitable and pleasing to God, whose affairs are at stake.

3. The better to preserve needed authority in spiritual things, they should try if possible to have requests made and temporal affairs handled by their friends rather than by themselves, or they should at least do this in such a way that that there is no wrong appearance of greed. To avoid all such concern, it would be better if a fixed resource could be settled for their support, although this should not be stated except in the proper manner and time.

4. They should give special attention to eventually acquiring, if they do not yet have one, a good, sizable piece of land, or one that can be expanded sufficiently for a house, church, and school; if possible, it should not be too far away from the activity [literally, "from the conversation"] of the city.

5. They should write weekly so that they can be given assistance and information in various matters.

(Translation by Martin Palmer, S.J.)

NOTES

FREQUENTLY USED ABBREVIATIONS

AHSI: Archivum Historicum Societatis Iesu.

ARSI: Archivum Romanum Societatis Iesu, Rome.

BAV: Biblioteca Apostolica Vaticana, Vatican City.

Chron: Polanco, J. *Vita Ignatii Loiolae et rerum Societatis Iesu Historia seu Chronicon.* (Monumenta Historica Societatis Iesu) 6 vols. Madrid, 1894–1898.

ConstEng: Constitutions of the Society of Jesus. Translated by G. Ganss, St. Louis, MO, 1970. For easier cross-referencing to other editions, the standard paragraph numbering is given instead of page numbers.

ConstMHSJ: Constitutiones et Regulae Societatis Iesu. (Monumenta Historica Societatis Iesu) 4 vols. Rome: 1934–1948.

EpistIgn: Sancti Ignatii de Loyola epistolae et instructiones (Monumenta Historica Societatis Iesu). 12 vols. Madrid, 1903–1911. References include volume number and letter number. Page number is given when text is cited.

EpistMixtae: Epistolae Mixtae ex variis Europae locis ab anno 1537 ad 1556 scriptae. (Monumenta Historica Societatis Iesu). 5 vols. Madrid, 1898–1901.

FD: Fontes Documentales de S. Ignatio de Loyola (Monumenta Historica Societatis Iesu). Rome, 1977.

First Jesuits: O'Malley, John. *The First Jesuits.* Cambridge MA: Harvard Univ. Press, 1993.

FN: Fontes Narrativi de S. Ignatio de Loyola et de Societatis Iesu Initiis (Monumenta Historica Societatis Iesu). 4 vols. Rome, 1943–1965.

Scripta: Scripta de S. Ignatio (Monumenta Historica Societatis Iesu). 2 vols. Madrid, 1904–1918.

SpEx: The Spiritual Exercises of St. Ignatius, A translation and commentary by George Ganss, S.J., St. Louis: Institute of Jesuit Sources, 1992. For easier crossreferencing to other editions, the standard paragraph

numbering is given instead of page numbers. Note that when the words "Spiritual Exercises" appear in *italic* type they refer to the book of the Exercises; when they appear in roman type, they refer to the entire dynamic or process of prayer, meditation, contemplation, and activity sketched out in the book.

Strategy: Lucas, Thomas, Editor. *Saint, Site, and Sacred Strategy: Ignatius, Rome, and Jesuit Urbanism.* Exhibition catalogue. Vatican City: Biblioteca Apostolica Vaticana, 1990.

StudiesSpir.: Studies in the Spirituality of Jesuits.

TV *Storia:* Tacchi Venturi, Pietro. *Storia della Compagnia di Gesù in Italia.* 2 vols, each in 2 parts, Rome: Edizioni Civiltà Cattolica, 1951.

CHAPTER ONE
LOCATION, LOCATION, LOCATION

1. Giacinto Gigli, *Il Diario,* BAV Vat. Lat 8717, fol. 50, author's translation.

2. Plutarchus, *Plutarch's Lives, Vol. 1,* translated by Bernadette Perrin, Loeb Classical Library, London: Wm. Heineman, 1967, pp. 120–21.

3. For exhaustive details of Javier's travels from Europe to India, see Georg Schurhammer, *Francis Xavier, Vol 2: India, 1541–1545,* translated by M. Joseph Costelloe, Rome: Jesuit Historical Institute, 1973, chapters 1–5. For purposes of consistency, the names of Ignatius' early companions will be given in their original spellings: hence, for example, Francisco Javier rather than Francis Xavier.

"Ignatius" was not the given name of Iñigo Lopez de Loyola, but a latinized version he assumed at Paris in 1529. For purposes of simplicity, he will be referred to as "Iñigo" for the period before his Parisian interlude, and as "Ignatius" afterward.

4. Dauril Alden, *The Making of an Enterprise, The Society of Jesus in Portugal, Its Empire, and Beyond, 1540-1750,* Stanford: Stanford Univ. Press, 1996, pp. 45, 77–78.

5. Michele Accolti, "A memorial of the journey to California," cited in John McGloin's *Jesuits by the Golden Gate, The Society of Jesus in San Francisco, 1849-1969,* San Francisco: Univ. of San Francisco Press, 1972, p. 1. Also see Gerald McKevitt, *The University of Santa Clara, A History, 1851-1977,* Stanford: Stanford Univ. Press, 1979, chapter 2.

6. Letter dated August 23, 1853, cited in John McGloin's *California's First Archbishop, The Life of Joseph Sadoc Alemany, O.P., 1814-1888,* New York: Herder & Herder, 1966, p. 193.

7. McGloin, *Jesuits by the Golden Gate,* pp. 11, 15.

8. McGloin, *California's First Archbishop,* pp. 205–06.

9. McGloin, *California's First Archbishop,* p. 211.

10. McGloin, *California's First Archbishop,* p. 258.

11. *Monumenta Peruana,* I, (1565–75), (MHSI), Rome, 1954, pp. 246–47.

12. *Monumenta Peruana,* I, p 243, 347.

13. *Monumenta Peruana,* II, pp. 143–44.

14. *Monumenta Peruana,* II, p. 617.

15. Harold Wethey, *Colonial Architecture and Sculpture in Peru.* Cambridge: Harvard Univ. Press, 1949, pp. 262–64.

16. José Montanha, "Apparatos para la Historia do Bispado de Macao," fol. 245, in the Arquivo Histórico Ultramarino, Lisboa.

17. For excellent brief histories of the Jesuit mission in Macao and its artistic impact, see Domingos Maurício Gomes dos Santos, "Macao, The First Western University in the Far East," and Gonçalo Couceiro, "Macao and the Art of the Society of Jesus in China," in *Review of Culture,* (Instituto Cultural de Macau), October–December 1994, pp. 5–26 and pp. 27–34 respectively.

18. See Couceiro, "Macao and the Art of the Society of Jesus in China," p. 33.

19. Pasquale M. D'Elia, *Fonti Ricciane, Documenti Origniali concernenti Matteo Ricci e la storia delle prime relazioni tra l'Europa e la Cina (1579-1615),* Rome: Libreria dello Stato, 1949, vol. 2, pp. 352–53.

20. Rachael Attwater, *Adam Schall, A Jesuit at the Court of China, 1592-1666,* Milwaukee: Bruce Publishing Company, 1963, p. 39.

21. Jean Charbonnier, *A Guide to the Catholic Church in China,* Singapore: China Catholic Communications, 1993, pp. 24–31.

22. Maryland Archives, XXVI: 160, cited in Timothy Riordan, Silas Hurry, and Henry Miller's *"A Good Brick Chappell" The Archeology of the c. 1667 Catholic Chapel at St. Mary's City, Maryland,* Historic St. Mary's City Archaeology Series No. 3: Alexander H. Morrison Fund Publication, 1995, p. 15.

23. Henry Miller, "Baroque Cities in the Wilderness: Archaeology and Urban Development in the Colonial Chesapeake," *Historical Archaeology,* 22, 1988, pp. 57–73.

24. Fr. Nicholas Russo, cited in an anonymous chronicle entitled "A Short History of the Mission of Our Lady of Loreto, New York," *Woodstock Letters,* 46, 2, 1917, p. 173.

25. "A Short History of the Mission," pp. 173–74.

26. "A Short History of the Mission," p. 181.

CHAPTER TWO
BETWEEN TWO WORLDS

1. Venerable Bede, *De temporum ratione,* in D. Woodward, "Reality, symbolism, time and space in medieval maps," *Annals of the Association of American Geographers,* 75, 1985, pp. 514–15.

2. For more detailed biographical and bibliographical information on the family, see Ricardo Garcia Villoslada, *San Ignacio de Loyola: Nueva Biografia.* Madrid: BAC, 1986, pp. 44–57; Cándido de

Dalmases, *Ignatius of Loyola, Founder of the Jesuits,* translated by Jerome Aixalá, St. Louis: Institute of Jesuit Sources, 1985, pp. 9–14; numerous articles in the MHSI volume *Fontes Documentales S. Ignatii.*

3. The *Autobiography,* entitled *Acta P. Ignatii ut primum scripsit P. Ludovicus Gonzales excipiens ex ore ipsius Patris,* was composed in Spanish and Italian beginning in 1553 and completed in 1555. It is far from complete: it covers in detail only the period from Ignatius' conversion until his settling in Rome (1521 to 1538). Integral text (even-numbered pages) and Annibale Coudreto's Latin (odd-numbered pages) appear in *FN* I, pp. 354–507. In the narration, Ignatius used the third person singular form and referred to himself as "the pilgrim." English translations are taken from Joseph O'Callaghan's 1992 Fordham Univ. Press edition of *The Autobiography of St. Ignatius Loyola.* "Given over to the vanities," p. 21.

4. Pedro de Leturia, "Notas criticas sobre la dama de Iñigo de Loyola" in *Estudios Ignacianos,* 2 vols. Rome: Institutum Historicum S.I., 1957, Vol. 1, pp. 87–96; Villoslada, *Nueva Biografia,* pp. 163–66; Pedro Ribadeneyra, *Vita Ignatii Loyolae* I, i, 2, in *FN* 4, p. 85.

5. Gauberto Fabricio Vagad's Spanish introduction to the *Flos Sanctorum,* cited in Leturia, "Jerusalén y Roma en los designios de San Ignacio de Loyola," *Estudios Ignacianos,* Vol. 1, p. 185.

6. Villoslada, *Nueva Biografia,* pp. 226–28. The interval at Manresa comprises a significant portion of Ignatius' *Autobiography,* some 15 numbered paragraphs out of a total of 101. *FN* 1, pp. 388–408, pp. 33–43 in O'Callaghan's translation.

7. *FN* 1, p. 410.

8. *FN* 1, pp. 410, 412; *Autobiography,* p. 42.

9. *FN* 1, p. 430; *Autobiography* p. 54.

10. *FN* 1, p. 450; *Autobiography,* p. 65. Between 1526 and 1538, Iñigo's orthodoxy was examined on eight different occasions by the Inquisition or other ecclesiastical and secular authorities. For his own account of his trials, see his 1545 letter to King John III of Portugal in *EpistIgn* 1, 81.

11. *FN* 1, pp. 456, 460. The interrogation at Salamanca is the first occasion when the text of the *Spiritual Exercises* came under direct scrutiny.

12. Twice in the *Autobiography* Ignatius used the image of closed doors to describe the effect of his encounters with the Spanish Inquisition: *FN* 1, p. 450,. 462. See *Autobiography,* p. 71.

13. G. Schurhammer, *Francis Xavier, Vol. 1, Europe 1506–1541,* translated by M. Joseph Costelloe, Rome: Jesuit Historical Institute, 1973, pp. 79, 85. Population figures are notoriously difficult to estimate. Schurhammer puts the population during Iñigo's stay at 300,000. Jean Delumeau in *La Civilisation de la Renaissance,* Paris: Arthaud, 1984, p. 261, estimates 200,000 inhabitants in 1500 and 300,000 in 1600. Chandler and Fox in *Studies in Population, 3,000 years of Urban Growth,* New York: Academic Press, 1974, p. 118, posit 225,000 inhabitants in 1500, 260,000 in 1553, and 220,000 in 1590.

14. Villoslada, *Nueva Biografia,* p. 320.

15. *FN* 1, p. 480; *Autobiography,* pp. 80–81.

16. Again, the text of the *Spiritual Exercises* was examined and found perfectly orthodox. Ignatius received a notarized copy of his acquittal. *FN* 1, p. 480.

17. For documents on Ignatius' works in Azpeitia, see *FD,* pp. 439–62.

18. Villoslada, *Nueva Biografia,* p. 385, n. 27. For an analysis of the importance of Vives' *De subventione pauperum* and its application in Italy, see P. Tacchi Venturi, *Storia della Compagnia di Gesù in Italia,* Rome: Edizioni Civiltà Cattolica, 1951, 1, i, pp. 421–26. Also see Polanco's *Vita P. Ignatii* in *FN* 2, p. 557.

19. *Scripta* 1, pp. 765–67.

20. *EpistIgn* 1, 6, p. 94.

21. Villoslada, *Nueva Biografia,* p. 402.

22. Known as "Theatines" because of the Latin name (*Teate*) of Carafa's diocese of Chieti.

23. For the full text of the letter, see *EpistIgn* 1, 11, pp. 114–18. For further commentary, see Georges Bottereau, "La 'Lettre' d'Ignace de Loyola à Gian Pietro Carafa," *AHSI* 44, 1975, pp. 139–42; Villoslada, *Nueva Biografia,* pp. 410–13.

24. Cited in P. Paschini, *S. Gaetano Thiene, Gian Pietro Carafa e le origini dei chierici regolari teatine,* Rome: Scuola Tipografica Pio X, 1926, p. 71.

25. The adversaries included Doctor Pedro Ortiz, who had denounced Ignatius to the Inquisition in Paris. Ortiz, former professor at Salamanca and Paris, was personal ambassador of Charles V to the Holy See. Ortiz later became one of Ignatius' most important supporters after he made the Spiritual Exercises under Ignatius in 1538. *Chron* 1, p. 64.

26. *FD,* p. 529, P. Togni in *Strategy,* p. 90.

27. *FN* 1, p. 494.

28. *FN* 1, p. 204.

29. *FN.* 1, p. 204.

30. *FN* 2, p. 133.

CHAPTER THREE
"BUT OF YESTERDAY"

1. For Rome, see Peter Partner, *Renaissance Rome, 1500–1559, A Portrait of a Society,* Berkeley & Los Angeles: Univ. of California Press, 1979, p. 82; for Jerusalem, see John Stambaugh and David Balch, *The Social World of the First Christians,* London: SPCK, 1986, p. 97.

2. Wayne Meeks, *The First Urban Christians.* New Haven: Yale Univ. Press, 1983, pp. 16–17. Meeks points out that because of the security and extension of Roman roads and sea lanes, travel in the western world would not again be so easy and convenient until the nineteenth century.

3. Meeks, *Urban Christians,* p. 34; Robert Grant, *Augustus to Constantine,* New York: Harper & Row, 1970, p. 48; Stambaugh and Balch, *Social World,* p. 53.

4. Robin Fox, *Pagans and Christians,* San Francisco: Harper & Rowe, 1986, pp. 281–82.

5. Pliny the Younger, *Letters,* II, Loeb Classical Library, London: Wm. Heineman, 1947, pp. 404–05.

6. See Revelations 17.1–18.24.

7. Tertullian, *On Prescription against Heretics,* vii, in *Latin Christianity: Its Founder, Tertullian.* In the series *The Ante-Nicene Fathers, Translations of The Writings of the Fathers down to A.D. 325,* Vol. III, edited by Alexander Robbers and James Donaldson, New York: Christian Literature Company, 1896, p. 246.

In the 380s, St. Jerome, repenting of his addiction to Ciceronian eloquence, eloquently echoed Tertullian: "What has Horace to do with the Psalter, Vergil with the Gospels, Cicero with Paul?" in Jerome's Letter XXII, 29, 30, in *Selected Letters,* Loeb Classical Library, 262, London: Wm. Heineman, 1924, p. 124 ff.

8. Tertullian, *Apology,* ch. xlii, in *Latin Christianity,* III, p. 49.

9. Tertullian, *Apology,* ch. xxxvii, in *The Ante-Nicene Fathers, Tertullian,* p. 45.

10. For a detailed analysis of Christianity's spread in rural regions, see Fox, *Pagans and Christians,* ch. 6, pp. 265–93.

11. *Epistle to Diognetus,* cited in Jaroslav Pelikan, *Jesus through the Centuries,* New Haven: Yale Univ. Press, 1985, pp. 49–50.

12. Peter Brown, *The World of Late Antiquity,* London: Thames & Hudson, 1971, pp. 93–94: "Christianity was essentially a 'Cockney' religion. It had clung to the contours of life throughout the empire. It was cockney, also, in assuming at least a minimal participation in literacy: the first thing an Egyptian peasant found himself being made to do, on joining a monastery, was learning to read–so as to understand the Bible. (The establishment of Christianity coincided, significantly, with a notable advance in book–production, by which the clumsy scroll was replaced by the compact codex)."

13. The letter of Cornelius is found in Eusebius, *The History of the Church,* translated by G. A. Williamson, Minneapolis: Augsburg Publishing House, 1975, 6, 43, p. 282 and p. 282, n.2.

14. Richard Krautheimer and Slobadan Curcic, *Early Christian and Byzantine Architecture,* Fourth Edition, Harmondsworth: Penguin, 1986, p. 25.

15. Brown, *The World of Late Antiquity,* p. 68.

16. Eusebius, *History,* 8, 1, p. 328; Markus, *Christianity,* p. 102.

17. Brown, *World,* p. 67.

18. T. Gannon and G. Traub, *The Desert and the City, An Interpretation of Christian Spirituality,* London: Collier–Macmillan, 1969, p. 23; Fox, *Pagans and Christians,* pp. 603–04.

19. For a concise and elegantly written summary of this move, see Peter Brown's essay entitled "Late Antiquity" in Paul Veyne's *A History of Private Life, I: From Pagan Rome to Byzantium,* translated by Arthur Goldhammer, Cambridge MA: Harvard Univ. Press, 1987, pp. 289–90: "Life in a city such as Antioch, the facts of sexuality, marriage, childbirth, solid and immemorial as they might seem, even to conventional Christians, appear now as no more than a confused eddy in a stream that was slipping fast from Paradise toward the Resurrection. Society . . . was an unplanned and impermanent accident of history. All human structure, all human society, all arts and building, cities and households, even the social definition of man and women as sexual beings destined for marriage and reproduction, were soon to come to rest in the vast hush of the presence of God. . . . Those who had adopted the life of monks and virgins on the edge of the city had anticipated the dawn of man's true nature. City, marriage, and culture, the 'necessary superfluities' of settled life, were but a passing interlude compared with that clear state, shorn of the 'cares of this life.' The monk on the hills outside the city strove to make that moment last a lifetime."

20. Fox, *Pagans and Christians,* p. 667.

21. The use of the word "pagans" to describe non–Christians is itself a Christian invention of the fourth century. In the literature of the time, it could either mean "rustic, country bumpkin" or "civilian" (one not inscribed in the city or state militia). It is interesting to note that either meaning has rather negative overtones in relationship to enfranchised urban life. For an exhaustive etymological discussion, see C. Mohrmann, "Encore une fois: paganus," in *Vigiliae Christianae,* 6, 1952, pp. 109–21.

22. Richard Krautheimer, *Three Christian Capitals: Topography and Politics,* Berkeley: Univ. of California Press, 1982, pp. 39–40, 60.

23. David Knowles, *From Pachomius to Ignatius,* Oxford: Oxford Univ. Press, 1966, pp. 4–5; Gannon and Traub, *The Desert and the City,* p. 34

24. Gannon and Traub, *The Desert and the City,* pp. 55 ff.

25. Jerome, *Ep.* 127, cited in Krautheimer, *Three Capitals,* p. 103.

26. Augustine, *City of God.* edited by Vernon J. Bourke.

New York: Doubleday Image Books, 1958, XV, i, p. 324. A note on language: given that the "City of God/City of Man" distych has so frequently echoed through theological writings, it seems defensible to forego here an inclusive translation. Augustine would most certainly not have excluded women from his human city destined for damnation.

27. Richard Sennett, *The Consciousness of the Eye: The Design and Social Life of Cities.* New York: Albert Knopf, 1990, p. 6.

28. Augustine, *City,* XV, i, p. 325.

CHAPTER FOUR
RENEGOTIATING THE PERSPECTIVE

1. The works of Peter Brown, in particular *The World of Late Antiquity* and his essay "Late Antiquity," in Veyne's *History of Private Life, I,* are particularly helpful for taking the spiritual temperature of the times.

2. Spiro Kostof, "The Architect in the Middle Ages, East and West," in *The Architect, Chapters in the History of the Profession,* edited by Spiro Kostof, Oxford and New York: Oxford Univ. Press, 1977. p. 67; Richard Krautheimer, *Rome, Profile of a City,* Princeton: Princeton Univ. Press, 1980, p. 4.

3. Krautheimer, *Rome, Profile,* p. 65; Robert Llewellyn, *Rome in the Dark Ages,* London: Faber and Faber, 1971, pp. 73–74.

4. Krautheimer, *Rome, Profile,* pp. 48–51.

5. Wolfgang Braunfels, *Urban Design in Western Europe: Regime and Architecture, 900–1900.* Translated by Kenneth J. Northcott. Chicago and London: Univ. of Chicago Press, 1988, p. 344; Krautheimer, *Rome, Profile,* pp. 56–58.

6. *Enchiridion Symbolorum Definitionum et Declarationum de rebus fidei et morum,* edited by H. Denzinger and A. Schönmetzer, 36th. edition, Rome, Barcelona and Friburg: Herder, 1976, no. 347.

7. Gregory's attitude towards the degradation of his city (he was, after all, a Roman, and grandson of Pope Felix III) is summarized in his *Sermon on Ezekiel,* II, 6: 22, 25: "Where now are those who exulted with joy over the glories of Rome? Where is their pride? Where now is the senate, where are the people? It has gone, and the people vanish. The

eagle has gone bald all over its body; growing old, it loses its feathers, even those of its wings." in *Sancti Gregorii Papae I cognomen Magni, Opera Omnia, Patrologia Latina,* Vol. 76, edited by J. P. Migne, Paris, 1849, pp. 1010–1011.

8. Krautheimer, *Rome, Profile,* pp. 71–75.

9. For the relationship between Benedict's *Rule* and the *Rule of the Master,* see David Knowles, "The *Regula Magistri* and the *Rule* of St. Benedict," in *Great Historical Enterprises,* London: Nelson, 1963, and *Christian Monasticism,* New York and Toronto: McGraw–Hill, 1969, pp. 33–35.

10. Wolfgang Braunfels, *Monasteries of Western Europe, The Architecture of the Orders,* Princeton: Princeton Univ. Press, 1972, p. 13.

11. Brown, "Late Antiquity" in *History of Private Life, I,* p. 292. On pp. 293–94, Brown continues: "The monastery was the first community prepared to offer a fully Christian training from boyhood up. The process of socialization as advocated in ascetic circles spelled the end of the ideal of the education by the city. For until the end of the fourth century, it was assumed that all boys, pagan and Christian, should be exposed to the magnificently noisy, artic-ulate, and extroverted 'shame culture' of competing peers, associating with the ancient rhetor's class-room on the edge of the forum. Now this would fall silent. . . . The ancient city, whose intimate disci-plines had molded the private and public identities of its upper–class members for centuries, threatened to dissolve into a mere confederation of families, each of which ensured for itself, in collaboration with clergymen and even monks living at some dis-tance from the city the true, that is the Christian grooming of the young male."

12. *RB 1980: The Rule of St. Benedict in Latin and English with notes,* edited by Timothy Fry, Collegeville: The Liturgical Press, 1980, ch. 66, p. 288–89.

13. Beginning in the seventh century, clusters of monas-teries sprang up around the four "major" basilicas of S. Pietro, S. Maria Maggiore, S. Paolo fuori le mura, and the Lateran, and the three "minor" basilicae of S. Lorenzo, S. Agnese, and S. Sebastiano. All seven basilicas were located on the periphery of the inhab-ited city center. These communities eventually evolved into collegiate or canons' communities charged with singing the office in the important shrines. While there were a few such communities

attached to central churches (i.e., S. Marco and S. Maria in Trastevere), the overwhelming preponder-ance were on the fringe of the *abitato.* See G. Ferrari, *Early Roman Monasteries: Notes for the History of the Monasteries and Convents at Rome from the V through the X Century,* Vatican City: Pontificio Istituto di Archeologia Cristiana, 1957, pp. 365–81. Llewellyn, *Dark Ages,* p. 136.

14. J. A. Jungmann, *The Mass of the Roman Rite: Its Origins and Development,* 2 vols., translated by Francis Brunner, Westminster, MD: Christian Classics, 1986, I, pp. 67–74.

15. Llewellyn, *Dark Ages,* p. 212.

16. Krautheimer, *Rome, Profile,* pp. 107–108.

17. Krautheimer, *Rome, Profile,* p. 114. For a good dis-cussion of the *Donation* see R.W. Southern, *Western Society and the Church in the Middle Ages,* Harmondsworth: Pelican, 1986, pp. 91–94, 97.

18. Knowles, *Pachomius to Ignatius,* pp. 8–9.

19. Braunfels, *Monasteries,* p. 31: "The monks [at Fulda] constantly complained to Charlemagne that they had entered the monastery for prayer and study, not as builder's mates." For St. Gall, see Walter Horn's magisterial *The Plan of St. Gall, A Study of the Architecture and Economy and Life in a Paradigmatic Carolingian Monastery.* 3 vols. Berkeley and Los Angeles: Univ. of California Press, 1979. Also see Braunfels, *Monasteries,* ch. 3, "The St. Gall Utopia", pp. 37–46; and Kostof, "The Architect in the Middle Ages, East and West, " in *The Architect,* pp. 71–73.

20. Braunfels, *Urban Design,* pp. 17–18 gives statistics based on the research of Albrecht Manan: in 855, Rome had 54 monasteries and convents; Paris and Ravenna 17; Lemans 15; Vienne and Lyons 10; Cologne, Milan, and Tours 8; Lucca, Metz, Orleans, Pavia, Trier 7; Auxerre, Venice, and Verona 6; Autun, Bourges, Chartres, Florence, Limoges, Reims, Sens, Soissons, and Spoleto 5. No statistics are available from the Eastern Carolingian Empire. Most of Spain at the time was under Islamic control.

21. See Braunfels, *Urban Design,* pp. 19–27 and *Monasteries,* pp. 176–79.

22. Braunfels, *Urban Design,* p. 19.

23. Krautheimer, *Rome, Profile,* p. 119.

24. Gannon and Traub, *Desert and City,* pp. 72–73, Krautheimer, *Rome, Profile,* pp. 148–51.

25. *PL* 188, col. 641.

26. Humbert Von Zeller, *The Benedictine Ideal,* London: Burns, 1959, p. 185.

27. Kostof, "The Architect in the Middle Ages, East and West," in *The Architect,* p. 93; Sennett, *Consciousness of the Eye,* p. 17.

CHAPTER FIVE
RESURGENCE AND RENAISSANCE

1. R. S. Lopez, "The Crossroad within the Wall," in *The Historian and the City,* Edited by O. Handlin and J. Burchard, Cambridge, MA: MIT Press, 1963, pp. 27–43. Lopez (p. 27) points out that the ancient hieroglyph for city, formed of a cross within a circle, is a graphic convention that shows the relationship between crossroads and town wall. Also, see Braunfels, *Urban Design,* p. 32.

2. Augustine's Letter 211. See B. Capelle, "L'Epître 211 et la règle de Saint Augustin," in *Analecta Praemonstratensia,* 3, 1927, pp. 369–78.

3. Southern, *Western Society,* pp. 244, 248.

4. Also known (in the singular) as *fratria, constorium corpus, societatas, fraternitas* in Latin, *etaria* in Greek. See G. G. Meersseman, *Ordo Fraternitatis: Contraternite e pietà dei laici nel medieovo,* Herder: Rome, 1977, p. 3–7, and Brown, *World,* pp. 63 ff.

5. In medieval Latin, *confraternitas, confratria,* and *fraterna* (a neologism), and in the vernaculars, *fraglia, confraduglia, confrarire, confrérie, charité, Brüderschaft,* and *brotherhood.*

6. John Bossy, *Christianity in the West, 1400–1700,* Oxford and New York: Oxford Univ. Press, 1985, pp. 62–63: "We should not regard the parish as necessarily a pre–existing datum into which fraternities were going to have to fit themselves somehow. Parochial formation and fraternity expansion were roughly contemporary processes, and though the parish network was substantially complete by 1400, there were plenty of gaps left at the Reformation. It was weak in the mountains, and in areas without much village settlement like Ireland. It preceded more rapidly on the virgin soil of the north than in Mediterranean Europe, where older forms of ecclesiastical structure preexisted. Hence fraternal institutions might often find no parish structure to compete with, and a brotherhood might form the original community of worship until such time as its chapel might be erected into a parish church."

7. Mariano Armellini, *Le Chiese di Roma dal secolo IV al XIX,* 2 vols., Rome: Edizioni R.O.R.E., 1942, I, p. 36, and Meersseman, *Ordo Fraternitatis,* p. 182–83.

8. Innocent III's verbal approval of Francis' way of life just preceded the Fourth Lateran Council's 1215 ban on new religious orders. That ban attempted to regulate a wild proliferation of religious and lay institutes. Rapid expansion led to papal establishment of minimum criteria for acceptance and formation of new members, and requirements for internal organization. Although Francis resisted attempts at codification of his brotherhood as long as he could, he was eventually forced to compose a written rule. In its 1223 form, the *Regula Bullata* was accepted by Pope Honorius III. It was the only rule to receive explicit papal approbation between Benedict and Ignatius' *Constitutions of the Society of Jesus.* For a short and cogent summary of the early constitutional history of the Franciscans, see Knowles, *From Pachomius to Ignatius,* pp. 44–46.

9. *Historia Occidentalis,* I, II, ch. 32, in *Fonti Francescane, Editio Minor,* Assisi: Editrici Francescane, 1990, [2214–2215] (hereafter *FontiFr;* references in square brackets are to numbered paragraphs).

10. In response to Lady Poverty's desire to see their cloister, the friars led her "up onto a hill, and they showed her all the world they were able to see, saying 'This, Lady, is our cloister.'" *Sacrum Commer-cium,* no. 63 in K. Esser, *The Origins of the Franciscan Order,* translated by A. Daly and I. Lynch, Chicago: Franciscan Herald Press, 1970, p. 112, n. 20; in the final approved version of the Rule, "The friars shall appropriate nothing to themselves, neither a house nor place nor anything. And as pilgrims and strangers in this world, serving the Lord in poverty, they shall live in faith on alms," *Regula Bullata,* [6], in *FontiFr* [90]. See also R. Huber, *A Documented History of the Franciscan Order,* Milwaukee: Nowiny, 1944, p. 10.

11. Raphael Huber, *Documented History,* p. 255; Southern, in *Western Society,* p. 286, estimates about 28,000 as the maximum Franciscan census.

12. For an exhaustive discussion of the controversies leading up to the Observant–Conventual division, see Huber, *Documented History,* ch. 8–36.

13. William Hinnesbusch, *The History of the Dominican Order,* New York: Alba House, 1966, pp. 41, 262–63, 330.

14. Prologue of the first Dominican constitutions, cited in Hinnesbusch, *The History of the Dominican Order,* p. 84.

15. Letter of James of Vitry, in *FontiFr* [2206]. Tommaso de Celano described Francis' own practice: "He often chose lonely places so that he could direct his soul completely to God; yet when he saw that the time was right, he was not reluctant to engage in activities and attend gladly to the welfare of his neighbor." I Celano 71, in *FontiFr* [445].

16. Buoncompagni the Rhetor, *Ars Rhetorica,* 2, in *FontiFr.* [2240].

17. James of Vitry, *Historia Occidentalis,* in Esser, *Origins of the Franciscan Order,* p. 139.

18. Esser, *Origins of the Franciscan Order,* p. 168. The earliest foundation outside of Assisi was in Bologna (1211) followed by Pisa, San Miniato near Florence, and San Giminiano. See Huber, *Documented History,* p. 19. As indicated above, the tension between ownership and rigorous poverty was the fundamental wedge that finally split the Conventual and Observant factions into two autonomous bodies in the fifteenth century. The later chapters of Huber's *Documented History* are particularly helpful for hacking through the very tangled branches and thickets of the Franciscan ramifications.

19. Hinnesbusch, *History of the Dominican Order,* pp. 151–58. The most complete survey of Dominic's own "building code" and early Dominican architecture is found in G. Meersseman, "L'architecture dominicaine au XIIIe siècle, législation et pratique," in *Archivum Fratrum Praedicatorum,* 16, 1946, pp. 136–90.

20. As regards the Franciscan shift towards academia, it is worth recalling along with Bonaventure the names of Alexander of Hales, Duns Scotus, and Roger Bacon and the impressive Franciscan faculties at Oxford and Paris. See Huber, *Documented History,* p. 42.

21. Enrico Guidoni, "Città e Ordini Mendicanti," in *La Città dal medioevo al rinascimento,* 3rd edition, Roma–Bari: Laterza, p. 126. R. Bonelli, analyzing early mendicant church construction, points out that the lengths of the early hall churches in central Italy, greatly exceeded those of the extant Romanesque cathedrals. See his article "Nuovi sviluppi di ricerca sull'edilizia mendicante," in *Gli Ordini mendicanti e la città: aspetti architettonici, sociali, e politici,* J. Raspi Serra, editor, Milan: Edizioni Gurinin, 1990, pp. 24–25. David Gillerman, "San Fortunato in Todi: Why the Hall Church," *JSAH* 48, June 1989, pp. 158–71 gives a good review of recent bibliography on the hall churches, as well as citing an example where the Franciscans managed to obtain a truly central location: "Rarely do we see the friars acquiring truly central properties; consistent with their evangelical ministry among the poor, they usually chose sites at the periphery, as in the case of S. Croce in Florence or S. Domenico in Perugia (begun in 1304). That the Franciscans veered from this practice in Todi suggests how highly they valued the S. Fortunato site." (p. 162).

22. Guidoni, "Città e Ordini Mendicanti," p. 128; Kostof, *A History of Architecture,* p. 373; G. Fanelli, *Firenze,* 4th edition, Rome–Bari: Laterza, 1988 pp. 24–29, and Guidoni, *Storia dell'urbanistica: Il Duecento,* Rome–Bari: Laterza, 1989, p. 307.

23. Braunfels, *Monasteries,* p. 137, Guidoni, "Città e Ordini Mendicanti," p. 131; Braunfels, *Urban Design,* p. 315.

24. Braunfels, *Monasteries,* pp. 128–30. Definitive studies on the diffusion of the mendicants have yet to be written. R. Emery's *The Friars in Medieval France,* New York: Columbia Univ. Press, 1972, is a very useful introduction to the question, and the general patterns sketched out in it serve not only for France but, *mutatis mutandis,* for the rest of Europe. For the Franciscans in Italy, see L. Pellegrini's "Gli insediamenti francescani nella evoluzione storica degli agglomerati umani e della circoscrizioni territoriali dell'Italia nel secolo XIII" in *Italia Sacra, Studi e Documenti di Storia Ecclesiastica,* 30, 1979, pp. 195–237, and "Insediamenti rurali e insediamenti urbani dei francescani nell'Italia del sec. XIII." *S. Bonaventura maestro di vita francescana e di sapienza cristiana. Atti del congresso internazionale per il VII centenario di S. Bonaventura da Bagnoregio, Roma 19–26 settembre 1974.* Rome, 1976, pp. 197–210. For the Dominicans, G. Villetti's's "Prospettive di ricerca sull'edilizia degli Ordini Mendicanti: il fondo 'Libri' nell archivio generale dell'Ordine dei Predicatori," *Architettura Archivi,* A I, I, 1982. LeGoff's "Apostolat mendiant et fait urbain dans la France médiévale: l'implantation des ordres mendiants," *Annales*

E.S.C., 22, 1968, pp. 335–55, and "Ordres mendiants et urbanisation dans la France médiévale," *Annales E.S.C.*, 25, 1970, pp. 924–46, are useful for understanding the relationship between mendicants and the money economy of the thirteenth century.

25. The Bull of Clement IV dated November 20, 1265, for Ascoli codified the determinations made in bulls of October 8, 1265, for Assisi and September 17, 1265, for Bologna. For the full developement of the rule of the *canne,* see Guidoni, "Città e Ordini Mendicanti," pp. 134–37, and notes.

26. Guidoni, "Città e Ordini Mendicanti," pp. 133–34.

27. For an exhaustive discussion of this argument with excellent bibliography and maps, see Guidoni, "Città e Ordini Mendicanti," pp. 145–51.

28. E. Rodocanachi, editor, *Una Cronica di Santa Sabina,* Rome: Fratelli Bocca 1899, p. 3. Also see Giulia Barone, "I francescani a Roma," *Storia della Città* 9, 1978, p. 34; Leonard Boyle, *San Clemente Miscellany I,* Rome: Collegio San Clemente, 1977, p. 2.

29. J. J. Berthier, *L'Eglise de la Minerve à Rome,* Rome: Cooperativa Tipografica Manuzio, 1910, pp. 6–9, Krautheimer, *Profile,* pp. 211, 275–76.

30. Krautheimer, *Profile,* p. 274. See also F. Castagnoli, Castagnoli et al., *Topografia e Urbanistica di Roma,* Bologna: Istituto di Studi Romani, 1958, p. 244.

31. Barone, "I francescani a Roma," p. 34. Braunfels, in *Urban Design,* p. 360, summarized medieval construction history of the Communal buildings on the Campidoglio. The various reconstructions of the Palazzo del Senatore were "a claim to authority . . . to which no actual power ever corresponded. Out of the material of history itself, a new reality was formed which spent, in the aesthetic sphere, what was really not its to spend. The pretext was the knowledge of the sacred meaning of the ancient capitol as the center of power." The most detailed—and visually most beautiful—history of the Campidoglio is Cesare Onofrio's *Renovatio Romae, Storia e urbanistica dal Campidoglio all'EUR,* Rome: Edizioni Mediterranee, 1973. Its chapters 4–8 deal with the medieval period.

32. Krautheimer, *Profile,* pp. 287–88.

33. Armellini (in *Le Chiese,* p. 667) identifies the *scalinata* as an ex–voto offering erected by the city in thanksgiving for having escaped total devastation in the plague of 1348. Krautheimer (*Profile,* pp. 228, 359) dates it to 1347, holding that it was constructed to "reflect the fantastic dream of Cola di Rienzo to establish a Roman republic, superior to Emperor and Pope, with its seat on the Capitol from which the world was once ruled." Onofrio (*Renovatio Romae,* p. 105) holds that it was constructed for the 1350 Jubilee.

34. See Krautheimer, *Profile,* pp. 359–60, for extensive analysis and bibliography on medieval population figures in Rome.

35. Francesco Petrarcha, *Letters on Familiar Matters, Rerum familiarium libri IX–XVI,* translated by Aldo Bernardo, Baltimore and London: Johns Hopkins Univ. Press, 1982, letter XI, 7, pp. 99–100.

36. Charles Stinger, *The Renaissance in Rome,* Bloomington: Indiana Univ. Press, 1985, p. 24. Alan Ceen, *The Quartiere de'Banchi: Urban Planning in Rome in the First Half of the Cinquecento,* Ann Arbor: University Microfilms, 1977, p. 141; Caroll Westfall, *In this most perfect Paradise: Alberti, Nicholas, and the Invention of Conscious Urban Planning in Rome, 1447–55,* University Park: Pennsylvania State Univ. Press, 1974, pp. 7, 130.

37. L. Schiaparelli, "Alcuni Documenti dei Magistri Aedificiorum Urbis," *Archivio della R. Società Romana di Storia Patria* 25, 1902, p. 16: "liberatione et reparatione gubernatione edificiorum, viarum et stratarum urbem."

38. Emilio Re, "Maestri di strada," *Archivio della R. Società Romana di Storia Patria* 43, 1920, p. 88: "rompere, mozare, tagliare et ruinare ogni cosa che occupasse strade, piazze, vicoli, fiumare, rivere et altri luochi publichi."

39. Ceen, *Banchi,* p. 95.

40. L. Ettlinger, "The Emergence of the Italian Architect in the 15th Century," in Kostof, *The Architect,* p. 98.

41. For a thorough survey of this architectural–theological synthesis, see Westfall, *Paradise,* ch. 1. Also see Stinger, *The Renaissance in Rome,* p. 256.

42. Guidoni, *La Città Europea, Formazione e significato dal IV all'XI Secolo,* Milan: Electa, 1978, pp. 133–34; P. Marconi, *La città come forma simbolica,* Rome: Bulzoni, 1973, pp. 33–35, 52–53; Stinger, *The*

Renaissance in Rome, pp. 66–67, 99. For a complete critical edition and analysis of the "Descriptio urbis Romae" see Luigi Vagnetti, "La Descriptio urbis Romae, uno scritto poco noto di Leon Battista Alberti," in *Quaderno,* Università degli Studi di Genova, Facoltà di Architettura 1, 1968, pp. 25–78.

43. Castagnoli et al, *Topografia,* p. 352.

44. On December 19 of the Jubilee year 1450, a traffic jam of horses and mules on the downtown end of the Ponte S. Angelo blocked a large procession leaving the Basilica of S. Pietro. Upwards of 200 pilgrims were trampled to death on the bridge or drowned in the Tiber. Delumeau, *Vie économique et social de Rome dans la seconde moitié du XVIe siècle.* Paris: E. de Boccard, 1957, p. 298; Stinger, *The Renaissance in Rome,* p. 32.

45. Krautheimer, *Profile,* p. 251.

46. Castagnoli et al, *Topografia,* pp. 356–57.

47. Stinger, *The Renaissance in Rome,* p. 78.

48. Partner, *Renaissance Rome,* p. 22; Delumeau, *Vie économique,* p. 300.

49. Giulio Argan, *The Renaissance City,* translated by Susan Bassnett, New York: George Braziller, 1969, p. 32: "[esiste] la macchina del tutto, ma senza ornamenti, e per dir così, l'ossa del corpo senza carne."

50. Stinger, *The Renaissance in Rome,* pp. 322–24. André Chastel's *The Sack of Rome,* Princeton: Princeton Univ. Press, 1983, is the best introduction to this complicated moment in the history of Cinquecento Rome.

51. Pio Pecchiai, *Roma nel Cinquecento,* Bologna: Istituto de Studi Romani, 1948, pp. 445–47. For details and analysis of the 1526 census, see D. Gnoli, "Descriptio Urbis, o Censimento della Popolazione di Roma avanti il sacco Borbonico," *Archivio della R. Società Romana di Storia Patria 17,* 1894, pp. 375–493.

52. Partner, *Renaissance Rome,* p. 174.

53. Stinger, *The Renaissance in Rome,* p. 104.

54. Stinger, *The Renaissance in Rome,* p. 257; see also Alan Ceen in *Strategy,* pp. 101–03. The Torre Farnese stood until 1888, when it was demolished to make way for the monument to Victor Emmanuel

II. See D. Coffin, *The Villa in the Life of Renaissance Rome,* Princeton: Princeton Univ. Press, 1979, pp. 27–34.

55. There is no adequate biography of Manetti, who is sometimes referred to as the "Renaissance Baron Haussmann." Some useful material can be found in Onofrio, *Renovatio Romae,* chs. 12 and 13, and in L. Dorez, *La Coeur du Pape Paul ·III,* Paris: n.p., 1932, ch. 3.

56. Ceen, *Banchi,* p. 96, and pp. 101–02. Manetti's tenure marks the apex of the powers of the *maestri.* Manetti adumbrated the era of the great papal architect planners like Domenico Fontana. When Sixtus V multiplied the number of *maestri* from two to 14 (one for each rione), the focus on planning shifted from the municipal office of *maestri delle strade* to the personal vision of the papal architect. See C. Scaccia Scarafoni, "L'antico statuto dei Magistri Stratarum e altri documenti relative a quella magistratura," *Archivio della R. Società Romana di Storia Patria 50,* 1927, p. 266.

57. Partner, *Renaissance Rome,* p. 174.

58. A. Proia and P. Romano, *Roma nel Cinquecento: Pigna (IX Rione),* Rome: Tipografia Agostiniana, 1936, p. 20.

59. Ceen, *Banchi,* pp. 159–60. See also Ceen in *Strategy,* pp. 138–39.

CHAPTER SIX
"A GOOD AND TRUE JERUSALEM"

1. Chronicle of Cornelio di Fine, in BAV, Cod Ott., 1614, p. 158 v. See also TV *Storia,* II, i, p. 163.

2. Polanco, "Sumario de las cosas más notables que a la institución y progresso de la Compañía de Jesús tocan," (ca. 1548) in *FN* I, pp. 199–200. Cf. *Chron,* 1, pp. 65–66.

3. Laínez, Letter of June 16, 1547 to Polanco, in *FN* I, p. 124. During the seventeenth century, the house was owned by the Collegio Romano. Located on what is modern Via S. Sebastianello, the site is presently occupied by the generalate of the Resurrectionist Fathers. See *FN* I, p. 124, n. 31.

4. Dalmases, *Ignatius Founder,* pp. 157–62. For the text of the sentence, see *FD,* pp. 556–57.

5. "Adhortationes Complutenses 1561," 3, in *FN* II, p. 169. During February 1538, Ignatius had given the Exercises to Doctor Ortiz at Montecassino. *Chron* I, p. 64.

6. While the first Jesuits sought to move towards the center of town, the first Theatines had moved out into the peace of the countryside. An early history of the Theatines cites the example of the early Theatine siting in Verona: they abandoned their house located on a busy piazza. "In front of the door of the church the people were celebrating with common games and profane dances; and since they [the Theatines] could not bear the confused din that arose from the promiscuous populace, and since they desired quiet, they preferred to distance themselves by departing from that place, rather than endure things so inappropriate and disrespectful that dishonored both their state of life and the holy place." B. Caraccioli, *Vita d. Cajetani*, cited in Paschini, *S. Gaetano Thiene*, p. 83. For the Theatines on the Pincio, see Paschini, pp. 57–58.

7. Rodrigues, "Commentarium de origine et progressu Societatis Iesu," (1577), [78–79], in *FN* III, p. 102.

8. *EpistIgn* 1, 18, p. 139.

9. Laínez, *Epistola* , *FN* I, p. 124. Javier was ill, and there is no mention of Codure or Broët. It is probable that Bobadilla preached at S. Celso on Via dei Banchi Vecchi. See *FN* I, p. 125, n. 32.

10. *Scripta*, II, 825. Ignatius once asked young Pedro de Ribadeneyra (who later became his first biographer) to write down all his mistakes in a given sermon. "I did this one day with pen and ink, and it was necessary to correct almost every word he spoke, and this seemed to me that this was a hopeless situation. I went forward and told our Father [Ignatius] what had occurred. With great humility and sweetness he said to me 'Pedro, what can we do for God?' meaning that since God had not given him more, he wished to serve with what he had been given." Ribadeneyra, *Vita* III, ii, 11, in *FN* IV, pp. 374–77.

11. John O'Malley, *The First Jesuits*, Cambridge MA: Harvard Univ. Press, 1993, p. 93 (hereafter *First Jesuits*); See also *Chron* 1, pp. 162, 222, 384; 2, pp. 113, 192–93; 3, p. 24; *EpistIgn* VI, 4124; VII, 4617; IX, 5673; X, 5827. For a full discussion of early Jesuit preaching, lecturing, and catechetical activities, see O'Malley, ch. 3.

12. Rodrigues' colorful account of the haunting is found in "Commentarium" [81], in *FN* III, p. 106.

13. Favre, "Memoriale Fabri," in *FN* I, p. 42. The favorable sentence was handed down on November 18, 1538, and Favre wrote of the offering in a letter dated November 23, so the meeting with the pope probably took place immediately after the acquittal. See A. Ravier, *Ignatius Loyola and the Founding of the Society of Jesus,* translated by M. J. and C. Daly, San Francisco: Ignatius Press, 1987, pp. 31–35, and 31, n. 23.

14. N. Bobadilla, "Autobiographia" [11] in *FN* III, p. 327.

15. *EpistIgn* I, p. 141, dated December 19, 1538.

16. *EpistIgn* I, pp. 132–33, dated November 23, 1538.

17. "Deliberatio primorum patrum" [1]; English translation in J. Toner, "The Deliberation That Started the Jesuits" in *Studies in the Spirituality of Jesuits* 6, 4, June 1974, pp. 185–86 [hereafter *StudiesSpir.*] The full text of the original is found in *ConstMHSJ* I, pp. 1–7.

18. "Deliberatio primorum patrum" [5–6] in Toner, "The Deliberation," pp. 196–97.

19. TV *Storia*, II, i, pp. 198–202.

20. Letter of Cardinal Gian Angelo de' Medici, June 25, 1540, in the Archivio di Stato di Parma, *Carteggio Farnesiano,* 1540, cited in TV *Storia* II, i, p. 222.

21. Ravier, *Founding*, pp. 98–101. 13 years later (1552), Ignatius himself would make one of his extremely rare trips out of Rome in an attempt to regularize the Colonna marriage, which "neither pope nor emperor nor other great princes had been sufficient to pacify." Although he elicited a promise of reconciliation from Doña Juana, his efforts ultimately proved fruitless. See Ribadeneyra, "Miscellanea" in *FN* II, p. 414.

22. The *Quinque Capitula* were incorporated into the text of *Regimini militantis ecclesiae*, found in *ConstMHSI* I, pp. 24–32.

23. *Chron* 1, pp. 81–82.

24. Ribadeneyra, *Vita,* III, 5, 20 in *FN* IV, p. 387. P. Tacchi Venturi, *Le Case abitate da S. Ignazio di Loiola in Roma secondo un inedito documento del tempo*. Rome: Tipografia Poliglotta della S.C. de Propaganda Fide, 1899, p. 39, (hereinafter TV *Case*) cites documents from the census of Leo X, 1517, for the parish census figure.

25. TV *Case*, pp. 28–29. Ignatius actually received title to the church and its buildings in a notarial document dated May 15, 1542. For the full text, see TV *Case*, pp. 54–55. In 1549, consistent with his evolving teaching on the necessity of absolute poverty for churches and professed houses, Ignatius renounced the fixed incomes of the benefice and arranged the transfer of the parochial responsibilities to the nearby church of S. Marco located within the papal palace. See Nadal, "Apologia contra censuram," VI, 129, and *ConstMHSJ* I, pp. 192–93. For the full text *Dudum postquam* (April 5, 1549) see J. Wicki, "Pfarrseelsorge und Armut der Professhäuser. Ein Motu proprio Paulus III aus der Vorgeschichte des Römischen Gesù (1549)," *Archivum Historicum Societatis Iesu* 11, 1942, pp. 69–82.

26. *FN* III, p. 178. Internal evidence dates the document between 1581 and 1584. There were a number of churches of S. Girolamo in Rome at the time. Without further evidence, it is impossible to determine which was offered to Ignatius. TV *Case*, p. 28, n. 1.

27. N. Orlandini, *Historiae Societatis Iesu prima pars,* Rome: Apud Bartholomeum Zannettum, 1614, I, III, 15, p. 76.

28. For the history of the Astalli family in the Rione della Pigna, see TV *Case*, pp. 22–26; for catalogues of Roman churches, see Armellini, pp. 55–73, esp. 58 and 66–67.

29. *EpistIgn* I, 208, pp. 616–17.

30. Ribadeneyra, *Vita* in *FN* IV, p. 385. Receipts for the rental payments can be found in ARSI *Hist Dom.Prof. I: Rom. 143.*

31. *Hist Dom. Prof. I: Rom. 143,* ARSI, cited in TV *Case,* p. 30, n.2.

32. Ceen has produced a very interesting rectification of the Bufalini plan of the neighborhood based on the more accurate Nolli plan of 1748. *Strategy,* pp. 110–11.

33. P. Pirri, "La Topografia del Gesù di Roma e le vertenze tra Muzio Muti e S. Ignazio secondo nuovi documenti," *AHSI* 10, 1940, pp. 186–87 (hereinafter: Pirri, "Topografia"); Hülsen, *Le Chiese de Roma nel Medio Evo,* Firenze, 1926, pp. 25 and 403; Proia and Romano, *Pigna,* pp. 24–25.

34. See "Stima dei lavori fatti esiguire da S. Ignazio di Loiola nella prima casa della Compagnia di Gesù in Roma [1544]" in TV *Case,* Appendix II, pp. 55–59.

35. *Chron* V, 21. For a brief account of the recent restoration work designed and directed by the author of the present work, see Thomas Lucas, "Le camere di Sant'Ignazio a Roma," *La Civiltà Cattolica* 1991, III, quaderno 3387–3388, pp. 280–86.

36. *EpistIgn* II, 366, pp. 132–33.

37. Pirri, "Topografia," pp. 178–81.

38. For the attribution and dating of the Bigio drawing see R. Bösel, *Jesuitenarchitektur in Italien 1540–1773. Die Baudenkmäler der römischen und der neapolitanischen Ordensprovinz,* 2 vols., Vienna, 1985–1986, II, pp. 162–63 and Doc. 1, p. 175; Pirri, "Topografia," p. 180; Vallery–Radot, *Le Recuil de plans d'édifices de la Compagnie de Jésus conservé à la Bibliotèque Nationale de Paris,* Rome: Institutum Historicum S.I., 1960, p. 21.

39. *EpistIgn* VII, 4529, 4531, 4617.

40. *Chron* V, p. 21.

41. Jesuit architect Giovanni Tristano was responsible for the construction of the *penitenciaria. EpistIgn* X, 6094.

42. For the *Fraternitas Romana* and the mendicant influence on late medieval–early Renaissance confraternities, see G. Barone, "Il movimento francescano e la nascita delle confraternite romane," in *Ricerche per la storia religiosa di Roma* 5, 1984, pp. 71–80. A good general introduction to the question of the confraternities during the Cinquecento with excellent recent bibliography is C. Black's *Italian Confraternities in the Sixteenth Century,* Cambridge and New York: Cambridge Univ. Press, 1989.

43. TV *Storia* I, ii, pp. 5–7.

44. P. Paschini *S. Gaetano Thiene,* pp. 12–20; P. Kunkel, *The Theatines in the History of Catholic Reform before the Establishment of Lutheranism.* Washington D.C.: Catholic Univ. Press, 1941, pp. 11–12, 17.

45. Ignatius' concern for the Theatines' future was not, in fact, unfounded. At the time of Ignatius' death, the Jesuits already numbered about 1,000 members; the Theatines, who had been in existence 15 years longer than the Jesuits, had about 35. The Theatines did not experience any kind of significant growth until one of the founders, Gian Pietro Carafa, was

elected Pope Paul IV in 1555. Paul IV gave them the church of S. Silvestro in Quirinale, and they received the territory of the present church of S. Andrea della Valle in 1582. Construction of S. Andrea began in 1591, eight years after the consecration of the Gesù. The Theatines did not open any houses outside Italy until the seventeenth century. G. Moroni, *Dizionario di Erudizione Storicio–Ecclesiastico,* Venice: Tipografia Emiliana, 1840–1861, vol 73, pp. 134–38, and Armellini, *Le Chiese,* p. 554.

In 1553, the Theatines appealed to be united with the Society of Jesus. They were politely yet firmly turned down by Ignatius. See *Chron* III, pp. 181–82, *EpistIgn* VI, 4007. He nevertheless tried to maintain friendly relations with them, even to the extent of offering to find them a suitable location in Rome for a house, *EpistIgn* V, 3815. Polanco left what O'Malley (*First Jesuits,* p. 81) calls a "somewhat self–serving but illuminating comparison between the Jesuits and the Theatines," pointing out that while the Jesuits were known for their open and friendly converse with all kinds of people, the Theatines were renowned for inspiring terror. *Chron* V, pp. 523–24.

46. *First Jesuits,* p. 295.

47. B. Pullan, *Rich and Poor in Venice: The Social Institutions of a Catholic State to 1620.* Cambridge MA: Harvard Univ. Press, 1971, pp 259–63. Emiliani's congregation is also known as the "Somaschi" for the city of Somasca near Milan where their headquarters was located. The Somaschi were briefly united with the Theatines (1546–1555), but Paul IV dissolved the union because the active life of the Somaschi was incompatible with the Theatine contemplative ideal. Kunkel, *The Theatines ,* p. 71; for Ignatius' negative judgment on the union, see *EpistIgn* I, p. 157; Tacchi Venturi, "S. Ignazio, di Loiola Apostolo di Roma," *Roma,* Agosto, 1940, p. 5.

48. *FN* I, p. 126, n. 34; Leturia, "Origine e senso sociale dell'apostolato di Sant'Ignazio di Loyola in Roma," *Estudios Ignacianos* 2, pp. 275–77. The boys' facility was located at S. Maria in Aquiro near the Pantheon, and the girls' orphanage, first located on Isola Tiberina, was transferred in 1560 to Ss. Quattro Coronati.

49. *First Jesuits,* pp. 185–88.

50. J. Reites, "St. Ignatius and the Jews," *StudiesSpir.* 13, 4, Sept., 1981, pp. 4–6.

51. Ribadeneyra, "Dicta et Facta S. Ignatii," I, 24, in *FN* II, 476; Reites, "St. Ignatius and the Jews," pp. 17–18.

52. M. Scaduto, *Storia delle Compagnia di Gesù in Italia III, L'Epoca di Giacomo Laínez, Il Governo 1556–1565,* Rome: Edizioni La Civiltà Cattolica, 1964, p. 124, notes 3 and 4. For the contemporary controversies on the admission of New Christians and Aquaviva's exclusion of their admittance after 1593, see Reites, "St. Ignatius and the Jews," pp. 18–30 and *First Jesuits,* pp. 188–89.

53. TV *Storia,* II, ii, pp. 152–54; Reites, "St. Ignatius and the Jews," p. 12; *FN* I, pp. 248–49, 304.

54. Villoslada, *Nueva Biografia,* pp. 537–38; Reites, "St. Ignatius and the Jews," pp. 12–13; TV *Storia,* I, ii, pp. 270–73, II, ii, pp. 149–60. The Church of S. Giovanni del Mercato or del Mercatello stood near the site of the open market which was held on the western flank of the Campidoglio until the fifteenth century. The house, as might be imagined, was much resented by the Jewish community. For the sad history of the house after Ignatius' leave–taking from the work, see Reites, p. 42, n. 46.

55. Delumeau, *Vie économique,* pp. 416–24, Stinger, *Renaissance in Rome,* p. 28. In O'Malley's *First Jesuits,* see notes 78–81 on p. 414 for excellent recent bibliography on prostitution in the late Middle Ages and early Renaissance.

56. Armellini, *Le Chiese,* pp. 696–97. That church was damaged during the sack of 1527 when a powder magazine in a nearby tower exploded. It was rebuilt by Gregory XIII, and given to the Poles as their national church.

57. Dalmases, *Ignatius, Founder,* pp. 181–82; O'Malley, *First Jesuits,* pp. 178–79. In medieval exegesis, Mary Magdalene was equated with the reformed prostitute who washed Jesus' feet with her tears; she was also thought to be the sister of Lazarus and Martha. Ignatius' substitution of Martha as patroness for his house for the prostitutes can be read as a gesture to lift some of the opprobrium from prostitutes who lived there.

58. *First Jesuits,* pp. 324, 359, and nn. 99, 103–05. "Although Ignatius is sometimes given credit for being the first person to conceive such an institution, a woman by the name of Laura Baliarda had labored to establish a seemingly similar one in

Modena in 1535. In 1542 Giammateo Giberti, the reforming bishop of Verona, made special provision for repentant prostitutes who did not want to become nuns. Ignatius may or may not have known about these precedents, if precedents they are. In any case, Santa Marta emerges with much clearer contours because we have more ample documentation about it; it is more important because under Jesuit inspiration similar houses were opened in other cities. Santa Marta was, even with possible antecedents, a strikingly original institution of social assistance." *First Jesuits,* pp. 183–84.

59. Ribadeneyra, *Vita* III, ix, 35 in *FN* IV, p. 411.

60. C. Chauvin, "La maison Sainte–Marthe," *Christus* 149, January, 1991, pp. 120–21. For the full membership list of the confraternity, see TV *Storia* I, ii, pp. 296–307. For Madama's support, see *EpistIgn* I, 85.

61. Ribadeneyra, "Dicta et Acta," in *FN* II, p. 346.

62. *Scripta* I, p. 662. For the full texts of the proceedings, see *Scripta* I, pp. 659–666. See also TV *Storia* II, ii, pp. 176–82. It is interesting to note, however, that at about this time the Society's involvement with the work decreased. Not long after the Jesuits withdrew from the work, the S. Marta property was divided into two sections, one for *convertite* who wanted to embrace the religious life and the other for women who were working towards an eventual reintegration into society. About ten years later the half–way house for non–religious women was moved to the chapel of S. Chiara, just behind the Pantheon.

63. *Chron* II, 147.

64. Brian Pullan, *Rich and Poor in Venice: The Social Institutions of a Catholic State to 1620,* Cambridge MA: Harvard Univ. Press, 1971, p. 390.

65. There are indications in the as yet unpublished research of Jesuit Pedro Miguel Lamet that Ignatius and Maria de Villarreal were the parents of Maria de Loyola. See A. Goldman, "Religion Notes: St. Ignatius and a Baby" in *The New York Times,* August 24, 1991, p. 23.

66. For the confraternity of the Dodici Apostoli that provided assistance to impoverished old people, see a document from the *Acta Beatificationis B.P. Ignatii* and a related document in TV *Storia* I, ii, pp. 321–24. Ignatius was also involved in the Confraternities of the Blessed Sacrament at the Minerva and of the Ospedale del Santo Spirito. From as early as the *Quinque Capitula* of 1539, work in a hospital for a full month was mandated for Jesuit novices. At Rome, they most often worked at the hospitals of S. Giacomo degli Incurabili (Via del Corso) and la Consolazione (on the southern flank of the Campidoglio). They were often called "Theatines" because of the memory of the Theatines' hospital work in Rome from 1524 to 1527. For a lurid account of Cornelius Wischaven's and other novices' harrowing experience–which included attempted seductions by a male nurse–see a document found in TV *Storia* I, ii, pp. 256–61, and *Storia* II, ii, pp. 29–37.

67. Such initiatives did not end with the early years of the Society, although with the shift into education the schools took on an ever–increasing importance as centers for confraternal and social assistance. One of the best documented Jesuit confraternities was *Confraternità dei carcerati* founded by Jean Tellier, a French Jesuit, in 1575. Headquartered at S. Giovanni della Pigna in Piazza della Pigna between the Gesù and the site of the Collegio Romano, the confraternity performed an impressive range of social and pastoral ministries for the imprisoned. See V. Paglia, *"La pietà dei carcerati:" Confraternite e società a Roma nei secoli XVI–XVIII.* Rome: Edizioni di Storia e Letteratura, 1980, pp. 3–80. Louis Chatellier's *L'Europe des Dévots,* St. Just La Pendue: Chirat, 1987 is an excellent chronicle of the evolution of confraternities into the Jesuit sodality movement.

CHAPTER SEVEN
THE MORE UNIVERSAL, THE MORE DIVINE

1. Augustine, Benedict, and Francis left sketches, *formulae vivendi,* for their respective orders, but the detailed constitutions were written after the founders' deaths. The Dominican Constitutions, adapted from the Rule of St. Augustine, were written by Dominic and the general chapters. Ignatius' Constitutions were approved after his death at the First General Congregation (1558).

2. There is a story in the oral tradition of the Society of Jesus about the construction of a large theology school–residence complex. (The attributions are various, but most often the story is told about the theologate at Woodstock, Maryland.) Because of the scale of the project, plans were sent to the Society's Curia in Rome for review. When the general's architectural consultant examined the plans, he discov-

ered that there were no toilets planned in the 200-room complex. He returned the plans to the local provincial with the dry interrogation: "Suntne angeli?"

3. A particularly eloquent treatment of the process of home design, and a delightful introduction to its place in architectural history, is Witold Rybczynski's *The Most Beautiful House in the World,* New York: Viking, 1990. John Padberg's fine essay "How We Live where We Live," in *StudiesSpir.* 20, 2, March, 1988 is the only available study of the historical and contemporary meaning of "home" in Jesuit communities.

4. For a good discussion of this metaphorical shift, see P. de Leturia, "Jerusalén y Roma en los designios de San Ignacio de Loyola" in *Estudios Ignacianos* 1, 1957, pp. 181–200. See J. Olin, "The Idea of Pilgrimage in the Experience of Ignatius Loyola," *Church History,* 48, 1979, pp. 387–97.

5. "The vow of stability is what made the man the monk, in other words, the promise to live his entire life in the monastery, where he would seek his own sanctification. The Jesuits' Fourth Vow was in essence a vow of mobility, that is, a commitment to travel anywhere in the world, for the 'help of souls.' The Fourth Vow was thus one of the best indications of how the new order wanted to break with the monastic tradition. The vow assumed, moreover, that the pope had the broad vision required for the most effective deployment in the 'vineyard of the Lord,' which by definition extended throughout the world. The implicit model . . . was Jesus sending his disciples–the 'vicar of Christ' (the vicar of Jesus) sending the Jesuits." *First Jesuits,* p. 299; cf. O'Malley's very important study "To Travel to Any Part of the World: Jerónimo Nadal and the Jesuit Vocation." *StudiesSpir.,* 16, 2, March 1984.

6. "Constituciones circa missiones" in *ConstMHSJ 1,* pp. 159–64, excerpt on p. 160. The "Constituciones circa missiones" served as the sketch for the seventh chapter of the *Constitutions of the Society of Jesus,* and is one of the oldest and most important texts on the missions of the Society.

7. *EpistIgn* 2, 581.

8. *MonNadal* 1 p. 144.

9. *MonNadal 5,* pp. 469–70. Cf. M. Scaduto, "La strada e i primi Gesuiti." *AHSI* 40, 1971, pp. 323–390.

Nadal extensively used this paradoxical image of the journey, mission, and pilgrimage as the "ideal house" and "most peaceful house" of the Society. O'Malley has laid out and explicated a number of these texts in "To Travel."

10. "Conclusiones septem sociorum" in *ConstMHSJ 1,* pp. 9–14. See Ravier, *Founding,* pp. 89–94.

11. *ConstMHSJ* 1, p. 13. English translation of this tortured text is by Ignacio Echániz in Aldama's *The Formula of the Institute, Notes for a Commentary,* St. Louis: Institute of Jesuit Sources and Rome: Centrum Ignatianum Spiritualitatis, 1990, pp. 77–78.

12. For a good analysis of the similarities and divergences between Jesuit and mendicant poverty, see Aldama, *The Formula,* pp. 77–79. He suggests that Ignatius, who was well acquainted with the Capuchins, might have assumed many of their practices concerning poverty. For the Dominicans' legislation against fixed revenues, see Hinnesbusch, *The History of the Dominican Order,* p. 153 ff.

13. *The Formula,* pp. 12, 14. For the Latin text of the *Quinque Capitula,* see *ConstMHSJ* 1, pp. 15–21. For the English translation by Ignacio Echániz see Aldama's *The Formula,* pp. 2–22 (even numbered pages).

14. *The Formula,* p 14.

15. For a brief but thorough introduction to the history of the composition of these documents, see Aldama's excellent *The Constitutions of the Society of Jesus: An Introductory Commentary on the Constitutions,* translated by Aloysius Owen, St. Louis: Institute of Jesuit Sources and Rome: Centrum Ignatianum Spiritualitatis, 1989, pp. 1–19. Aldama's "La composición de las Constituciones de la Compañía de Jesús," *AHSI* 42, 1973, pp. 211–45, is useful for understanding the important role of Ignatius' secretary Juan de Polanco in the composition process. Chapter 2 of Ravier's *Founding* is also useful, although the English translation is very unreliable. Ganss' "Technical Introduction to the Constitutions of the Society of Jesus" in *ConstEng* pp. 35–59 is most helpful for sorting out the nuances of the legal vocabulary of "constitutions," "declarations," "formulae," etc.

16. Partner, *Renaissance Rome,* p. 76. Interpretation of the census figures for 1526–1527 (the only detailed census of the 16th century), allow for estimates of

approximately 25% Romans, 55% non–Roman Italians, and 20% non–Italians.

17. *SpEx* [23].

18. *The Formula*, p. 20.

19. *The Formula*, p. 18 For the difficulties which these exceptions to common practice caused, see Ravier, *Founding*, pp. 107–16; Aldama, *Formula*, pp. 28–33.

20. *Constitutions of the Society of Jesus and their Complementary Norms. A Complete English Translation of the Official Latin Texts*. St. Louis: Institute of Jesuit Sources, 1996, pp. 3–4.

21. See *First Jesuits*, chapter 7 and Aldama, *Formula*, pp. 40–45 for the impact on the order of the Jesuits' apostolic work among the Protestants.

22. Aldama, *Formula*, p. 42.

23. Nadal, *Orationis Observationes*, edited by Michael Nicolau, Rome: Institutum Historicum S.I., 1964, #316.

24. See Polanco, in *Chron* 1, p. 286; *First Jesuits*, p. 74,

25. Chapter 6 of O'Malley's *First Jesuits* gives a complete analysis of the problematic of the Jesuits' move into higher education. He also provides an excellent review of recent bibliography, esp. n. 2, pp. 418–19. See P. Grendler, *Schooling in Renaissance Italy: Literacy and Learning, 1300–1600,* Baltimore and London: Johns Hopkins Univ. Press, 1989, pp. 363–81.

26. *The Formula*, p. 14.

27. *First Jesuits*, p. 202.

28. *ConstMHSJ* 1, p. 47.

29. For a detailed study of the Parisian methodology and its implications, see *First Jesuits*, pp. 215–25; Villoslada, *Nueva Biografia*, pp. 890–92.

30. For Goa, see Ribadeneyra, *Vita, FN* 4, III, v, 19, p. 385; Villoslada, *Nueva Biografia*, pp. 880–81. For Ingolstadt, see Villoslada, *Nueva Biografia*, pp. 883–84.

31. Cf. *Chron* 1, p. 249.

32. *EpistMixtae* 1, pp. 454–56.

33. Although it is not exhaustive, *EpistIgn* 4, 2226, (Polanco writing on commission of Ignatius to Antonio Araoz, Dec. 1, 1551) does provide a list of 15 benefits–for the Society, for the students, and for the locality–that derive from the foundation of colleges.

34. *Chron* 5, p. 535; Cf. *Chron* 2, pp. 19, 651.

35. *EpistIgn* 4, 2227, p. 10; *EpistIgn* 12, 50 (Appendix 1) p. 310.

36. P. Grendler, *Schooling*, p. 365.

37. *Chron* 5, pp. 561–562. For an analysis of the social milieu of the colleges during Ignatius' lifetime, see *First Jesuits*, pp. 208–12.

38. Ravier, *Chroniques*, pp. 200–06 even, 224, 246.

39. *EpistIgn* 5, 3939, 3940. These rulings were codified in Decree 73 of the First General Congregation (1558), requiring four or five teachers, two or three priests for pastoral ministry, a few others to substitute in cases of need, and two lay brothers. *Institutum Societatis Iesu,* 2, Florence: Tipographia a Ss. Conceptione, 1893, p. 171. Also *Monumenta Paedogogica Societatis Iesu, I, 1540–1556,* (Monumenta Historica Societatis Iesu) Rome, 1965, pp. 446–49, English translation in *For Matters of Greater Moment, The First Thirty Jesuit General Congregations, A Brief History and A Translation of the Decrees,* St. Louis: Institute of Jesuit Sources, 1994, pp 86–87.

40. This Chronology was devised from a close reading of Ravier's *Chroniques* and Villoslada's *Nueva Biografia,* esp. pp. 894–95. Where there were discrepancies, the later date was chosen because of the frequent gaps between written approval of a work and its actual realization.

41. *The Formula*, p. 14.

42. For a good discussion of the technical vocabulary of ecclesiastical economics of the period, see Ganss' notes 13, 14, and 15 in *ConstEng* pp. 78–79.

43. "Constitutiones anni 1541," *ConstMHSJ* 1, pp. 34–38; "De collegis fundandis," *ConstMHSJ* 1, p. 62.

44. The *Spiritual Diary* is a unique document among the corpus of written *ignatiana*: it is an autograph account of Ignatius' reflections, prayer, and mystical visions, for a period of one year while he was com-

posing what would become the core of the *Constitutions*. It is also important to recall that at the same moment he was building a new house for thirty Jesuits who lived in Rome, organizing the Casa S. Marta for the Prostitutes, negotiating the foundation of the house for Jewish catechumens. Original text in *ConstMHSJ* 1, pp. 86–158.

45. For texts on the professed houses, see *ConstEng* [4, 5, 289, 322–25, 330, 400, 422, 554–558, 570, 572, 575, 587, 589, 603, 636, 636–651, 680, 743, 762, 763, 827].

46. *ConstEng* [554, 555, 557].

47. *ConstEng* p. 166, n. 19.

48. *EpistIgn* 9, 5399, p. 83. For a short, clear exposition of Ignatius' ability to change his mind on important issues like this one, see J. O'Malley's "How the Jesuits Changed: 1540–56." *America*, 165, 2, July 20–27, 1991, pp. 28–32.

49. For a very detailed analysis of this text, its history, and solid bibliography, see Aldama's *The Constitutions of the Society of Jesus: Part VII Missioning*, translated by I. Echaniz, Anand, India: Gujarat Sahitya Prakash and Rome: Centrum Ignatianum Spiritualitatis, 1990. The text of Part VII is an amplification of Ignatius' "Constituciones circa missiones" of 1544–1545, found in *MHSJConst* 1, pp. 159–64.

50. All English translations of the *Constitutions* are from Ganss' *ConstEng*. For simplicity, references are given directly in the text using the standard text numbering in square brackets.

51. In the 51 paragraphs, the idea of the universal (or more universal) good appears at least eight times [613, 615, 618, 622a, 622d, 623e, 626, 650], "more universal benefits" four times [618, 623a, 623f, 624]. The "greater glory" and/or "greater service of God" is the most characteristic phrase of the document: it appears in 18 places [twice in 603, twice in 605, 608, 609, thrice in 618, 622a, 623a, 623g, twice in 624k, 634, 645, 647, 650]. The comparative adjective "greater" (*mejor*) appears another 25 times in the chapter in the following contexts: aid to souls [605], devotion [610, 622b], spiritual fruit [615 and 622b], facility [618], security and safety [618, 619], need [622a, 631], indebtedness [622c], perfection [twice in 623 b], confidence [624 a], bodily labors [624b], spiritual dangers [624c], edification [625c, 645], importance of those to whom the Society is sent [626, 638], and care proportionate to the nature of the work [629].

52. The metaphor of the "vineyard" or "Christ's vineyard" for the world appears 15 times in the *Constitutions*. See Aldama, *Missioning*, pp. 4, 73.

53. *SpEx* [177]. The details of the "election of the third time" are spelled out in *SpEx* [178–88].

54. *ConstEng* [622, 623] pp. 274–78.

55. Polanco identified the importance of urban and university ministry for attracting recruits to the Society: "Living in large and well-traveled locations–after universities, we ought to prefer for this goal [promoting vocations] large centers where there is great transit of able people, and among many cities there are some in particular, such as Rome and Venice in Italy, Valladolid, Toledo, Sevilla, and the Court in Spain, etc." *Polanci Complementa,* (Monumenta Historica Societatis Iesu), Madrid, 1916–1917, I, p. 726.

56. Nadal, *Scholia in Constititiones S.I.,* edited by Manuel Ruiz Jurado, Granada: Faculdad de Teologia, 1976, p. 175. English translation in O'Malley's "To Travel," pp. 7–8.

57. *MonNadal* 5, p. 470. English translation in Aldama's *Missioning*, p. 133.

58. *MonNadal* 5, p. 469.

59. For example, masses were celebrated daily, other devotions and confessions throughout the week, sermons and lectures generally reserved to Sundays and Holy Days, etc., Aldama, *Missioning*, p. 136.

CHAPTER EIGHT
GOD IN THE DETAILS

1. Delumeau, *Vie économique et social de Rome dans la seconde moitié du XVIᵉ siècle,* Paris: E. de Boccard, 1957, I, pp. 45–51; Scaduto, "La corrispondenza dei primi gesuiti e le poste italiane," *AHSI* 19, 1950, pp. 237–53, esp. charts on pp. 250–53, give figures for Italy gleaned from the correspondence of Ignatius. For the Javier correspondence, see Ravier, *Les Chroniques,* p. 176.

2. Delumeau, *Vie économique,* I, pp. 37–38.

3. *EpistIgn* 1, 208, p. 609

4. The word *hijuela* literally means "drainage canal"; by extension it is used to signify a subordinate item.

EpistIgn 1, 31, 32, 58. In July 1547, Juan de Polanco, Ignatius' indefatigable secretary, wrote an instruction and rules on letter–writing that were distributed to the entire Society. They covered 20 points, including style, content, frequency, the question of confidential materials, and postal strategy. The documents are most useful for understanding the strategic importance of letters to the early Society. *EpistIgn* 1, 179–80.

5. D. Bertrand, *La Politique de Saint Ignace de Loyola,* Paris: Editions du Cerf, 1985, p. 39. For sources of the data, see p. 36, n. 57.

6. Bertrand, *La Politique,* pp. 37, 38.

7. *EpistIgn* 1, 169.

8. *EpistIgn* 5, 3521; 8, 5122.

9. *EpistIgn* 6, 4227; 9, 5637.

10. *EpistIgn* 6, 4319; 11, 6510.

11. *EpistIgn* 8, 5137, p. 338.

12. *EpistIgn* 9, 5422; 11, 6246.

13. *EpistIgn* 6, 4389; 10, 5902.

14. See Hugo Rahner, *Letters to Women,* translated by K. Pond and S. Weetman, Freiberg, Herder, and Edinburgh–London: Nelson 1960, part 3, pp.169–246.

15. cf. *EpistIgn* 11, 6420, 6592; 12, 6651, 6632. The last letter in the series (12, 6731), which confirmed the transaction, was sent six days prior to Ignatius' death.

16. *EpistIgn* 12, 6731–6741.

17. The Database follows the text in Appendix A, pp. 175–88.

18. See the categories "Gen. Fin." (general finances) and "Rome Fin." (Roman finances) in the data base.

19. See the category "Com. Luogo" (*commodo luogo,* or convenient location) in the database.

20. *EpistIgn* 7, 4487, p. 48

21. *EpistIgn* 7, 4794, pp. 536–37; see *Chron,* 4, 452.

22. *EpistIgn* 4, 2225 dated December 1, 1551, served as the model for 4, 2227, 2228, 2229, 2234, 2238, and 2239."Instruction del modo de proceder mandata a Ferrara, et quasi del medesmo tenore a Firenze et Napole et Modena, mutando alcune cose," *EpistIgn* 3, 1941 relates that copies of this document were sent to Alcalá, Palermo, Paris, and to Nadal. Similar documents are *EpistIgn* 11, 5099 (on urban ministry) and 12, 6565 "circa la fundatione materiale et temporale." A second category was addressed to the actual organization and curricular development of new colleges, as well as rules for the spiritual and temporal life of the students.

23. *EpistIgn* 3, 1899, pp. 542-50.

24. *EpistIgn* 3, 1899, p. 542.

25. *EpistIgn* 3, 1899, p. 548.

26. *EpistIgn* 3, 548.

27. *Chron* 4, p. 179.

28. *EpistIgn* 7, 4567.

29. *Chron* 6, pp. 374–75; Bösel in *Strategy,* pp. 145–46. For Vienna, see *Chron* 3, p. 260, and *EpistIgn* 7, 4867.

30. *EpistIgn* 12, 6645, p. 67.

31. *EpistIgn* 5, 3728, p. 446–47

32. *EpistIgn* 5, 3805, p. 554. Perhaps because of his own delicate health, Ignatius was particularly sensitive to the needs of the sick. See *ConstEng* [303, 304, 580, 595, 596, 826]. Ignatius also approved the purchase of suburban villas for care of the sick and for recreation. See *ConstEng* [559], *EpistIgn* 8, 5097, 5161, 5171, 5219; 10, 6058.

33. *EpistIgn* 9, 5415, p. 120.

34. *EpistIgn* 6, 3973. For another 43 references, see the "manpower" entries in the database.

35. For Granada, see *EpistIgn* 9, 5430, for Naples, 3, 1729, 1730.

36. *EpistIgn* 6, 4113.

37. *EpistIgn* 6, 4064, p. 175; see *Chron* 4, 83.

38. *EpistMixtae* 5, p. 240.

39. For a good summary of the correspondence and Laínez's complicated relationship with Eleonora, see H. Rahner's *Letters to Women,* pp. 93–107.

40. *Polanco Complementa,* 1, p. 25.

41. *EpistIgn* 1, 152, pp. 458–59.

42. *Chron* 2, p. 177.

43. See *EpistIgn* 4, 2335, p. 77. See also *EpistIgn* 3, 2186, 2188, 2189, (esp. p. 719 on courtly manners); 6, 4084; 7, 4474, p. 28 (on the Infanta Juana). Juana, in fact, was the only woman ever to be a permanent member of the Society of Jesus. Queen of Portugal from 1552 until her sickly husband João Emmanuel's death in 1554, Juana was made regent of Spain by Charles V for five years during Philip's marriage to Mary Tudor of England. Juana, a close friend of Francisco Borja, insisted on being admitted to the Society in 1554, and Ignatius reluctantly allowed her to profess first vows in secret. She remained a member of the Society until her death in 1573. See H. Rahner, *Letters to Women,* pp. 52–67, for a thorough treatment of Juana's singular relationship to the Society.

44. *EpistIgn* 3, 2047, pp. 637–38.

45. For the construction history of the college of S. Giovannino, see P. Pirri, "L'architetto Bartolomeo Ammannati e i Gesuiti," *AHSI* 12, 1943, pp. 5–57 and C. Carmagnini and P. Matracchi, "Il Collegio di San Giovannino in Firenze: Rilievo Architettonico e Interpretazione delle Vicende Costruittive dal progetto di Bartolomeo Ammannati ad Oggi," *Ricerca, Bollettino degli Scolopi Italiani,* 1976, pp. 295–347.

46. *EpistMixtae* 4, p. 222.

47. Although the foundation in Milan was not established until five years after Ignatius' death, it is included in this list because of its great importance as a center for the Society's diffusion in Northern Italy. The Church of S. Fedele near the Duomo was given to the Society in 1567, and the nearby Collegio di Brera was founded in 1573. For Milan, see A. Scurani, "Ieri e oggi dei Gesuiti a Milano" in *Terra Ambrosiana,* 6, novembre–dicembre 1990, pp. 52–59; and G. Castellani, "I primi tentativi per l'introduzione dei Gesuiti a Milano (1545–1559), *AHSI* 3, 1934, pp. 36–47.

48. *Chron* 5, pp. 387–409; A. Astrain, *Historia de la Compañía de Jesús en la Asistencia de España, Tomo I, San Ignacio de Loyola, 1540–1556,* Madrid: Sucesores de Rivadeneyra, 1902, pp. 438–64. For Ignatius' own reflections on the situation, see *EpistIgn* 10, 5866.

49. *EpistMixtae* 4, 770; *Chron* 5, p. 397.

50. For example, cf. *EpistIgn* 6, 4196, 4270; 7, 4828; 10, 5985; for a full listing, see the category "Mend. Rule" in the database.

51. For the full text of *Etsi ex debito,* see *Institutum Societatis Iesu,* Vol. 1, Florence: Ex Typographia a Ss. Conceptione, 1892, pp. 31–4; for *Salvatoris Domini,* see *Institutum,* Vol. 1, pp. 63–7.

52. *EpistIgn* 10, 5897, p. 115.

53. *EpistIgn* 12, 6677, p. 119.

54. *EpistIgn* 5, 3816, p. 567.

CHAPTER NINE
LANDMARKING

1. *Synopsis Historiae Societatis Iesu,* Louvain: Typis ad Sancti Alphonsi, 1950, pp. 34, 82, 122; *Imago Primi Saeculi Societatis Iesu a Provincia Flandro-Belgica eiusdem societatis repraesentata,* Antwerp, 1640, p. 248.

2. For building plans, see *EpistIgn* 7, 4019, 4088, 4524, 4796; 8, 5071. For the 40 letters dealing with the granting or denying of the "local option," see that category in the data base. For blank letters, see Aldama, *Constitutions,* p. 269.

3. *Institutum* 2, no. 113, p. 182, English translation in *For Matters of Greater Moment,* p. 98.

4. P. Pirri, *Giovanni Tristano e i primordi della architettura gesuitica,* Rome: Institutum Historicum S.I., 1955, pp. 40–42. Among Tristano's distinguished successors in the post were Giovanni di Rosis, Orazio Grassi, Benedetto Molli, and Andrea Pozzo.

5. *Institutum,* 2, no. 84, p. 210. Thereafter, a very large collection of drawings of Jesuit buildings was assembled in the Jesuit Archives in Rome. Much of the archive, including the drawings of Jesuit buildings, was dispersed at the time of the suppression of the Society in 1773. Now, however, 1,222 of the drawings are in the Cabinet des Estampes of the

Bibliotèque Nationale de Paris, and another volume from that same original collection, with 311 pages of documents and drawings, was recently discovered in the National Library of Malta. See Vallery-Radot, *Le Recuil*, pp. 3*–7*; the Malta discovery was reported by P. Iapelli at a conference in Milan entitled "L'architettura della Compagnia di Gesù, XVI–XVIII sec.," October 24–27, 1990.

6. E. Guidoni and A. Marino, *Storia dell'urbanistica: Il Cinquecento,* Rome and Bari: Laterza, 1982, pp. 614–15.

7. Connors, *Borromini and the Roman Oratory, Style and Society,* Cambridge MA: The MIT Press, 1980, pp. 3, 82.

8. For the original correspondence among Farnese, Borja, and Vignola see Pirri, *Tristano,* pp. 228–29.

9. Pirri, *Tristano,* p, 138–54.

10. Tacchi Venturi, *Le Case,* p. 52.

11. P. Pirri and Di Rosa, "Il P. Giovanni de Rosis (1538–1610) e lo Sviluppo dell'Edilizia Gesuitica," *AHSI* 14, 1975, p 28–30.

12. Letter of Claudio Aquaviva to P. Alagona, Oct. 6, 1612, in Pirri, *Tristano,* p. 266.

13. *EpistIgn* 11, 6228.

14. "De Collegio Romano, 1551–61," in Rinaldi, *La fondazione del Collegio Romano,* Arezzo: n.p., 1914, p. 67.

15. Pirri, *Tristano,* p. 29.

16. When Pius IV entrusted the newly founded Seminario Romano to the Jesuits in 1563 and ordered its students to attend classes at the Collegio Romano, one auxilliary bishop complained "it is intolerable to entrust the education of Roman youths to Germans and Spaniards, that is, to heretics and marrani (Jewish converts)." F. Sacchini, *Historiae Societatis Iesu pars tertia sive Borgia,* Rome: Typis Manelfi Manelfii, 1649, p. 303.

17. In the Avvisi (the equivalent of newspapers) of Nov. 27, 1582, it was suggested that the Jesuits were building "more a fortress than a school." Cf. BAV, Urb. lat. 1050, fol. 453 A, 271. For a detailed analysis of the planning and construction of the Collegio Romano complex, see the articles by E. Levy and R. Bösel in *Strategy,* pp. 161–71.

18. Delumeau, *Vie économique,* 2, p. 765.

19. Connors, *Borromini,* p. 146, n. 46.

20. Villoslada, *Storia del Collegio Romano dal suo inizio (1551) alla soppressione della Compagnia di Gesù (1773),* Rome: Gregorian Univ. Press, 1954, p. 153.

21. L. Montalto, "Il Problema della cupola di Sant'Ignazio da Padre Orazio Grassi e Fratel Pozzo a oggi." *Bolletino del centro di studii per la storia dell'' architettura,* 11, 1957, pp. 33–62.

22. For Molli, see Bösel, *Strategy,* pp. 173–74; for Bernini and S. Andrea, see Morello, *Strategy,* pp. 192–93; for Alexander VII and the Collegio Romano, see R. Krautheimer, *The Rome of Alexander VII, 1655–1667,* Princeton: Princeton Univ. Press, 1985, pp. 84–7.

23. K. Rahner, *Theological Investigations,* Vol. 14, translated by David Bourke, New York: Seabury, 1976, p. 169.

24. John O'Malley's "How the Jesuits Changed: 1540–56." *America,* 165, 2, July 20–27, 1991, pp. 28–32.

25. For an excellent exposition of this Jesuit "theology" of conversation, see John Padberg, "The Jesuit question," *The Tablet,* September 22, 1990, pp. 1189–91.

26. Alden, *Empire,* p. 19.

27. A detailed history of the Suppression has yet to be written. Chapters 5 and 6 of William Bangert's 1972 *A History of the Society of Jesus.* St. Louis: Institute of Jesuit Sources, provide a useful introduction to this complicated thematic.

28. Some examples of separate incorporations and geographic relocations include: Georgetown University and Georgetown Prep, Washington, DC; St. Joseph's University and St. Joseph's Prep, Philadelphia; Loyola College and Loyola Blakefield Prep, Baltimore; University of San Francisco and St. Ignatius Prep, San Francisco; Santa Clara University and Bellarmine Prep, San Jose; St. Louis University and St. Louis University High School; Seattle University and Seattle Prep.

29. *Documents of the Thirty-fourth General Congregation of the Society of Jesus,* St. Louis: Institute of Jesuit Sources, 1995, [110], pp. 61–62.

30. *EpistIgn* 10, 5985, p. 288; *Chron* 5, pp. 47–48.

31. *EpistIgn* 9, 5388, p. 66.

BIBLIOGRAPHY

Acta sanctorum quotquot toto orbe coluntur, vel a catolicis scriptoribus celebrantur, notis illustravit I. Bollandus *Societatis Iesu theologus, oper et studius contulit* G. Henschenius *eiusdem Societatis theologus.* Venetiis, 1734-1770.

ALDAMA, ANTONIO DE. *Vestigia Sanctorum Societatis Iesu in Urbe Roma.* Rome: Postulatio Generalis Soc. Iesu, 1953.

ALDAMA, ANTONIO DE. "La composición de las Constituciones de la Compañía de Jesús." *AHSI* 42, 1973, pp. 211-245.

ALDAMA, ANTONIO DE. *The Constitutions of the Society of Jesus: An Introductory Commentary on the Constitutions.* Translated by Aloysius Owen. St. Louis: Institute of Jesuit Sources and Rome: Centrum Ignatianum Spiritualitatis, 1989.

ALDAMA, ANTONIO DE. *The Constitutions of the Society of Jesus: Part VII Missioning.* Translated by I. Echaniz. Anand, India: Gujarat Sahitya Prakash and Rome: Centrum Ignatianum Spiritualitatis, 1990.

ALDAMA, ANTONIO DE. *The Constitutions of the Society of Jesus: The Formula of the Institute: Notes for a Commentary.* Translated by Ignacio Echaniz. St. Louis: Institute of Jesuit Sources and Rome: Centrum Ignatianum Spiritualitatis, 1990.

ALDEN, DAURIL. *The Making of an Enterprise, The Society of Jesus in Portugal, Its Empire, and Beyond, 1540-1750.* Stanford: Stanford University Press, 1996.

ANONYMOUS. "A Short History of the Mission of Our Lady of Loreto, New York," *Woodstock Letters,* 46, 2, 1917.

Ante-Nicene Fathers, The. Translations of the Writings of the Fathers down to A.D. 325. Edited by Alexander Roberts and James Donaldson. New York: Christian Literary Company, 1896: Vol. III: *Latin Christianity: Its Founder, Tertullian.* Vol IV: *Tertullian, Part Fourth; Minucius Felix; Commodian, Origen Parts First and Second.*

Archivum Romanum Societatis Iesu. *Hist Dom Prof, I;*
Rom. Templ. Dom Prof. 143, 144; Roma 1028, I, 1. Rome: Borgo S. Spirito 4.

ARGAN, GIULIO C. *The Renaissance City.* Translated by Susan Bassnett, New York: George Braziller, 1969.

ASTRAIN, ANTONIO. *Historia de la Compañía de Jesús en la Asistencia de España. Tomo I, San Ignacio de Loyola. 1540-1556.* Madrid: Sucesores de Rivadeneyra, 1902.

AUGUSTINE. *The City of God.* Translated by Gerald G. Walsh et al. New York: Image, 1958.

AUGUSTINE. *The Rule of St. Augustine, masculine and feminine versions.* Translated by Raymond Canning. Introduction and Commentary by Tarsicius Van Bavel. London: Darton, Longman & Todd, 1984.

BALDOVIN, JOHN F. *The Urban Character of Christian Liturgy: The Stational Liturgy of Jerusalem, Rome, and Constantinople.* Rome: Orientalia Christiana Analecta, 1987.

BANGERT, WILLIAM V. *A History of the Society of Jesus.* St. Louis: Institute of Jesuit Sources, 1972.

BARONE, GIULIA. "I francescani a Roma." *Storia della Città* 9, 1978, pp. 33-35.

BARONE, GIULIA. "Il movimento francescano e la nascita delle confraternite romane." *Ricerche per la storia religiosa di Roma* 5, 1984, pp. 71-80.

BARTOLI, DANIELLO. "Vita del P. Pietro Codaccio che fu il primo d'Italiani che entrasse nella compagnia de Giesù," Ms in ARSI: *Epp. NN.* 98.

BATLLORI, MIGUEL. "Economia e Collegi" in *Domanda e Consumi.* Atti della Sesta Settimano di Studio, Istituto Internazionale di Storia Economica "F. Datini." Firenze, 1978.

BATLLORI, MIGUEL. "Le città italiane e i collegi gesuitici." in *Cittá Italiani del '500 tra Riforma e Controriforma.* (Atti del Convegno di Internazionale di Studi, Lucca, 13-15 ottobre, 1983). Lucca: Pacini Fazzi, 1988, pp. 293-97.

BATLLORI, MIGUEL. *Cultura e Finanze: Studi sulla Storia dei Gesuiti da S. Ignazio al Vaticano II.* Rome: Edizioni di Storia e Letteratura, 1983.

BATLLORI, MIGUEL. "Tipologia de las fundaciones económicas de los colegios de los jesuitas en los siglos XVI y XVII" in *Homenaje a Julián Marías.* Madrid: España Calipe, 1984, pp. 85-94.

BENEVOLO, LEONARDO. *The Architecture of the Renaissance.* 2 vols., Translated by Judith Landry. Boulder: Westview Press, 1978.

BENEVOLO, LEONARDO. *La Città Italiana nel Rinascimento.* Milan: Edizioni Il Polifilo, 1990.

BERTHIER, J. J. *L'Eglise de la Minerve à Rome.* Rome: Cooperativa Tipografica Manuzio, 1910.

BERTRAND, DOMINIQUE. *La Politique de S. Ignace de Loyola.* Paris: Cerf, 1985.

BÉRENCE, FRED. *Les Papes de la Renaissance.* Paris: Editions du Sud, 1966.

BOLLATI, S., CANIGGIA, M., and CANIGGIA, G. *Esperienze operative sul tessuto urbano di Roma,* Rome: Università degli studi di Roma, 1963.

BONDANELLA, PETER. *The Eternal City: Roman Images in the Modern World.* Chapel Hill: University of North Carolina Press, 1987.

BONELLI, RENATO. "Nuovi sviluppi di ricerca sull'edilizia mendicante" in *Gli Ordini mendicanti e la città: aspetti architettonici, sociali, e politici,* Edited by J. Raspi Serra, Milan: Edizioni Gurinin, 1990.

BORSI, STEFANO. *Roma di Sisto V: La pianta di Antonio Tempesta, 1593.* Rome: Officina Edizioni, 1986.

BOSSY, JOHN. *Christianity in the West, 1400-1700.* Oxford: Oxford University Press, 1985.

BOTTEREAU, GEORGES. "La 'Lettre' d'Ignace de Loyola à Gian Pietro Carafa." *AHSI* 44, 1975, pp. 139-52.

BÖSEL, RICHARD. *Jesuitenarchitektur in Italien 1540-1773. Die Baudenkmäler der römischen und der neapolitanischen Ordensprovinz.* 2 vols. Vienna, 1985-1986.

BOYLE, LEONARD E. *San Clemente Miscellany I.* Rome: Collegio San Clemente, 1977.

BRAUDEL, FERNAND. *The Mediterranean and the Mediterranean World in the Age of Philip II.* 2 vols. Translated by Sian Reynolds. London: Collins, 1973.

BRAUNFELS, WOLFGANG. *Monasteries of Western Europe, The Architecture of the Orders.* Princeton: Princeton University Press, 1972.

BRAUNFELS, WOLFGANG. *Urban Design in Western Europe: Regime and Architecture, 900-1900.* Translated by Kenneth J. Northcott. Chicago & London: University of Chicago Press, 1988.

BRICARELLI, C. "Il Palazzo di Venezia in Roma da Paolo II a Pio VII." *Roma,* 8, 1930.

BRODRICK, JAMES. *St. Ignatius Loyola, The Pilgrim Years, 1491-1538.* New York: Farrer, Straus, & Cudahy, 1956.

BRODRICK, JAMES. *The Origin of the Jesuits.* New York: Longmans, 1960.

BROWN, PETER. *Augustine of Hippo, a Biography.* London: Faber & Faber, 1967.

Bullarium Franciscanum. 4 vols. Edited by J.H. Sbaralea. Rome, 1758-1768.

Bullarium Romanum. 24 vols. Turin, 1857-1872.

BURROUGHS, C. *From Sign to Design: Environmental Process and Reform in Early Renaissance Rome.* Cambridge MA: The MIT Press, 1990.

CAMPBELL, TONY. *The Earliest Printed Maps.* Berkeley: University of California Press, 1987.

CANCELLIERI, FRANCESCO. *Storia dei Solenne Possessi.* Rome, 1802.

Canones Congregationum Generalium Societatis Iesu cum aliis nonnullis ad praxim pertinentibus. Rome: In Collegio Societatis Iesu, 1581.

CAPELLE, B. "L'Epître 211 et la règle de Saint Augustin." *Analecta Praemonstratensia* 3, 1927, pp. 369-78.

CARMAGNINI, CARLO, and MATRACCHI, PIETRO. "Il Collegio di San Giovannino in Firenze: Rilievo Architettonico e Interpretazione delle Vicende Costruittive dal progetto di Bartolomeo Ammannati ad Oggi." *Ricerca, Bollettino degli Scolopi Italiani,* 1976, pp. 295-347.

CASTAGNOLI, F., CECCHELLI, C., GIOVANNONI, G., and ZOCCA, M. *Topografia e Urbanistica di Roma.* Bologna: Instituto di Studi Romani, 1958.

CASTELLANI, G. "I primi tentativi per l'introduzione dei Gesuiti a Milano (1545-1559)." *AHSI* 3, 1934, pp. 36-47.

CEEN, ALLAN. *The Quartiere de'Banchi: Urban Planning in Rome in the first Half of the Cinquecento.* Ann Arbor: University Microfilms, 1977.

CHANDLER, T., and FOX, G. *Three Thousand Years of Urban Growth.* New York: Academic Press, 1974.

CHARBONNIER, JEAN. *A Guide to the Catholic Church in China.* Singapore: China Catholic Communications, 1993.

CHASTEL, ANDRÉ. *The Sack of Rome.* Princeton: Princeton University Press, 1983.

CHATELLIER, LOUIS. *L'Europe des Dévots.* St. Just La Pendue: Chirat, 1987.

CHAUVIN, CHARLES. "La maison Sainte-Marthe." *Christus* 149, January, 1991, pp. 117-126.

CHENU, M.D. "Fraternitas." *Revue d'histoire de la spiritualité* 49, 1973, pp. 385-400.

CLAIR, C. *La Vie de Saint Ignace de Loyola.* Paris: Plon, Norrit et Cie., 1891.

COFFIN, DAVID. *The Villa in the Life of Renaissance Rome.* Princeton: Princeton University Press, 1979.

CONANT, K.J. "The Afterlife of Vitruvius in the Middle Ages," in *Journal of the Society of Architectural Historians,* 27, 1968, pp. 33-38.

CONNORS, JOSEPH. *Borromini and the Roman Oratory, Style*

and Society. Cambridge MA: The MIT Press, 1980.

Constitutiones et Regulae Societatis Iesu (Monumenta Historica Societatis Iesu). 4 vols. Rome, 1934-48.

Constitutions of the Society of Jesus and their Complementary Norms. A Complete English Translation of the Official Latin Texts. St. Louis: Institute of Jesuit Sources, 1996.

CONWELL, JOSEPH. "The Kamakazi Factor: Choosing Jesuit Ministries." *Studies in the Spirituality of Jesuits* 11, 5, 1979.

COUCEIRO, GONÇALO. "Macao and the Art of the Society of Jesus in China." *Review of Culture,* (Instituto Cultural de Macau), October-December 1994, pp. 27-34.

D'AMATO, JOHN F. *Renaissance Humanism in Papal Rome.* Baltimore: Johns Hopkins University Press, 1983.

DALMASES, CÁNDIDO DE. "Los estudios de San Ignacio en Barcelona (1524-1526)." *AHSI* 10, 1941, pp. 283-93.

DALMASES, CÁNDIDO DE. *Ignatius of Loyola, Founder of the Jesuits.* Translated by Jerome Aixalá. St. Louis: Institute of Jesuit Sources, 1985.

DE NICHOLAS, ANTONIO. *Ignatius of Loyola: Powers of Imagining, a philosophical hermeneutic of imagining through the collected works of Ignatius of Loyola.* New York: SUNY Press, 1983.

D'ELIA, PASQUALE M. *Fonti Ricciane, Documenti Originali concernenti Matteo Ricci e la storia delle prime relazioni tra l'Europa e la Cina (1579-1615).* 2 vols. Rome: Libreria dello Stato, 1949.

DELLI, SERGIO. *Le Strade di Roma.* Rome: Newton Compton, 1983.

DELUMEAU, JEAN, *Vie économique e social de Rome dans la seconde moitié du XVIe siècle.* 2 vols. BEFAR, 184, Paris: E. de Boccard, 1957.

DELUMEAU, JEAN. *La Civilisation de la Renaissance.* Paris: Arthaud, 1984.

DENZINGER H. and SCHÖNMETZER A., Editors. *Enchiridion Symbolorum Definitionum et Declarationum de rebus fidei et morum.*, 36th. edition. Rome, Barcelona and Friburg: Herder, 1976.

DICKENSON, ROBERT. *The West European City, A Geographical Interpretation.* London: Routledge & Kegan Paul Ltd., 1951.

Dizionario Encyclopedico di Architettura e Urbanistica. 6 vols. Rome: Instituto Editoriale Romano, 1968-9.

Documents of the Thirty-fourth General Congregation of the Society of Jesus. St. Louis: Institute of Jesuit Sources, 1995.

DOREZ, L. *La Coeur du Pape Paul III.* Paris: n.p., 1932.

DUDON, PAUL. *St. Ignatius of Loyola.* Translated by William Young, Milwaukee: Bruce, 1949.

EGGER, HERMANN. *Römische Veduten,* 2 vols. Wien, Leipzig: F. Wolfrum, 1911-1931.

EHRLE, FRANCESCO. *La Pianta di Roma du Perác-*

Lafréry. Rome: Danesi, 1908.

EHRLE, FRANCESCO. *Roma ai Tempi di Giulio III, La Pianta di Roma di Leonardo Bufalini del 1551.* Rome: Danesi, 1911.

EMERY, RICHARD. *The Friars in Medieval France.* New York: Columbia University Press, 1972.

ENDEAN, PHILLIP. "Who Do You Say Ignatius Is? Jesuit Fundamentalism and Beyond." *Studies in the Spirituality of Jesuits* 19, 5, November 1987.

Epistolae Mixtae ex variis Europae locis ab anno 1537 ad annum 1556 scriptae. (Monumenta Historica Societatis Iesu). 5 vols. Madrid, 1898-1901.

ESSER, KAJATAN. *The Origins of the Franciscan Order.* Translated by A. Daly and I. Lynch. Chicago: Franciscan Herald Press, 1970.

EUSEBIUS. *The History of the Church.* Translated by G.A. Williamson. Minneapolis: Augsburg Publishing House, 1975.

Exercitia Spiritualia S. Ignatii. et eorum Directoria. (Monumenta Historica Societatis Iesu). Revised edition. Rome, 1969.

FAGIOLO, MARCELLO, and MADONNA, MARIA LUISA, Editors. *Roma Sancta, La città delle basiliche.* Rome: Gangemi, 1985.

FANELLI, GIOVANNI. *Firenze.* 4th ed. Rome-Bari: Laterza, 1988.

FARINA, S. "I conventi mendicanti nel tessuto urbanistico di Bologna." *Storia della Città* III, 9, pp. 56-61.

FERRARI, G. *Early Roman Monasteries: Notes for the History of the Monasteries and Convents at Rome from the V through the X Century.* Vatican City: Pontificio Istituto di Archeologia Cristiana, 1957.

FIORANI, LUIGI, Editor. "L'esperienza religiosa nelle confraternite romane tra cinque e seicento." *Ricerche per la storia religiosa di Roma,* 5, 1984, pp. 155-196.

Fontes Documentales de S. Ignatio de Loyola (Monumenta Historica Societatis Iesu). Rome, 1977.

Fontes Narrativi de S. Ignatio de Loyola et de Societatis Iesu Initiis (Monumenta Historica Societatis Iesu). 4 vols. Rome, 1943-1965.

Fonti Francescane, Editio Minor. Assisi: Editrici Francescane, 1990.

FORCELLA, VINCENZO. *Feste in Roma nel Pontificato di Paolo III, 1534-1545.* Rome: n.p., 1885.

FOSS, MICHAEL. *The Founding of the Jesuits, 1540.* London: Hamish Hamilton, 1975.

FOX, ROBIN LANE. *Pagans and Christians.* San Francisco: Harper & Rowe, 1986.

FREER, ARTHUR. *The Early Franciscans and Jesuits; a study in constrasts.* London: SPCK, 1922.

FREGNA, R., and POLITO, S. "Fonti di Archivio per una storia edilizia di Roma, I Libri delle case dal '500 al '700: forma ed esperienza della Città." *Controspazio* 9, 1971, 2-20

FROMMEL, CHRISTOPH L. "Papal Policy: The Planning of Rome during the Renaissance" in *Art and History, Images and Their Meaning*. Edited by Robert Rotberg and Theodore Rabb. Cambridge: Cambridge University Press, 1988.

FRUTAZ, AMATO PIETRO. *Le Piante di Roma*. 3 vols. Rome: Instituto di Studi Romani, 1962.

GANNON, THOMAS, and TRAUB, GEORGE. *The Desert and the City: An Interpretation of Christian Spirituality*. London: Collier-Macmillan, 1969.

GANSS, GEORGE. *St Ignatius' Idea of a Jesuit University*. Milwaukee: Marquette University Press, 1956.

GIGLI, GIACINTO. *Diario Romano (1608-1670)*. Edited by Giuseppe Ricciotti. Rome: Tumminelli, 1958.

GILLERMAN, DAVID. "San Fortunato in Todi: Why the Hall Church." *Journal of the Society of Architectural Historians* 48, June 1989, pp. 158-171.

GIROUARD, MARK. *Cities & People: A Social and Architectural History*. New Haven: Yale University Press, 1985.

GNOLI, DOMENICO. "Descriptio Urbis, o Censimento della Popolazione di Roma Avanti il Sacco Borbonico." *Archivio della R. Società Romana di Storia Patria* 17, 1894, pp. 375-493.

GOLDMAN, ARI L. "Religion Notes: St. Ignatius and a Baby." *New York Times,* August 24, 1991, p. 23.

GOMES DOS SANTOS, DOMINGOS MAURÍCIO. "Macao, The first western university in the Far East." *Review of Culture,* (Instituto Cultural de Macau), October-December 1994, pp. 5-26.

GRANT, ROBERT. *Augustus to Constantine: The Thurst of the Christian Movement into the Roman World*. New York, Evanston, and London: Harper & Row, 1970.

GRENDLER, Paul. *Schooling in Renaissance Italy: Literacy and Learning, 1300-1600*. Baltimore and London: Johns Hopkins University Press, 1989.

GUIDONI, ENRICO and MARINO, ANGELA. *Storia dell'urbanistica: Il Cinquecento*. Rome-Bari: Laterza, 1982.

GUIDONI, ENRICO. "Strada e isolato. D'alto medioevo al settecento." *Lotus International* 19, 1978, pp. 4-10.

GUIDONI, ENRICO. *La Città Europea, Formazione e significato dal IV all'XI Secolo*. Milano: Electa, 1978.

GUIDONI, ENRICO. *La città dal Medioevo ad Rinascimento*. 3d Edition. Rome-Bari: Laterza, 1989.

GUIDONI, ENRICO. *Storia dell'urbanistica: Il Duecento*. Rome-Bari: Laterza, 1989.

HALL, JAMES. *A History of Ideas and Images in Italian Art*. San Francisco: Harper and Row, 1983.

HALLMAN, BARBARA. *Italian Cardinals, Reform and the Church as Property*. Berkeley: University of California Press, 1985.

HAMY, ALFRED. *Documents pour Servir à L'Histoire des Domiciles de la Compagnie de Jésus dans le Monde Entier de 1540 à 1773*. Paris: Picard, n.d.

HAWLEY, JOHN STRATTON, Editor. *Saints and Virtues*. Berkeley: University of California Press, 1987.

HEYDENREICH, LUDWIG, and LOTZ, WOLFGANG. *Architecture in Italy, 1400 to 1600*. Translated by Mary Hottinger. Harmondsworth and Baltimore: Penguin, 1974.

HIBBERT, CHRISTOPHER. *Rome, the Biography of a City*. New York and London: W.W. Norton, 1985.

HINNESBUSCH, WILLIAM. *The History of the Dominican Order*. New York: Alba House, 1966.

HOHENBERG, PAUL, and LEES, LYNN. *The Making of Urban Europe 1000-1950*. Cambridge MA: Harvard University Press, 1985.

HORN, WALTER *The Plan of St. Gall, A Study of the Architecture and Economy and Life in a Paradigmatic Carolingian Monastery*. 3 vols. Berkeley: University of California Press, 1979.

HUBER, RAPHAEL. *A Documented History of the Franciscan Order*. Milwaukee: Nowiny, 1944.

HUBERT, J. "Evolution de la topografie et de l'aspect des villes de Gaulle du Ve au Xe siècle." In *La città nell'alto Medioevo (Settimana di Studio del centro italiano di Studi sull'alto Medioevo VI)*. Spoleto: 1959, pp. 529-558.

HÜLSEN, CHRISTIAN and EGGER, HERMANN. *Die Römischen Skizzenbücher von Marten Van Heemskerck*. 4 vols. Berlin: Im Verlag Von Julius Bard, 1913.

HÜLSEN, CHRISTIAN. *Le Chiese de Roma nel Medio Evo*. Firenze, 1926.

IGNATIUS LOYOLA. *The Autobiography of St. Ignatius Loyola with related documents*. Translated by Joseph O'Callaghan. New York: Harper and Row, 1974.

IGNATIUS LOYOLA. *The Constitutions of the Society of Jesus*. Translated by George Ganss. St. Louis: Institute of Jesuit Sources, 1970.

IGNATIUS LOYOLA. *The Spiritual Exercises of St. Ignatius, A translation and commentary by George Ganss, S.J.* St. Louis: Institute of Jesuit Sources, 1992.

Imago Primi Saeculi Societatis Iesu a Provincia Flandro-Belgica eiusdem societatis repraesentata. Antwerp, 1640.

INSOLERA, ITALO. *Roma Immagini e Realtà del X al XX secolo*. 3rd. ed. Rome-Bari: Laterza, 1985.

Institutum Societatis Iesu. 3 vols. Florence: Typographia a Ss. Conceptione, 1892-1893.

IPARRAGUIRRE, I., *Historia de los Ejercicios Espirituales de S. Ignacio*. 2 vols. Rome: Institutim Historicum Societatis Jesu and Bilbao: El Mensajero del Corazón de Jesús, 1947-1955.

ISERLOH, ERWIN, GLAZIK, JOSEPH, and JEDIN, HUBERT. *History of the Church,* Translated by Anselm Biggs and Peter Becker. New York: Seabury, Vol V: *Reformation and Counter Reformation,* 1980.

JEROME. *Selected Letters*. Loeb Classical Library, 262. London: Wm. Heineman, 1924.

JUNGMANN, JOSEF. A. *The Mass of the Roman Rite: Its Origins and Development.* 2 vols. Translated by Francis Brunner. Westminster MD: Christian Classics, 1986.

KAGAN, RICHARD L. "Philip II and the Art of the Cityscape." In *Art and History, Images and Their Meaning.* Edited by Robert Rotberg and Theodore Rabb. Cambridge: Cambridge University Press, 1988.

KEAVENEY, R. *Views of Rome.* London: Scala Publications with the Biblioteca Apostolica Vaticana and Smithsonian Institution Travelling Exhibition Service. 1988.

KELLY, J.N.D. *The Oxford Dictionary of Popes.* Oxford and New York: Oxford University Press, 1986.

KNOWLES, DAVID. "The *Regula Magistri* and the *Rule* of St. Benedict." In *Great Historical Enterprises,* London: Nelson, 1963.

KNOWLES, DAVID. *From Pachomius to Ignatius.* Oxford: Oxford University Press, 1966.

KNOWLES, DAVID. *Christian Monasticism,* New York and Toronto: McGraw-Hill, 1969.

KOSTOF, SPIRO, Editor. *The Architect.* New York: Oxford University Press, 1977.

KOSTOF, SPIRO. *A History of Architecture, Settings and Rituals.* Oxford: Oxford University Press, 1985.

KOSTOF, SPIRO. *The City Shaped: Urban Patterns and Meanings through History.* Boston, Toronto, & London: Bullfinch Press, 1991.

KÖNIG-NORDHOFF, URSULA. *Ignatius von Loyola, Studien zur Entwicklung einer neuen heiligen Ikonographie in Rahmen einer Kanonisationskampagne um 1600.* Berlin: Gebr. Mann Verlag, 1982.

KRAUTHEIMER, RICHARD and CURCIC, SLOBADAN. *Early Christian and Byzantine Architecture.* Fourth Edition, Harmondsworth: Penguin, 1986.

KRAUTHEIMER, RICHARD. "Alberti and Vitruvius." In *Studies in Early Christian, Medieval, and Renaissance Art.* New York: New York University Press, 1969, pp. 323-32.

KRAUTHEIMER, RICHARD. *Rome, Profile of a City.* Princeton: Princeton University Press, 1980.

KRAUTHEIMER, RICHARD. *Three Christian Capitals: Topography and Politics.* Berkeley & Los Angeles: University of California Press, 1982.

KRAUTHEIMER, RICHARD. *The Rome of Alexander VII, 1655-1667.* Princeton: Princeton University Press, 1985.

KUNKEL, PAUL. *The Theatines in the History of Catholic Reform before the Establishment of Lutheranism.* Washington D.C.: Catholic University Press, 1941.

La Canonizazione dei Santi Ignazio di Loyola, Fondatore della Compagnia di Gesù e Francesco Saverio Apostolo dell'Oriente, a cura del comitato romano ispano per le centenarie onoranze. Rome: n.p., 1922.

LANCIANI, RODOLFO. *The Golden Days of the Renaissance in Rome.* Boston and New York, n.p., 1906.

Latin Christianity: Its Founder, Tertullian. In *The Ante-Nicene Fathers, Translations of The Writings of the Fathers down to A.D. 325,* Vol. III, Edited by Alexander Roberts and James Donaldson. New York: Christian Literature Company, 1896.

LE GOFF, J. "Apostolat mendiant et fait urbain dans la France médiévale: l'implantation des ordres mendiants." *Annales E.S.C.,* 22, 1968, pp. 335-355.

LE GOFF, J. "Ordres mendiants et urbanisation dans la France médiévale." *Annales E.S.C.,* 25, 1970, pp. 924-946.

LETURIA, PEDRO DE. *El gentilhombre Iñigo López de Loyola en su patria y en su siglo.* Barcelona: Editorial Labor, 1941.

LETURIA, PEDRO DE. *Estudios Ignacianos.* Edited by P. Iparraguirre. 2 vols. Rome: Institutum Historicum S.I., 1957.

LEWINE, M.J. *The Roman Church Interior, 1527-1580.* Ann Arbor: University Microfilms, 1960.

LLEWELLYN, PETER. *Rome in the Dark Ages.* London: Faber and Faber, 1971.

LOPEZ R. S. "The Crossroad within the Wall." In *The Historian and the City.* Edited by O. Handlin and J. Burchard. Cambridge MA: MIT Press, 1963.

LUCAS, THOMAS, Editor. *Saint, Site, and Sacred Strategy: Ignatius, Rome, and Jesuit Urbanism.* Vatican City: Biblioteca Apostolica Vaticana, 1990.

LUCAS, THOMAS. "Le camere di sant'Ignazio a Roma." *La Civiltà Cattolica* 1991, III, quaderno 3387-3388, pp. 280-286.

MAFFEIUS, JOANNES. *De vita et moribus Ignatii Loiolæ qui Societatem Iesu fundavit, Libri III,* Rome: F. Zannettum, 1585.

MARCONI, PAOLO. *La città come forma simbolica.* Rome: Bulzoni, 1973.

MARKUS, ROBERT. *Christianity in the Roman World.* New York: Charles Scribner's Sons, 1974.

MAROCCO, MARCELLO. "Il Quartiere del Rinascimento." *Studi Romani* 31, 1983, 1, pp. 34-48.

MARTIN, GREGORY. *Roma Sancta (1581).* Edited by G. B. Parks. Rome: Edizioni di Storia e Letteratura, 1969.

MARTÍN, LUIS FERNANDEZ. "El hogar donde Iñigo de Loyola se hizo hombre." *AHSJ,* 49, 1980, pp. 21-94.

MARTINI, A. "Da chi fu hospite S. Ignazio a Venezia nel 1536." *AHSI* 18, 1949, pp. 253-60.

MCGLOIN, JOHN B. *California's First Archbishop, The Life of Joseph Sadoc Alemany, O.P., 1814-1888.* New York: Herder & Herder, 1966.

MCGLOIN, JOHN B. *Jesuits by the Golden Gate, The Society of Jesus in San Francisco, 1849-1969.* San Francisco: University of San Francisco Press, 1972.

MCKEVITT, GERALD. *The University of Santa Clara, A History, 1851-1977.* Stanford: Stanford University Press, 1979.

MEEKS, WAYNE. *The First Urban Christians.* New Haven: Yale University Press, 1983.

MEERSSEMAN, GILLES GERARD. "L'architecture dominicaine au XIIIe siècle, législation et pratique." *Archivum Fratrum Praedicatorum,* 16, 1946, pp. 136-190.

MEERSSEMAN, GILLES GERARD. *Ordo Fraternitatis: Contraternite e pietà dei laici nel medievo.* (Series *Italia Sacra, Studi e documenti di storia ecclesiastica, no. 24)* Rome: Herder, 1977.

MILLER, HENRY. "Baroque Cities in the Wilderness: Archaeology and Urban Development in the Colonial Chesapeake." *Historical Archaeology,* 22, 1988, pp. 57-73.

MILLER, M. *Chartres Cathedral.* Andover U.K.: Pitkin Pictorials, 1990.

Mirabilia Urbis Romæ, Nova recognita et emendata, Anno Iubilei MDL. Rome: n.p., 1550.

MOHRMANN, C. "Encore une fois: paganus." *Vigiliae Christianae* 6, 1952, pp. 109-121.

MONTALTO, LISA. "Il Problema della cupola di Sant'Ignazio da Padre Orazio Grassi e Fratel Pozzo a oggi." *Bolletino del centro di studii per la storia dell'architettura,* 11, 1957, pp. 33-62.

MONTANHA, JOSÉ. "Apparatos para la Historia do Bispado de Macao", fol. 245, in Arquivo Histórico Ultramino, Lisboa.

Monumenta Paedagogica Societatis Iesu, Vol. I (1540-1556) (Monumenta Historica Societatis Iesu). Rome, 1965.

Monumenta Peruana (Monumenta Historica Societatis Iesu). 4 vols. Rome, 1954-1966.

MOORMAN, JOHN. *A History of the Franciscan Order from its origins to the year 1517.* Oxford: Clarendon, 1968.

MORONI, GAETANO. *Dizionario di Erudizione Storicio-Ecclesiastico.* 131 vols. Venice: Tipografia Emiliana, 1840-1861.

MURATORI, S., Editor. *Studi per un operante storia urbana di Roma.* Rome, 1963.

NADAL, GERONIMO. *Epistolae et monumenta P. Hieronymi Nadal.* (Monumenta Historica Societatis Iesu). 5 vols. Madrid and Rome, 1898-1962.

NADAL, GERONIMO. *Orationis Observationes.* Edited by Michael Nicolau. Rome: Institutum Historicum S.I., 1964.

NADAL, GERONIMO. *Scholia in Constititiones S.I.* Edited by Manuel Ruiz Jurado. Granada: Faculdad de Teologia, 1976.

NAVENNE, F. DE . *Le palais Farnèse et les Farnèse.* Paris: n.p., 1914.

New Cambridge Modern History, The. Edited by A.W. Ward et al. 12 vols. Cambridge: Cambridge University Press, 1957-1968.

NORBERG-SCHULTZ, CHRISTIAN. *Baroque Architecture.* London: Rizzoli, 1986.

O'MALLEY, JOHN W. "The Jesuits, St. Ignatius, and the Counter Reformation, Some Recent Studies and Their Implications for Today." *Studies in the Spirituality of the Jesuits,* 14, 1, January 1982.

O'MALLEY, JOHN W. "To Travel to Any Part of the World: Jeronimo Nadal and the Jesuit Vocation." *Studies in the Spirituality of the Jesuits,* 16, 2, March 1984.

O'MALLEY, JOHN W. "How the Jesuits Changed: 1540-56." *America,* 165, 2, July 20-27, 1991, pp. 28-32.

O'MALLEY, JOHN W. *The First Jesuits.* Cambridge, MA: Harvard University Press, 1993,

OLIN, JOHN C.*The Catholic Reformation: Savonarola to Ignatius Loyola—Reform in the Church, 1495-1540.* New York: Harper & Row, 1969.

OLIN, JOHN C. "The Idea of Pilgrimage in the Experience of Ignatius Loyola." *Church History,* 48, 1979, pp. 387-397.

ONOFRIO, CESARE. *Renovatio Romae, Storia e urbanistica dal Campidoglio all'EUR.* Rome: Edizioni Mediterranee, 1973.

Origine et Summario delle opere pie di Roma. Edited by M. Armellini. In *Cronachetta mensuale di scienze naturali e d'archeologia ,* 19, 1885.

ORLANDINI, N. *Historiae Societatis Jesu prima pars,* Rome: Apud Bartholomeum Zannettum, 1614.

PADBERG, J. "How we live where we live." *Studies in the Spirituality of the Jesuits,* 20, 2, March, 1988.

PADBERG, J. "The Jesuit question," *The Tablet,* September 22, 1990, pp. 1189-1191.

PADBERG, JOHN W., O'KEEFE, MARTIN, AND McCARTHY, JOHN L., Editors and translators. *For Matters of Greater Moment: The First Thirty Jesuit General Congregations, A Brief History and a Translation of the Decrees,* St. Louis: Institute of Jesuit Sources, 1994.

PAGLIA, V. "Vita Religiosa nella Confraternita della Pietà dei carcerati (sec. XVI-XVII)." *Richerche per la storia religiousa di Roma,* 2, 1978, pp. 51-96.

PAGLIA, V. *"La pietà dei carcerati:" Confraternite e società a Roma nei secoli XVI-XVIII.* Rome: Edizioni di Storia e Letteratura, 1980, pp. 3-80.

PARTNER, PETER. *Renaissance Rome 1500-1559, A Portrait of a Society.* Berkeley & Los Angeles: University of California Press, 1979.

PASCHINI, P. *S. Gaetano Theine, Gian Pietro Carafa e le origini dei chierici regolari teatine.* Rome: Scuola Tipografica Pio X, 1926.

PASTOR, LUDOVICO. *Storia dei Papi dal Fine del Medio Evo, Paolo III.* Vol. V, Translated by Angelo Mercati. Rome: Desclée & C. Editori Pontifici, l959.

PATETTA, LUCIANO, *Storia e tipologia, cinque saggi sull'architettura del passato.* Milan: clup, 1989.

PECCHIAI, PIO. *Roma nel Cinquecento.* (Storia di Roma,

Vol XIII). Bologna: Istituto de Studi Romani, 1948.

PECCHIAI, PIO. *Il Gesù di Roma.* Rome: Società Grafica Romana, 1952.

PELIKAN, JAROSLAV. *Jesus through the Centuries.* New Haven: Yale Univ. Press, 1985.

PELLEGRINI, L. "Insediamenti rurali e insediamenti urbani dei francescani nell'Italia del sec. XIII." *S. Bonaventura maestro di vita francescana e di sapienza cristiana. Atti del congresso internazionale per il VII centenario di S. Bonaventura da Bagnoregio, Roma 19-26 settembre 1974.* Rome, 1976, pp. 197-210.

PELLEGRINI, L. "Gli insediamenti francescani nella evoluzione storica degli agglomerati umani e della circoscrizioni territoriali dell'Italia nel secolo XIII." *Italia Sacra, Studi e Documenti di Storia Ecclesiastica*, 30, 1979, pp. 195-237.

PETRARCHA, FRANCESCO, *Letters on Familiar Matters, Rerum familiarium libri IX-XVI.* Translated by Aldo Bernardo, Baltimore and London: Johns Hopkins University Press, 1982.

PIERI, P. *Il Rinasciamento e la crisi militare italiana.* Turin: n.p., 1952.

PIETRANGELI, CARLO, Editor. *Guide Rionali di Roma: Rione IX–Pigna.* 3 vols. Rome: Fratelli Palombi, 1980.

PINTO, JOHN A. "Origins and Development of the Ichnographic City Plan." *Journal of the Society of Architectural Historians* 35, 1976, pp. 34-50.

PIRRI, PIETRO, and DI ROSA, PIETRO. "Il P. Giovanni de Rosis (1538-1610) e lo Sviluppo dell'Edilizia Gesuitica." *AHSI* 14, 1975, pp. 3-104.

PIRRI, PIETRO. "La Topografia del Gesù di Roma e le vertenze tra Muzio Muti e S. Ignazio secondo nuovi documenti." *AHSI* 10, 1941, pp. 177-217.

PIRRI, PIETRO. "L'architetto Bartolomeo Ammannati ed i Gesuiti." *AHSI* 12, 1943, pp. 5-57.

PIRRI, PIETRO. *Giovanni Tristano ed i Primordi della Architettura Gesuitica.* Rome: Institutum Historicum S.I., 1955.

PLINY THE YOUNGER. *Letters.* Vol. 2. Loeb Classical Library, London: Wm. Heineman, 1947.

POLANCO, JOANNES ALPHONSUS DE. *Polanci Complementa. Epistolae et commentaria Patris Ioannis Alphonsi de Polanco e Societate Iesu.* (Monumenta Historica Societatis Iesu) 2 vols. Madrid, 1916-1917.

POLANCO, JOANNES ALPHONSUS DE. *Vita Ignatii Loiolae et rerum Societatis Iesu seu Chronichon.* (Monumenta Historica Societatis Iesu) 6 vols. Madrid: 1894-1898.

PONNELLE, LOUIS and BORDET, LOUIS. *Saint Philippe Neri et la Société romaine de son temps, 1519-1595.* Paris: Librairie Bloud & Gay, 1929.

PORTOGHESI, PAOLO. *Rome of the Renaissance.* Translated by Pearl Sanders. New York: Phaidon, 1972.

PORTOGHESI, PAOLO. *Roma Barocca.* Rome-Bari: Laterza, 1982. [also available in English, translated by Barbara Luigia La Penta. Cambridge MA: MIT Press 1970.]

PROIA, A, and ROMANO, P. *Roma nel Cinquecento: Pigna (IX Rione).* Rome: Tipografia Agostiniana, 1936.

PULLAN, BRIAN. *Rich and Poor in Venice: The Social Institutions of a Catholic State to 1620.* Cambridge MA: Harvard University Press, 1971.

RAHNER, HUGO, and VON MATT, LEONARD. *St. Ignatius of Loyola, A Pictorial Biography.* Translated by John Murray. London: Longmans Green & Co., 1956.

RAHNER, HUGO. *Letters to Women.* Translated by K. Pond and S. Weetman. Frieberg: Herder, and Edinburgh-London: Nelson 1960.

RAHNER, KARL. *Theological Investigations.* Vol. 14. Translated by David Bourke. New York: Seabury, 1976.

RASPI SERRA, JOSELITA, Editor. *Gli ordini mendicanti e la città. Aspetti archetettonici, sociali, e politici.* Milan: Edizioni Guerini Studio, 1990.

RAVIER, ANDRÉ. *Les Chroniques: S. Ignace de Loyola.* Paris: Nouvelle Librairie de France, 1973.

RAVIER, ANDRÉ. *Ignatius Loyola and the Founding of the the Society of Jesus.* Translated by M. J. and C. Daly. San Francisco: Ignatius Press, 1987.

RB 1980: The Rule of St. Benedict in Latin and English with notes. Edited by Timothy Fry. Collegeville: The Liturgical Press, 1980.

RE, EMILIO. "Maestri di strada." *Archivio della R. Società Romana di Storia Patria* 43, 1920, pp. 5-102.

Regulae Societatis Iesu (Monumenta Historica Societatis Iesu). Rome, 1948.

REITES, JAMES W. "St. Ignatius and the Jews." *Studies in the Spirituality of the Jesuits,* 13, 4, September, 1981.

RINALDI, E. *La fondazione del Collegio Romano.* Arezzo: n.p., 1914.

RIORDAN, TIMOTHY, HURRY, SILAS, AND MILLER, HENRY. *"A Good Brick Chappell" The Archeology of the c. 1667 Catholic Chapel at St. Mary's City, Maryland,* Historic St. Mary's City Archaeology Series No. 3: Alexander H. Morrison Fund Publication, 1995.

ROBERTSON, CLARE. *'Il Gran Cardinale' Alessandro Farnese, Patron of the Arts.* New York and New Haven: Yale University Press, 1992.

RODOCANACHI, E., Editor. *Una Cronica di Santa Sabina.* Rome: Fratelli Bocca,1899.

ROMANI, M. *Pellegrini e viaggiatori nell'economia di Roma dal XIV al XVII secolo.* Milano, 1948.

ROSE, S. *St. Ignatius and the Early Jesuits.* London: Burns and Oates, 1891.

RUSCONI, ROBERTO. "Gli ordini mendicanti tra rinascimento e controriforma: eremi e riforme, conventi e città, missioni e campagne." In *Città Italiane del '500 tra Riforma e Controriforma.* (Atti del Convegno di

Internazionale di Studi, Lucca, 13-15 ottobre, 1983). Lucca: Pacini Fazzi, 1988, pp. 267-281.

RYBCZYNSKI, WITOLD. *The Most Beautiful House in the World*. New York: Viking, 1990.

RYKWERT, JOSEPH. *The Idea of a Town: The Anthropology of Urban Form in Rome, Italy, and the Ancient World*. Princeton: Princeton University Press, 1976.

SACCHINI, FRANCESCO. *Historiae Societatis Iesu pars tertia sive Borgia*. Rome: Typis Manelfi Manelfii, 1649.

Sancti Gregorii Papae I cognomen Magni, Opera Omnia, Patrologia Latina, Vol. 76. Edited by J. P. Migne. Paris, 1849.

Sancti Ignatii de Loyola epistolæ et instructiones (Monumenta Historica Societatis Iesu). 12 vols. Madrid, 1903-1911.

SCACCIA SCARAFONI, C. "L'antico statuto dei Magistri Stratarum e altri documenti relative a quella magistratura." *Archivio della R. Società Romana di Storia Patria* 50, 1927, pp. 239-308.

SCADUTO, MARIO. "La corrispondenza dei primi gesuiti e le poste italiane." *AHSI* 19, 1950, pp. 237-253.

SCADUTO, MARIO. *Storia delle Compagnia di Gesù in Italia III, L'Epoca di Giacomo Lainez, Il Governo 1556-1565*. Rome: Edizioni La Civiltà Cattolica, 1964.

SCADUTO, MARIO. "La strada e i primi Gesuiti." *AHSI* 40, 1971, pp. 323-390.

SCADUTO, MARIO. *Storia delle Compagnia di Gesù in Italia IV, L'Epoca di Giacomo Lainez, L'Azione, 1556-1565*. Rome: Edizioni La Civiltà Cattolica, 1974.

SCHIAPARELLI, L. "Alcuni Documenti dei Magistri Aedificiourm Urbis." *Archivio della R. Società Romana di Storia Patria* 25,1902, pp. 5-59.

SCHURHAMMER, GEORG. *Francis Xavier, his life, his times*. 4 vols. Translated by M. Joseph Costelloe. Rome: Jesuit Historical Institute, 1973-1980. Vol I: *Europe, 1506-1541*; Vol II: *India, 1541-1545*; Vol. III: *Indonesia and India, 1545-1549*.

Scripta de Sancto Ignatio (Monumenta Historica Societatis Iesu). 2 vols. Madrid, 1904-1918.

SCURANI, A. "Ieri e oggi dei Gesuiti a Milano." *Terra Ambrosiana*, 6, novembre-dicembre 1990, pp. 52-59.

SENNETT, RICHARD. *The Conscience of the Eye: The Design and Social Life of Cities*. New York: Albert Knopf, 1990.

SOUTHERN, R.W. *Western Society and the Church in the Middle Ages*. Harmondsworth: Pelican, 1970.

STAMBAUGH, JOHN and BALCH, DAVID. *The Social World of the First Christians*. London: SPCK, 1986.

STINGER, CHARLES. *The Renaissance in Rome*. Bloomington: Indiana University Press, 1985.

Synopsis Historiae Societatis Iesu. Louvain: Typis ad Sancti Alphonsi, 1950.

TACCHI VENTURI, PIETRO. *Le Case abitate da S. Ignazio di Loiola in Roma secondo un inedito documento del tempo*. Rome: Tipografia Poliglotta della S.C. de Propaganda Fide, 1899.

TACCHI VENTURI, PIETRO. *L'azione di S. Ignazio di Loiola nella vita italiana del cinquecento*. Vatican City: Tipografia Poliglotta Vaticana, 1931.

TACCHI VENTURI, PIETRO. "S. Ignazio di Loiola, apostolo di Roma." *Roma,* Agosto, 1940, pp. 1-20.

TACCHI VENTURI, PIETRO. *La Prima Casa di S. Ignazio in Roma, o Le Sue Cappellette al Gesù*. Rome: Società Grafica Romana, 1951.

TACCHI VENTURI, PIETRO. *Storia della Compagnia di Gesù in Italia*, 2 vols, each in 2 parts, Rome: Edizioni Civiltà Cattolica, 1951.

TOMEI, PIETRO. *L'architetture a Roma nel quattrocento*. Rome, 1942.

TONER, JULES. "The Deliberation That Started the Jesuits." *Studies in the Spirituality of Jesuits*, 6, 4, June 1974.

TOSTI-CROCE, MARINA. "Gli esordi dell'architettura francescana a Roma." *Storia della Città*, 9, 1978, pp. 28-32.

URBANELLI, C. "Caratteristiche degli insediamenti cappuccini nei primi cinquanta anni della riforma." in *Le origini della riforma cappuccina 1525-1536*. (Atti del Convegno di studi storici, Camerino, 18-21 settembre, 1978). Ancona, 1979, pp. 171-199.

VACCARO, P. *Tessuto e tipo edilizio a Roma dalla fine del XIV secolo fin'alla fine del XVIII secolo*. Rome, 1968.

VAGNETTI, LUIGI. "La 'Descriptio Urbis Romae.'" *Quaderno del Istituto di elementi di architettura e rilievo dei monumenti di Genova*, 1, 1968, pp. 25-88.

VALLERY RADOT, JEAN. *Le Recuil de plan d'édifices de la Compagnie de Jésus conservé à la Biblioteque Nationale de Paris*. (Bibliotheca Inst. Hist. S.I.,Vol. XV). Rome: Institutum Historicum S.I., 1960.

VERSFELD, MARTINUS. *A Guide to* The City of God. London and New York, 1958.

VEYNE, PAUL, Editor. *A History of Private Life, I. From Pagan Rome to Byzantium*. Translated by Arthur Goldhammer. Cambridge MA: Harvard University Press, 1987.

VILLETTI, G. "Prospettive di ricerca sull'edilizia degli Ordini Mendicanti: il fondo 'Libri' nell'archivio generale dell'Ordine dei Predicatori." *Architettura Archivi*, A I, I, 1982.

VILLOSLADA, RICARDO GARCIA. *Storia del Collegio Romano dal suo inizio (1551) alla soppressione della Compagnia di Gesù(1773)*. Rome: Gregorian University Press, 1954.

VILLOSLADA, RICARDO GARCIA. *San Ignacio de Loyola: Nueva Biografia*. Madrid: BAC, 1986.

VON ZELLER, HUMBERT. *The Benedictine Ideal*. London: Burns, 1959.

WESTFALL, CARROLL WILLIAM. *In this most perfect*

Paradise: Alberti, Nicholas, and the Invention of Conscious Urban Planning in Rome, 1447-55. University Park: Pennsylvania State University Press, 1974.

WETHEY, HAROLD. *Colonial Architecture and Sculpture in Peru.* Cambridge: Harvard University Press, 1949.

WICKI, J. "Pfarrseelsorge und Armut der Professhäuser. Ein Motu proprio Paulus III aus der Vorgeschichte des Römischen Gesù (1549)." *AHSI* 11, 1942, pp. 69-82.

WITTKOWER, R., and JAFFE, I. *Baroque Art: The Jesuit Contribution.* New York: Fordham University Press, 1972.

WOODWARD, D. "Reality, symbolism, time and space in medieval maps." *Annals of the Association of American Geographers, 75, 1985*, pp. 514-515.

WOODWARD, KENNETH L. *Making Saints.* New York: Simon and Schuster, 1990.

WÖLFFLIN, HEINRICH. *Renaissance and Baroque.* Translated by Kathrin Simon. Ithaca: Cornell University Press, 1964.

ZUCKER, PAUL. "Space and Movement in High Baroque City Planning." *JSAH* 14 , 1955, pp. 8-13.

ZUCKER, PAUL. *Town and Square, From the Agora to the Village Green.* New York: Columbia University Press, 1959.

FIGURE CREDITS

The author gratefully acknowledges the following institutions and persons for granting permission to reprint images:

Biblioteca Apostolica Vaticana. From *Saint, Site, and Sacred Strategy, Ignatius, Rome, and Jesuit Urbanism,* Edited by Thomas M. Lucas. Vatican City: Biblioteca Apostolica Vaticana, 1990: p. v, Figs. 1.4, 2.1; 2.4; 2.6; 5.4,5.8; 6.5; 6.6; 8.5; 8.8; 8.9; 9.1; 9.2; 9.3; 9.4; 9.5; 9.6.

Biblioteca Apostolica Vaticana facsimile editions: Figs 1.1; 4.1; 6.4.

Itaru Takahara and Diego Yuuki, S.J., Fig. 1.2.

Jesuit Community Archive, University of San Francisco: Fig. 1.3.

Leal Senado de Macau: Fig. 1.5.

Arquivo Oltremar, Lisbon, Fig. 1.6.

John Podsiadlo, S.J.: Fig. 1.8.

Henry Miller: Fig. 1.7.

Casa Professa, Rome: Fig. 2.2; 2.6; 6.3; 7.1.

Elizabeth O'Keefe: compass rose, Figs. 2.3; 2.5; 8.1.

Princeton University Press. From Wolfgang Braunfels, *Monasteries of Western Europe, The Architecture of the Orders.* Princeton: Princeton University Press, 1972: Figs. 4.2; 4.3; 4.4.

Princeton University Press. From Richard Krautheimer, *Rome, Profile of a City.* Princeton: Princeton University Press, 1980: Fig. 5.5.

University of Chicago Press. From Wolfgang Braunfels, *Urban Design in Western Europe: Regime and Architecture, 900-1900.* Translated by Kenneth J. Northcott. Chicago & London: University of Chicago Press, 1988: Figs. 5.1; 5.6.

Oxford University Press. From Spiro Kostof, *A History of Architecture, Settings and Rituals.* Oxford: Oxford University Press, 1985: Fig. 5.7.

Edizioni Il Polifilo. From Leonardo Benevolo, *La Città Italiana nel Rinascimento.* Milan: Edizioni, 1990: Figs. 8.12; 8.13; 8.14; 8.15; 8.16; 8.17; 8.21; 8.22; 8.23.

Edizioni Laterza. From Enrico Guidoni, *La Città dal medioevo al rinascimento.* Rome and Bari: Gius. Laterza & Figli Spa., 1989: Figs. 5.2; 5.3.

Thomas M. Rochford, S.J.: Fig. 8.2.

Don Doll, S.J.: Fig. 9.6.

Author: cover, Figs. 5.9; 6.1; 6.2; 6.4; 6.5; 6.7; 6.8; 7.2; 7.3; 7.4; 7.5; 8.3; 8.4; 8.10; 8.11; 8.18; 8.19; 8.20; 8.21.

INDICES

INDEX OF NAMES AND PLACES

SUBJECT INDEX

LANDMARKING

Book and Cover design by Elizabeth M. O'Keefe and Thomas M. Lucas S.J., *in aedibus S.I.* Composed in 10 pt Adobe Baskerville with display lines in Adobe Trajan. Initial Caps from Franciscan Fra Luca de Pacioli's *De Divina Proportione* (1509), the first serious treatise containing diagrams of the true shapes and proportions of classical Roman letters. Cover art is Valerién Regnard's 1684 engraving of the facade and interior perspective of the Chiesa del Gesù, Rome, the Mother Church of the Society of Jesus.

MCMXCVII.